MULTICULTURAL CLASSROOMS

Multicultural Classrooms

PERSPECTIVES FOR TEACHERS

LOUIS COHEN AND LAWRENCE MANION

CROOM HELM
London & Canberra

© 1983 Louis Cohen and Lawrence Manion
Croom Helm Ltd, Provident House, Burrell Row,
Beckenham, Kent BR3 1AT

British Library Cataloguing in Publication Data

Cohen, Louis
    Multicultural classrooms.
    1. Minorities—Education—Great Britain
    I. Title   II. Manion, Lawrence
    371.97   LC3747.G7

    ISBN 0-7099-0747-8
    ISBN 0-7099-0719-2 Pbk

Typeset in Great Britain on Compugraphic Editwriter by
Pat and Anne Murphy Typesetters, Highcliffe, Dorset
Printed and bound in Great Britain by
Biddles Ltd, Guildford and King's Lynn

CONTENTS

Prudent men should judge of future events
by what has taken place in the past
and what is taking place in the present.

Miguel de Cervantes (1547–1616)
Persiles and Sigismunda

PREFACE

Our purpose in writing this book is to present teachers with a
series of perspectives on multicultural classrooms. By
perspective, we simply mean a point of view, a way of looking at
things. The perspectives we shall be adopting in our study we
may designate loosely as *social science* ones. We say 'loosely' for
two reasons: first, social science subsumes a number of
distinctive disciplines each with its own set of characteristic
perspectives and, second, we shall at times have recourse to other
points of view — historical and philosophical, for example —
which lie beyond the scope of social science as we choose to
define it.

Of those disciplines making up the social sciences, psychology,
social psychology and sociology are of prime interest to us in our
study of multicultural classrooms. For the most part, these three
approaches to the study of human behaviour and action share
the same scientific basis although, as we shall see, differences
exist both within and between them. Limiting ourselves for the
moment to the more obvious differences *between* them we may
say that *psychology* has as its chief object of study the individual
organism shaped by combinations of heredity and environment,
the behaviour of which is determined primarily by personal
rather than situational factors. *Social psychology*, on the other
hand, is concerned with the social nature of the individual and
the influences other people have upon his beliefs, attitudes and
behaviour. The prime focus of social psychology is upon two
factors — the behaviour of the individual as a participant in a
social situation and the social processes underlying this
behaviour. In contrast to both psychology and social psychology,
sociology examines the effects of social structure on human
behaviour as it is manifested through social controls, social
stratification and social institutions.

But why adopt social science perspectives at all readers may
well ask? Why not organise a colloquium in which suggested
solutions to the problems of multicultural classrooms could be
freely debated? Or could not one simply indulge in armchair
theorising about important issues in contemporary multicultural
society?

The utility of such approaches notwithstanding, we believe that the social sciences will better assist us to develop a conceptual weaponry to observe, analyse and think about what goes on in multicultural classrooms; to attain greater understanding of the issues involved; to arrive at explanations for teacher and pupil behaviour and to identify causes and consequences of actions. In brief, to establish a more secure knowledge base on which to conduct the *profession* of education, the ultimate aim being facilitation of the teaching-learning process and improvement of the overall functioning of the school as it relates to the needs and the aspirations of all its members.

1 MULTICULTURAL BRITAIN: THE BACKGROUND

Introduction

A casual glance at the literature on race relations shows the
confusion surrounding the use of terms such as *race, ethnicity,
racism, ethnocentrism* and *prejudice.* Contemporary Britain is
variously described as *multiracial, multi-ethnic,* or *multicultural*
and teachers are exhorted to explore the implications of
multiracial, multi-ethnic or multicultural[1] education for their
classroom organisation and practice. There exists, to quote one
observer:

> A confused and differential notion of race as used by human
> biologists, social scientists, lawyers, demographers and the
> man-in-the-street; a blurred distinction between 'racial' and
> 'ethnic' . . . and a confusion between criteria of colour,
> geographical origin, national origin, religion, culture and
> ethnic affiliation.

Given such a state of affairs the first task of a book on
multicultural classrooms must surely be to clarify the meanings
of terms commonly found in the literature of race relations. That
done, a second requirement is to place multicultural classrooms
within the wider context of multicultural society. To do this we
look back over the past 20 years or so and show how
immigration has brought about fundamental changes in our
society. Britain is now a racially-mixed and culturally-varied
nation. In consequence, our institutions have had to adapt in
order to reflect and to cater for the many racially-mixed
communities that now exist throughout the land. Schools in
particular have had to adapt and change. Whether the changes
and adaptations in philosophy, organisation and practice that
have already occurred are sufficient to ensure that the education
system adequately reflects and caters for the needs and
aspirations of all members of our multicultural society is a
central question of the book.

11

Race

It hardly needs saying that the category, *race*, is a human
invention and that the designation of race is quite an arbitrary
matter. Because racial groups are distinguished by socially-
selected physical traits, definitions of race vary widely according
to the perceptions and the expectations of those doing the
defining. Some authorities,[2] for example, have chosen to
recognise as many as 30 races while others identify only three.
On several matters to do with the concept of race, however,
biological experts seem to be in general accord:[3]

1. Race as a taxonomic concept is of limited utility as a way
   of classifying human beings.
2. The genetic diversity *within* racial groups is probably as
   great as that *between* groups.
3. All men living today belong to a single species and are
   derived from a common stock.
4. The capacity to advance culturally is one shared by all
   members of *Homo sapiens* and is of far greater significance
   for the evolution of the species than biological or genetic
   evolution.

Clearly, the concept of race as used by biologists has little or
no relevance to our understanding of the social, economic and
political differences among men.[4] But, since the whole notion of
race and *racism* (see below) is bound up with such differences, it
is to social scientists rather than life scientists that we must turn
for further clarification.

Ethnicity

Ethnicity is a word that appears frequently in the literature on
race relations. Because it is often confused with race, it is
important that we look closely at the meaning of the term. To
begin with, ethnicity is not a euphemism for race, nor is it
sufficient in differentiating between the two terms to say simply
that 'whereas racial groups are distinguished by socially selected
physical traits, ethnic groups are distinguished by socially
selected *cultural* traits'.[5] The fact is that physical appearance can

also serve as one of the many possible criteria that feature in ethnic divisions.

Culture or Shared Customs

A more fruitful line of analysis,[6] which might be thought of as a political approach to ethnicity, argues that alliances based on ethnicity function as informal interest groups operating through *shared customs* or *culture.* For example, the various Polish communities in Great Britain are generally perceived as distinct ethnic-minority groups; they are not distinguished as racial minorities nor do they see themselves as such. Regular religious and social events serve to preserve a national and *cultural identity* among the Poles, marking them off as an ethnic group rather than an ethnic category such as the Welsh in England or the Scots in Canada. This leads us to a final point, that 'there is ethnicity and ethnicity';[7] — 'it cannot be measured, yet there is an obvious difference between the ethnic consciousness generated by a group of Latvians who meet periodically to dance in London and the ethnic allegiance manifested by Northern Ireland Catholics.'

Ethocentrism and Racism

Earlier we defined race in terms of the differentiating of certain groups by socially-selected physical characteristics. When, subsequently, distasteful distinctions are drawn between such groups by others, or by themselves, then we have *ethnocentrism.* Ethnocentrism is *in-group glorification*;[8] that is a process of invidious comparison in which the symbols and values of one group becomes objects of attachment and pride while the symbols and values of another become objects of disparagement and contempt. Ethnocentrism in the sense that we have chosen to define it is a form of minimal racism.[9] What then is maximum racism? We shall retain the term *racism* (that is maximum racism) to describe an 'ideology of racial domination and exploitation that (i) incorporates beliefs in a particular race's cultural and/or inherent biological inferiority and (ii) uses such beliefs to justify and to prescribe inferior or unequal treatment for the group'.[10] Racism manifests itself at three levels:

1. The continuing racial discrimination by numerous institutions of society represents the structured aspect of racial ideology. We refer to this as *institutional racism*.
2. The existence of informal group norms that serve to reinforce occasional collective acts of racial discrimination we refer to as *collective racism*.
3. The beliefs of a particular person about the cultural and/or biological inferiority of a minority group and his discriminatory behaviour towards members of that group we refer to as *individual racism*.

Prejudice

The many definitions of prejudice in the literature on race relations need not concern us here. Two broad areas of agreement about the nature of prejudice, however, are of immediate importance. First, prejudice is an intergroup phenomenon which is negatively oriented and is something undesirable.[11] Second, prejudice is an attitude and as such is learned, rather than innate, behaviour.

Several approaches to the study of prejudice can be identified; these form the substance of Chapter 2. For present purposes it is sufficient to note that sociologists account for racial discrimination and prejudice in terms of social-stratification theories. One explanation, for example, argues that race-relations problems arise when conquerors use those whom they subjugate to exploit newly-acquired lands and resources. In such circumstances a social structure begins to emerge in which different racial groups constitute separate classes, lower-status racial groups being debarred from almost all forms of social interaction with members of the dominant group.[12]

Social psychologists approach the problem of prejudice from a rather different perspective. They see prejudice as a matter of conforming to social norms. Here, explanations centre upon the basic ethnocentrism of every group, the argument being that 'in-group glorification' is functionally related to group formation, cohesion and intergroup competition.

Psychologists' explanations of prejudice are couched in terms of individual pathologies. One theory, for example, sees prejudice as rooted in the personality of the individual. Prejudice, it is argued, serves to satisfy the psychological needs of the person who manifests it. Thus, frustration-aggression theory proposes that the disappointment resulting from the blocking of some goal generates aggression. When that aggression cannot be directed towards the true source of the frustration it is displaced on to some relatively defenceless scapegoat.

As we shall see, no one theory provides an adequate explanation of racial prejudice.

The Background

Mention the word 'immigrant' to the man-in-the-street and it is fairly certain that he will call to mind a coloured person from Jamaica or the Indian subcontinent rather than a white person from Poland or the Republic of Ireland. That the average Englishman *does* respond in this way provides much of the impetus for writing this book.

It seems to us that it is of the utmost importance that we understand the reasons for the social and political responses that greeted the arrival of Afro-Caribbean and Asian migrants to this country, responses incidentally that are still commonly made both to them and to their first- and second-generation offspring. To grasp the problem we need to look at migration to Britain within the broader perspective of migratory movements occurring throughout Western Europe at the end of the Second World War.

Social scientists try to explain migration in several ways. One popular view[13] that we shall shortly illustrate employs a 'push-pull' model, the 'push' arising out of economic circumstances in the migrants' homelands, the 'pull' representing employment opportunities abroad.

Another explanation of migration argues that it can only be understood within the context of international capitalism.[14] In a Marxist analysis, labour migration is described as a 'form of development aid given by poor countries to rich countries'. The ruling classes of Europe, it is concluded, actively manipulate the concept of race in order to divide the working class.

For Rex,[15] it is the colonial background of migration that is the key to our understanding of present day racial discrimination and racial prejudice. New kinds of economy and new forms of social relations involving both *colonisers* and *colonised*, Rex asserts, were brought into being as a result of the conquest of poor, underdeveloped countries by technologically advanced nations during the nineteenth century. As the age of colonialism passed and the plantations, the peasant production, the mining operations of the former colonial territories ceased to be profitable, colonial people left their own countries in search of work in the rich urban-industrial societies of the metropolitan countries. But the history of the respective countries remains; the memory of military conquest or military action against an insurrection. In addition, Rex argues, there is always a disparity of technological levels between the colonising and colonised peoples which renders the latter dependent on the former. Inevitably the colonial nation is seen as defeated and educationally and technologically backward and this view becomes stabilised by the development of racist theories in the metropolitan countries themselves.

Migrant Workers in Europe[16]

One consequence of 30 million deaths during the Second World War was a chronic shortage of labour to help in the enormous task of rebuilding industry and commerce in war-ravaged Europe. Once hostilities were over, refugees and displaced persons were a ready-made source of labour. Britain, for example, welcomed some two hundred thousand European Volunteer Workers who made a substantial contribution to depleted manpower reserves.

As the economies of Western Europe recovered and expanded so did their manpower needs. Countries were forced to look further afield for workers. Britain turned for help to the West Indies, to India and to Pakistan. France looked to Tunisia and Algeria; Holland to Indonesia. Nations like West Germany, Switzerland and Luxembourg which had no former colonies began to recruit labour in the poorer, non-industrialised areas of Southern Europe. Greek, Turkish, Italian, Yugoslav, Spanish and Portuguese migrant workers flocked northwards to fill jobs in industry, construction and the service industries. In 1974, an EEC Report estimated that some fifteen million migrant workers and their families were living in Western Europe.

Typically, migrant workers in continental Europe have taken the worst jobs — those that cannot be filled from indigenous manpower reserves — the dirty jobs, the hard jobs, those with poor conditions, low rates of pay and high accident rates. For the most part, the same holds true for those immigrants who came to Britain from the former colonies in the West Indies and the Indian subcontinent.

Coloured Immigrants in Britain

The 1971 Census showed that there were just under three million immigrants living in Britain; *immigrants* denoting people who are now resident but were born overseas. Box 1.1. shows where those immigrants originated.

Box 1.1: Immigrants in Britain: The 1971 Census Data

The Republic of Ireland	703,235
Europe	677,295
India and Pakistan	461,930
The West Indies	304,070
Africa	164,205
Australia and New Zealand	78,155
Other countries	594,250

Source: Adapted from 1971 Censuses of Population (HMSO).

The category 'Other countries' in Box 1.1 refers to places such as Cyprus, Hong Kong and Malta. Whilst accounts[17] of the lives of immigrants from these countries contain important and valuable insights, from hereon we focus attention on newcomers to Britain who originate from the New Commonwealth[18] and Pakistan (NCWP). The vast majority of these immigrants are *coloured*, the term we shall now employ to describe people of Afro-Caribbean and Asian descent. In brief, we are solely concerned with West Indians, Indians and Pakistanis who began arriving in Britain from 1951, 1955 and 1957 respectively.

Although there have been coloured people living in Britain for many years, particularly in and around major seaports like

Liverpool, Bristol and Cardiff, the total number of people was always insignificant, that is until the passing of the McCarren-Walter Act in 1952 by the United States of America, the intention of which was to restrict immigration from the Caribbean. West Indians, particularly Jamaicans,[19] had for a long time moved from their islands in order to improve their economic situation. One hundred thousand Jamaicans, for example, went to Panama in 1905 to help build the canal; thousands went to Cuba in the early 1920s during the sugar boom; and many more were recruited to work in the United States of America during the Second World War. In 1952, however, the United States passed the McCarren-Walter Act once more[20] restricting immigration to West Indians. In consequence, Britain became the favoured destination and the rapid increase in immigration from the West Indies dates from that time.

Home Office[21] estimates show that net Commonwealth (ie NCWP) immigration numbers were 42,700 in 1955, 46,830 in 1956 and 42,400 in 1957, the majority of immigrants coming from the West Indies. Emigration to Britain followed what is termed 'chain migration',[22] that is the man in the family came first followed by his wife and children, although children were often left with grandparents or other relatives until funds were saved to cover the costs of their journey. Typically, immigrant labour from the West Indies filled the low-paid, physically-arduous jobs whose anti-social hours were unattractive to indigenous 'British' workers.

During the late '50s such concern was expressed over the growing number of coloured immigrants entering Britain and settling in particular metropolitan areas that following the 1958 racial disturbances in London and Nottingham there was considerable pressure to reduce the overall intake of Caribbean immigrants to Britain. The net effect of all this was to stimulate immigration, would-be immigrants seeking to beat restrictions that might be imposed through Parliamentary legislation.

There followed an unprecedented increase in the annual rate of immigration. Figures for NCWP immigrants rose to 136,400 in 1961, the number swelled by people from the Asian[23] sub-continent who, like West Indians, feared the impending imposition of restrictive controls.

Control came under the provisions of the 1962 Commonwealth Immigration Act. Up until 1962 it had been the case that aliens

were subject to immigration control whilst citizens of the
Commonwealth countries and of the United Kingdom and
colonies had the right of free entry into Britain. From 1962 all
Commonwealth citizens seeking to work and settle in Britain
were required to obtain work vouchers, the stated intention being
to ensure that would-be immigrants had skills that were in
current demand. Successive government acts in the 1960s resulted
in a sharp decline in the net inflow of NCWP immigrants.

Since 1973, when the 1971 Immigration Act came into operation, few NCWP groups have been allowed entry. Those entitled
to enter and settle include:[24]

1. Commonwealth citizens whose parents or grandparents
   were born in Britain. These people are called *patrials* and
   come mainly from countries such as Canada and Australia.
   Non-patrials is the term used to denote Commonwealth
   citizens without a parent or grandparent born in Britain.
   Non-patrials are subject to strict immigration control.
2. Wives, husbands, fiance(e)s, children under 18 years of age
   and certain other dependants of Commonwealth citizens
   who are already settled in Britain.
3. Persons who have United Kingdom passports and who have
   no other citizenship. This group is largely composed of
   Asians from East Africa.

In summary, under the 1971 Immigration Act, non-patrial
Commonwealth citizens, usually from the West Indies and the
Asian subcontinent, are subject to strict immigration control in
similar fashion to aliens.

A complex and controversial British Nationality Act passed
early in 1981 replaced the British Nationality Act 1948 by
creating three new categories of citizenship. The three new
categories defined in the Act are (1) British Citizenship,
(2) Citizenship of the British Dependent Territories and
(3) British Overseas Citizenship. Only British citizens would have
the right to live in Britain.

Category 1 (British Citizenship) is acquired by those born in
the United Kingdom to a British citizen or to a person settled in
the UK. People born here to non-British parents who were in the
United Kingdom only temporarily do not necessarily have
citizenship, but they will still be allowed to register as British

citizens if either parent later becomes a citizen or settles in Britain, or if the child has spent the first ten years of its life in the country. Children born abroad to British citizens will not automatically acquire British Citizenship, particularly where the parents themselves are British citizens by descent rather than by birth. In brief, the general principle of the Act is that a child born abroad will be a British citizen by descent if either the father or mother was born or adopted in Britain or acquired citizenship by registration or naturalisation.

Category 2 (Citizenship of British Dependent Territories) and *Category 3* (British Overseas Citizenship), that is to say British subjects and British protected persons settled in Britain will be entitled to be registered as citizens after five years' residence. Other Commonwealth citizens and foreign nationals will be able to apply for naturalisation after five years' residence, but this is not a right, it should be noted; rather, it rests on the discretion of the Home Secretary.

The new Act also changes the law which gives the wife of a citizen of Britain and colonies the right to be registered as a citizen herself but no corresponding right in the case of a foreign husband who marries a British woman. Henceforth, the husband or wife of a British citizen will have to apply for naturalisation, but they will be able to do so after three, rather than five, years of residence.

Category 2 (Citizenship of British Dependent Territories) covers some three million people living in Britain's remaining colonies. They will have the right to enter and live in their own territories but not in Britain. Where they are admitted to Britain on a temporary basis and allowed to stay for five years, they will then be entitled to register as British citizens.

Category 3 (British Overseas Citizenship) applies to any present citizen of Britain and its colonies who does not become either a British citizen or a citizen of British Dependent Territories. The majority of persons falling into this category are those of Chinese origin living in Malaysia who at the time of Malaya's independence opted to remain British. The 200,000 East African Asians waiting to enter Britain under the voucher system are also included here.

The British Nationality Act (1981) has already provoked considerable controversy, some decrying its racialist overtones, others its nightmarish complexity to administer. Retraining of

Home Office staff and extensive administrative changes will be
required to cope with the provisions of the new Act, which is
unlikely to be in force before January 1983.

Meanwhile, at the time of writing, confusion about the
implications of the Act has led to a deluge of applications for
registration and naturalisation before the Act becomes law. In
the first five months of 1981, applications increased to 37,000 as
compared with 22,000 for the same period in 1980. In the last
few months of 1981, Home Office staff were reported to be
faced with a backlog of some 60,000 cases.

The Present Position

The most up-to-date statistics on Britain's colour population are
contained in a publication of the Runnymede Trust.[25] Box 1.2
shows the estimated population of NCWP ethnic origin in
Britain to the year 1978.

Box 1.2: NCWP Coloured Population in Britain

Mid year	Estimated numbers	Percentage of population in Britain
1972	1,453,000	2.7
1973	1,547,000	2.8
1974	1,615,000	3.0
1975	1,691,000	3.1
1976	1,771,000	3.3
1977	1,846,000	3.4
1978	1,921,000	3.5

Source: Adapted from Runnymede Trust.[26]

The demographic characteristics of the above population are as
follows:[27]

1. *Age Structure*
   Compared with the total population of Britain the coloured
   population is very young, a consequence of the youthful-
   ness of past immigrants.
2. *Sex Ratios*
   Compared with the total population of Britain (where there
   are roughly equal numbers of males and females) there are

more males than females in the coloured population, a
consequence of past immigration patterns.

3. *Birthrates*

The overall pattern of declining birthrates in Britain (i.e.
until 1977) is also reflected in the coloured population,
where the rate of decline is greater for this group than for
the total population of England and Wales. Within the
coloured population, the birthrate among those of West
Indian origin has shown a particularly steep decline.

4. *Deathrates*

Very few deaths occur, relatively speaking, among the
coloured population. Compared with a deathrate of about
twelve per thousand for Britain as a whole in 1978, the
deathrate for persons born in the NCWP was about six per
thousand, a consequence of the youthful age structure of
the NCWP-born population.

We turn now to present brief portrayals of the backgrounds of
members of Britain's coloured population.[28]

The West Indians

West Indians[29] constitute the largest of the coloured immigrant
groups in Great Britain. The 1971 Census estimated that the
number of West Indian-born people in Britain was just over 1
per cent of the population, a proportion that remained stable
over recent years, although currently the number of West Indian
born people leaving Britain exceeds the number of those
entering. Box 1.3 shows the islands of the Antillean archipelago
which, together with British Honduras in North America and
Guyana in South America, comprise the British Caribbean,
commonly referred to as the West Indies.

'Push-pull' models have been used to explain West Indian
migrations, some observers stressing the primacy of 'push'
factors,[30] others the potency of 'pulls'.[31] Probably both push and
pull forces best account for West Indian emigration to Britain;
Foner's[32] research on Jamaicans, for example, pointing to a
combination of 'pushes' — overpopulation, lack of jobs and
patterns of land distribution — and 'pulls' — better jobs in post-
war Britain and better educational opportunities for children.

Box 1.3: West Indians in Britain: The Major Islands of British Caribbean

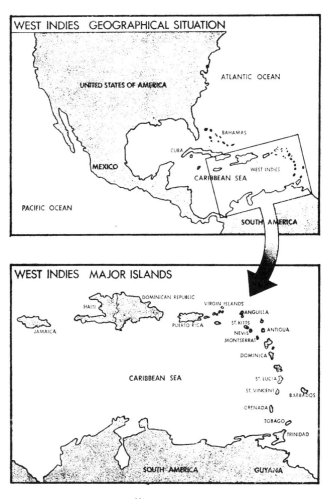

Source: Adapted from Hill.[33]

In the early stages of migration to Britain, skilled and semi-skilled workers constituted the majority of those leaving the West Indies. Most of these people took up jobs in transport and in the building industries, their wives or common-law wives finding employment in service and catering industries or in hospital work.

It might be supposed that because West Indians share our language, our faith and significant aspects of our culture, they would have experienced less difficulty in coming to terms with British society than perhaps Indian or Pakistani immigrants. For a variety of reasons this has not been the case. One reason in particular is pre-eminent — skin colour.

'The black immigrant', notes Lewis,[34] '[came] to feel less like a West Indian in English society and more like a black man in a white society'. For most West Indian migrants, Foner[35] observes, coming to England was a shock, for whatever their shade of skin colour or their achievements, they tended to be viewed by most English people as lower class and inferior.

Colour has long been associated with status in the West Indies. The common experience of colonialism, slavery and the plantation system are identified as fundamental elements in Creole culture.[36] *Creole* refers to 'things, habits and ideas native to the West Indies'. It describes a social system that emerged in the West Indies following the emancipation of slaves, a system that was rooted in the political and economic dominance of Great Britain. The strong adherence to European culture and a white ruling class ensured that the European element of Creole culture became the most highly valued. The 'white bias' that for the most part still continues to characterise Caribbean society accounted to a considerable extent for immigrants' orientation towards British society and their aspirations, on arrival, to be part of it. Bagley[37] describes a rigid stratification system in Jamaica which motivated many black rural Jamaicans to come to Britain to escape from a society in which white, oriental and fair people had power and privilege. What they experienced, however, Foner[38] observes was 'systematic exploitation at every level in British society — in employment, housing, education, and the social services'.

Later in the book, when we come to look at coloured pupils' self identities and achievement, we discuss several pieces of research that see the power of the European 'model' and European 'ways' as instrumental in West Indian psychology in causing a rejection of all that is West Indian. Such self-rejection, it is suggested, produces low feelings of self worth which in turn affect subsequent attitudes and behaviour. That is one side of the coin. An alternative point of view[39] argues that the unequal treatment that West Indians have experienced as a result of their skin colour has led many to reject the 'inferiority' of blackness. Furthermore, it is because second generation West Indians, born and bred in Britain, are rejected by white society and are bitter and frustrated by the racial prejudice and discrimination they experience that they look with pride to their blackness as the basis for identification with fellow blacks.

The Indians

The Indians, who constitute the second largest coloured minority group in Britain, can be divided into two separate occupational groupings: professionals such as doctors, teachers, businessmen, etc., who originate from all parts of India and are distributed all over the United Kingdom; and semi-skilled or unskilled workers, originating largely from the rural Punjab or from Gujarat (see Box 1.4) and now located in a number of our major cities. Members of this latter Indian group may speak Punjabi, Gujurati, Tamil or other Indian languages and practise Hinduism

Box 1.4: Indians in Britain: Areas of Major Emigration to the United Kingdom

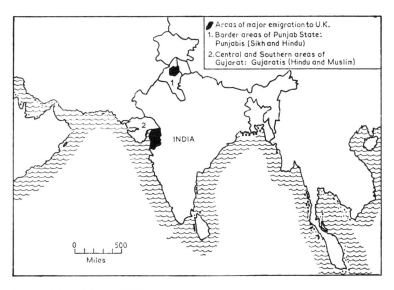

Source: Adapted from Hill.[40]

or Sikhism, with a minority following the teachings of Islam or of Christianity.

Like Asians who came to Britain in the late 1950s from Pakistan and what is now Bangladesh, Indian immigrants were also prepared to undertake the tedious, unpleasant jobs that indigenous white workers were unwilling to do. Their pattern of settlement in this country has been described[41] as consisting of several distinct phases of development, one of which was the characteristic institution of the *all-male household* set up shortly after arrival in Britain. The all-male household served several important functions. It enabled newcomers to minimise living expenses and maximise savings. Savings went to support family and kin back to India and to pay off accumulated debts there (often the reason for emigration). Later, those savings also enabled many immigrants to invest in decaying Victorian and Edwardian terraced houses so that they too could increase their capital by eliminating rent payments and accumulating additional income from new arrivals. Those who bought houses, the Ballards note,[42] did not usually see themselves as putting down roots in Britain. Rather, their intention was to make a temporary investment that could be sold whenever necessary in order to buy land back in their villages in India.

The decision to bring wives and children over to Britain marked the next stage in the immigrant's pattern of settlement. Indian family structure is of the extended type and is founded on stable conjugal unions. Despite the lengthy separation of husbands and wives, the latter, who remained in the migrants' home villages, were in no sense abandoned; they were part of the extended household and under the care of a father or a brother of the absent husband. Hill[43] explains that compared with the average British family, the Indian family is larger and more complex. The individual Indian perceives himself surrounded not by concentric circles containing wives and children, close friends and acquaintances but by his immediate family (which includes all his brothers and sisters as well as his own children), then by kin, including distant relatives, then by members of his village and finally by his linguistic group. Because most Indians are accustomed to living surrounded by their kinsmen, it is understandable that they should try to recreate similar environments in Britain by setting up small communities in the style of the old country.

The strength of the Indian extended family network and its socialising effects is central to an account[44] of the ability of second-generation Asians to maintain and adapt traditional 'Indian' values despite external pressures to the contrary. Ballard concludes that young Asians, like most adolescents, are adept at making compromises enabling them to deal with two parallel worlds. Let one of Ballard's interviewees, a pharmacology student, speak for himself.

> I've learned to behave as two different people. I'm quite another person when I'm away from home with English people than when I'm here with my family and my Punjabi friends. I'm so used to switching over that I don't even notice.

We take up the important question of the self-identities of pupils from coloured minority groups in Chapter 4.

The Pakistanis

Most Pakistani immigrants to Britain come from small village communities in the northern part of Pakistan or from Bangladesh, both of these areas being characterised by similar systems of agrarian land tenure and family organisation. The great majority of immigrants have had little or no formal education. Like the larger Indian immigrant group, the Pakistanis are found in unskilled and semi-skilled occupations in Britain. Pakistanis, according to Khan,[45] are the most encapsulated and home-orientated of Asian migrants in Britain. Men wear Western dress but the women retain their traditional costumes. Sexual segregation is strictly enforced, women rarely being allowed out to work. Pakistanis are Moslem by religion and religious observances are strictly adhered to. The majority of Pakistanis in Britain come from Mirpur, a District of Azad Kashmir, Campbellpur, a District of Punjab Province, other Districts of Punjab Province and the North-west Frontier Province (see Box 1.5). All except the last category speak some form of Punjabi and are Punjabi in culture. A few immigrants in Britain from villages in the North-west Frontier Province are Pathans who speak Pushto. Educated villagers and people from the cities speak Urdu, the national language.[47]

Box 1.5: Pakistanis in Britain: Areas of Major Emigration to the United Kingdom

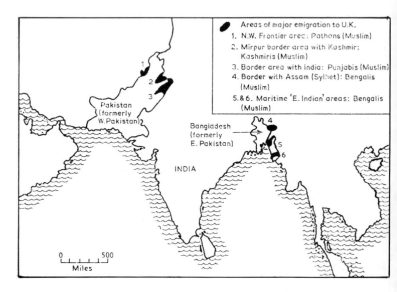

Source: Adapted from Hill.[46]

Khan's account of the Pakistanis in Bradford shows how the village-kin network, an extension of that in the homeland, serves to segment this group of immigrants from the indigenous population. Men who work long hours in the textile mills on all-Pakistani night shifts have little time for relaxation and what time is available is spent with friends and kinsfolk. Moreover, the nature of the migration process itself tends to reinforce the encapsulation of the group:

> Migrants came to join friends or relatives, they depended on their support and this directed them into certain occupations. The natural tendency to trust and interact only with people of one's own village-kin network . . . has increased in Britain as numbers have increased . . . Encapsulated in their own world, the skills required for communication and participation could not be acquired so easily and mutually rigid views developed to hinder (or justify) the segregation between the migrants and the majority society.

To the extent that Pakistani families maintain close contact and allegiance to the extended family and kin group in the homeland and plan to return to Pakistan at some time in the future, their encapsulation from the indigenous population is further strengthened.

Khan identifies sources of stress and anxiety arising out of the transition from close face-to-face relationships in the village communities of Pakistan to the impersonality and large scale of city life in England where lack of facility in language and lack of knowledge of mannerisms and customs hinder communication and increase the likelihood of misunderstanding. The strict nature, regularity and uniformity of the factory shift-work system bears no relation to the previous work experience of most Pakistani males. Moreover, Khan observes, this new type of economic activity indirectly causes Pakistani women to be subject to a stricter form of *purdah* than they experienced in home villages, the men being away from the household unit for long periods of time and the unit itself transposed from a village to an urban environment. As a social anthropologist Khan shows that although the principles regulating the daily routine of Pakistani immigrants have been modified and altered in significant ways, they remain firmly rooted in the main institutions of village life and have served to protect this particular minority group for longer than other immigrant communities from the effects of blatant prejudice and discrimination.

What of the children of the Pakistani immigrants who were born in Britain and are now in early adulthood? How does this second generation cope? In a perceptive paper, the Ballards[48] warn us against an oversimplified view of increasingly irresolvable conflicts between children and their parents arising out of the incompatibility of Asian and Western cultures and the discontinuities and contradictions in the behaviour and aspirations of the two generations. The Ballards' study shows the 'cultural conflict' viewpoint to be inaccurate and, incidentally, a good example of ethnocentrism in its implicit assumption that young Asians would like to 'be like us' if their parents would only let them! We take up this important issue in Chapter 4 where we discuss the self-identities, the feelings and the aspirations of coloured pupils as revealed in the words of the children themselves.

Notes

1. We adopt the term *multicultural* throughout the text in light of our remarks about *race, ethnicity* and *culture* on pages 12 and 13.

2. W.T. Keeton (1980) *Biological Science*, London: W.W. Norton and Company.

3. UNESCO, Paris (1950, 1951, 1964, 1967) *Statements on Race and Race Prejudice* quoted in J. Rex (1970), *Race Relations in Sociological Theory*, London: Weidenfeld and Nicolson.

4. J. Rex (1970) *Race Relations in Sociological Theory*, London: Weidenfeld and Nicolson.

5. W. J. Wilson (1973) *Power, Racism and Privilege*, New York: The Free Press.

6. J. L. Watson (ed.) (1977) *Between Two Cultures*, Oxford: Basil Blackwell.

7. A. Cohen (ed.) (1974) *Urban Ethnicity*, London: Tavistock Publications.

8. D. L. Noel (1972) 'Slavery and the Rise of Racism' in D. L. Noel (ed.), *The Origins of American Slavery and Racism*, Columbus, Ohio: Merrill.

9. R. Schermerhorn (1970) *Comparative Ethnic Relations: A Framework For Theory and Research*, New York: Random House.

10. Rex, *Race Relations*.

11. G. K. Verma and C. Bagley (1975) *Race and Education Across Cultures*, London: Heinemann.

12. P. Cohen (1976) 'Race Relations as a Sociological Issue' in G. Bowker and J. Carrier (eds) *Race and Ethnic Relations: Sociological Readings*, London: Hutchinson.

13. D. H. Wrong (1961) *Population and Society*, New York: Random House.

14. S. Castles and G. Kosack (1973) *Immigrant Workers and Class Structure*, London: OUP for the Institute of Race Relations.

15. J. Rex (1973) *Race, Colonialism and the City*, London: Routledge and Kegan Paul.

16. Our account draws on the pamphlet *Our People* produced for the Thames TV series (January 1979) giving an overview of multicultural Britain.

17. There are a number of studies of these immigrant groups in Britain to choose from: G. Dench (1975) *Maltese in London: A Case Study in the Erosion of Ethnic Consciousness*, London: Routledge and Kegan Paul; Ng Kwee-choo (1968) *The Chinese in London*, London: Oxford University Press for the Institute of Race Relations; S. Paine (1974) *Exporting Workers: The Turkish Case*, London: Cambridge University Press; E. Krausz (1971) *Ethnic Minorities in Britain*, London: MacGibbon and Kee; S. Patterson (1964) 'Polish London' in R. Glass and J. Westergaard (eds), *London: Aspects of Change*, London: MacGibbon and Kee.

18. *New Commonwealth* refers to those former British colonies that have attained independence and joined the Commonwealth since 1945. It does not include the Old Commonwealth — Canada, Australia and New Zealand. We include Pakistan although it left the Commonwealth in 1973. Until 1972 Pakistan consisted of two widely-separated parts of the Indian sub-continent. What was West Pakistan is now the Republic of Pakistan and what was East Pakistan is now Bangladesh. For purposes of exposition, we consider Pakistan and Bangladesh together, referring to immigrants from these countries as Pakistanis.

19. N. Foner (1977) 'The Jamaicans: Cultural and Social Change among Migrants in Britain' in Watson, *Between Two Cultures*.

20. Immigration restrictions were imposed on West Indians in 1924 by the United States. Since the McCarren-Walter Act of 1952, new immigration laws passed in 1965 have permitted emigration to the United States from the West

Indies, particularly for more highly-skilled and professional men and women.

21. We are indebted to K. Thomas (1980) for the immigration statistics: K. Thomas (1980) 'A Study of Stereotypes, Peer Group Friendship Patterns and Attitudes in a Multiracial School', unpublished PhD dissertation, University of Nottingham.

22. Foner, 'The Jamaicans'.

23. Thomas, in 'A Study of Stereotypes', points out that as late as 1959, the net combined inflow from India and Pakistan was estimated to have been as low as 3,800.

24. Thames TV series, *Our People.*

25. The Runnymede Trust and the Radical Statistics Race Group (1980) *Britain's Black Population*, London: Heinemann Educational Books.

26. Ibid.

27. Ibid.

28. Our brief portrayal of the backgrounds of Caribbean and Asia immigrants draws on the work of D. Hill (1976) *Teaching in Multiracial Schools*, London: Methuen; E. de Lobo (1978) *Children of Immigrants To Britain*, London: Hodder and Stoughton; C. Bagley (1979) 'A Comparative Perspective on the Education of Black Children in Britain', *Comparative Education,* **15** (1), 63–81; Foner, 'The Jamaicans'; V.S. Khan (1977) 'The Pakistanis: Mirpuri Villagers at Home and in Bradford' in Watson, *Between Two Cultures*; V. S. Khan (1979) 'Miripuris in Bradford' in V. S. Khan (ed.), *Minority Families in Britain*, London: The Macmillan Press.

29. Whilst we are aware of the richness and variety in the customs, values and social organisation of the many separate societies that go to make up the West Indies, purely for purposes of exposition we talk of West Indian immigrants as a homogeneous group.

30. D. Lawrence (1974) *Black Migrants: White Natives*, Cambridge: Cambridge University Press.

31. C. Peach (1968) *West Indian Migrants to Britain*, London: Oxford University Press.

32. Foner, 'The Jamaicans'.

33. Hill, *Teaching in Multiracial Schools.*

34. G. Lewis (1971) 'An introductory note to the study of Race Relations in Great Britain', *Caribbean Studies,* **11**, 5–29.

35. Foner, 'The Jamaicans'.

36. Ibid.

37. Bagley, 'The education of Black Children in Britain'.

38. Foner, 'The Jamaicans'.

39. Ibid.

40. Hill, *Teaching in Multiracial Schools.*

41. R. Ballard and C. Ballard (1977) 'The Sikhs: The Development of South Asian Settlements in Britain' in Watson, *Between Two Cultures.*

42. Ibid.

43. Hill, *Teaching in Multiracial Schools.*

44. C. Ballard (1979 Conflict, Continuity and Change: Second Generation Asians' in V.S. Khan (ed.), *Minority Families in Britain*, London: The Macmillan Press.

45. Khan, 'The Pakistanis'; Khan, 'Mipuris in Bradford'.

46. Hill, *Teaching in Multiracial Schools.*

47. Khan, 'The Pakistanis'; Khan, 'Mipuris in Bradford'.

48. Ballard and Ballard, 'The Sikhs'.

2 THE ORIGINS OF PREJUDICE

Introduction

Prejudice means, literally, *judgement in advance*. In the context of race relations, prejudice has been described as a negative attitude towards some group of people which is applied to all members of that group in the absence of, or in the face of, evidence to the contrary.

Definitions couched in these terms typically emanate from psychologists endeavouring to explain why certain individuals evince negative attitudes and hostility towards members of certain groups. Sociologists, as we shall see, are generally less concerned with individual pathologies. They focus upon structural, demographic and economic factors that underpin minority group/majority group relations. In this way they try to explain social interaction in terms of underlying social processes.

We begin our account of the origins of prejudice with the contribution of psychologists. They advance several explanations of the phenomenon, one of which we have already identified as frustration-aggression theory (page 15). Closely related to a *frustration-aggression* interpretation of prejudice is the idea of *defence mechanisms* by which prejudiced individuals are said to shield themselves from their own anxieties and tensions by accusing minority groups of motives that they themselves possess. Allied to defence-mechanism theory is the notion of the *authoritarian personality*, an explanation that emphasises basic personality differences between highly-prejudiced and less-prejudiced people. Finally, an important tradition in the psychological study of prejudice is research into stereotyping.

We discuss each of these psychological approaches in turn before examining the contributions of social psychologists and sociologists to our understanding of discrimination and prejudice.

Psychological Explanations of Prejudice

Frustration-aggression Theory

As the name implies, this explanation proposes that frustration may lead to aggression, which in turn may manifest itself in a

32

variety of ways including hostility towards ethnic minority groups. Thus, racial prejudice has been interpreted as displaced aggression resulting from the frustration of unemployment and unstable economic circumstances. Dollard and his associates,[1] for example, argue that Negro lynchings in America earlier in the century were not the result of frustration with blacks as blacks. Rather, Negroes were made *scapegoats*, innocent victims of displaced aggression on the part of whites who were frustrated by financial disasters in the cotton economy of the Southern States.

Nearer home, Verma and Bagley's[2] study of nine hundred black and white adolescents in British secondary schools identified highly-prejudiced pupils in terms of such personality characteristics as emotional instability, tension, alienation from school and a generally jaundiced view of life. According to the researchers:

These students perhaps express their resentment against various ethnic targets. It could be that [their personality difficulties] lead to alienation from a wide range of moral and social institutions in society and are concomitant with feelings of unworthiness which are perhaps alleviated by the scapegoating of available ethnic targets.

Support for the 'scapegoating' theory of racial prejudice is also claimed from laboratory-type studies such as the one conducted by Wilson[3] with some 90 or so university students roughly equally divided by sex. The researcher administered a well-known projective test which purports to measure different types of aggression along with a scale for identifying various dimensions of social attitudes such as *conservatism, puritanism, punitiveness, ethnocentrism* and so on. Some interesting relationships emerged between social attitudes and projective aggression, one of which is of particular relevance to the present discussion. *Racial prejudice* was significantly associated with *ego-defensiveness*, a finding which was interpreted as support for a scapegoat explanation of prejudice in that the expression of hostility towards foreigners and ethnic minorities is said to function as a means of preserving self-respect, an interpretation, one should note, that might just as easily arise from our account of the role of defence mechanisms which follows shortly.

Frustration-aggression theory has also been used to explain the supposed relationship between *status-inconsistency* and racial prejudice. The term status-inconsistency refers to 'the extent to which an individual's rank positions on given status hierarchies are at a comparable level' — a somewhat abstruse definition which can be more simply explained as follows. If status-inconsistency *is* related to racial prejudice then it might be predicted that a well-educated white person who is poorly paid and engaged in a low status occupation will exhibit racial prejudice. 'Inconsistency' in this particular person's various statuses is said to arise because he is neither high on all of them nor low on all of them. 'Consistency', it is argued, is present when the statuses *white, good education, white-collar occupation* and *high income* are present or when *black, poor education, blue-collar occupation* and *low income* occur together.

A test of the status-inconsistency and racial-prejudice hypothesis was undertaken in five English boroughs by Bagley[4] who claims support for the proposed relationship. Individuals who exhibit status-inconsistency, he says, are:

> People who believe that they should achieve some status in society but are prevented from doing so by certain structural factors . . . [In consequence] they may be especially prejudiced on this account. Placing ethnic minorities below themselves may be a way of enhancing status for such individuals.

Various studies, according to Bagley and Verma,[5] show that feelings of relative deprivation are important in influencing racial attitudes: subjectively-deprived individuals are likely to be more prejudiced than others.

The frustration-aggression explanation of prejudice has been criticised on several grounds.[6] First, it is too broad in scope in that many situations may be defined as frustrating by those involved and those situations may then be invoked to account for prejudiced attitudes. In other words, the perception of frustration may be a *product* of prejudice rather than a *cause* of it. Second, the frustration-aggression interpretation is often a *post hoc* explanation which is impossible to verify after the event. Third, it is difficult to generalise from the attitudes that arise from frustrating experiences to the actual expression of aggressive behaviour since the effects of frustration are frequently diverted into alternative channels. In a word, frustration-aggression is too much of a 'catch-all' explanation of prejudice.

Defence Mechanisms

In our introduction to the chapter we said that the idea of defence mechanisms is closely related to frustration-aggression and to the notion of the authoritarian personality (which we discuss shortly). All three explanations of prejudice draw upon assumptions about the role of the *unconscious* in everyday behaviour, none perhaps more directly than the concept of defence mechanisms as proposed by that most famous of all psychologists, Sigmund Freud.

Box 2.1 summarises some basic principles of Freud's theory of the mind. They help us to grasp the role of defence mechanisms in relation to prejudice.

Box 2.1: Freud's Theory of Mind

The mind is divided into three parts. The *id*, unconscious, is the repository of basic drives, sex and aggression, and what has been repressed into it. The id is the source of mental energy, demanding immediate expression. This, however, in modern society cannot be permitted. The id is controlled therefore by two other mental provinces, namely the *ego*, the repository of our conscious life and moral values (these being those of our parents as seen at about the age of five when the *super-ego* develops).

Mental health depends upon the correct balance of these three systems: too much control and the individual leads a narrow inexpressive life. If the *super-ego* is too strong we feel guiltridden and anxious, yet if there is too little control we become psychopathic criminals. The *ego* maintains control by the use of mechanisms of defence which satisfy the conflicting demands of *id* and *super-ego* and which are unconscious. The system of defences we use profoundly affects our behaviour.

Successful defences, (sublimation) allow expression of the instinctual, forbidden *id* drive. Unsuccessful defences prevent its expression. But since an instinctually-barred expression still demands outlet, unsuccessful defences are used over and over again. This is the basis of the tension and weariness of neurotic illness.

Source: Adapted from Kline.[7]

Freud describes several ego-defence mechanisms — *repression, denial, projection, reaction-formation, regression, isolation* and *undoing*. Successful defence mechanisms, that is sublimations, allow good ego-control; unsuccessful ones, he contends, produce anxiety and conflict.

In psycho-analytical terms, prejudice may be seen as an

unsuccessful defence mechanism, a *projection* on to others of what is wrong in the person as a way of denying inner conflict. But why inner conflict in the first place, the reader may well ask?

In a cogently-argued case for psycho-analytical approach to the understanding of racial prejudice, Jahoda[8] has suggested one possible source of such inner conflict. Prejudice, Jahoda says, is a negative judgement on the part of a person or a group of persons made on the basis of inadequate reality testing. Reality testing, she contends, demands not only contact with other groups but also reliance on the opinions of authoritative others. And herein lies the difficulty. Take the case of the child nurtured and raised by prejudiced parents.[9] The young child trusts them and accepts the authority of their beliefs on many issues, including the merits of various ethnic minorities. For this particular child, prejudice is 'natural' because from the very outset of his socialisation he has been assured that this is so. For him, prejudice has deep-seated, unconscious roots psycho-logically-laden with strong feelings for the agents of socialisation (love, hate, admiration, disdain, etc.). It is these feelings, at various levels of consciousness, that accompany the growing child into adulthood. Trying to eradicate prejudice by rational means (information, reasoned argument, etc.) is likely to fail in cases like this for such people distort reality-testing procedures and are unable to perceive situations accurately which might serve to reduce their prejudice. For them, prejudice becomes self-confirming.

So much for a psycho-analytical account of *projection* and *prejudice*. What are the objections to Freudian explanations such as this? Apart from more obvious questions to do with the data themselves, their representativeness and the methods used in their analysis, there are more fundamental problems that bear upon the ill-defined terms in which Freudian theory is propounded and, most importantly, the inability of falsifying Freudian theory. This last point is illustrated as follows:[10]

A theory is held to be scientific if it is capable of being falsified, that is, if it can be put to some crucial test which might prove it wrong. But Freudian theory undertakes to explain completely opposing facts: if a patient loves his mother it is because of his Oedipus complex; if he hates her, it is a reaction-formation to his Oedipus complex; if he is indifferent to her, he has repressed his Oedipal feelings.

Readers who find this final critique somewhat impartial may care to follow the spirited defence of Freud's theory in the Open University article itself.[11]

The Authoritarian Personality

The idea that highly-prejudiced people have different personalities to less-prejudiced individuals arose directly out of concern over the Nazi persecution of Jews. In their attempts to identify persons predisposed towards Hitler-type fascism, psychologists proposed that basic tendencies towards anti-semitism, ethnocentrism and politico-economic conservatism were linked to a more fundamental personality disposition which they termed *authoritarianism*. This they determined to measure directly with a Fascism (F) Scale. A seminal book, *The Authoritarian Personality*,[12] was the outcome of their reseach.

The authoritarian personality, the research suggests, is characterised by toughmindedness, rigid adherence to authority and conventional values, exaggerated concern with sexuality and a strong hostility towards those who infringe sexual mores. We illustrate these propensities with selected items from the California F-scale (see Box 2.2), the instrument used by Adorno and his co-workers in their research.

Box 2.2: Selected Items from the California F-scale

What youth needs most is strict discipline, rugged determination and the will to work and fight for family and country.

Obedience and respect for authority are the most important virtues that children should learn.

The wild sex life of the old Greeks and Romans was tame compared to some of the goings-on in this country even in places where people might least expect it.

Sex crimes such as rape and attacks on children deserve more than mere imprisonment; such criminals ought to be publicly whipped or worse.

Source: Adapted from Adorno *et al.*[13]

Adorno and his colleagues draw upon psycho-analytical theory to explain the origins and dynamics of the authoritarian personality. Authoritarians, they say, acquire their personal dispositions largely as a result of the ways they are treated by their parents. Early in childhood they learn a style of behaviour which involves both rigid obedience to parental authority and idealisation of parental demands for perfection. These demands are systematically reinforced by punishment for failure or non-compliance. Children reared under such a regime emerge as obsessive, guilt-ridden, anxious adults, sexually inhibited, acquiescent to authority, low in their tolerance of ambiguity and high in their propensity for imposing authority upon those subordinate to themselves.

Adorno and his co-workers explain the association of authoritarianism and racial prejudice as follows. The authoritarian has a weak ego controlled by a strict super-ego. Because of the weak ego's reluctance to accept responsibility for feelings and actions, the hostility that has been generated towards overdemanding parents during childhood is now displaced on to defenceless minorities such as Jews. Both the strong super-ego and the weak ego are blamed for the punitiveness and toughmindedness that typify the authoritarian personality.

Despite the considerable criticism levelled at the Adorno team's interpretation of their findings, *The Authoritarian Personality* has generated a spate of studies into personal correlates of prejudice and a crop of new concepts has emerged (conservatism, dogmatism, toughmindedness, Machiavellianism) that seem to share a good deal in common.

The problem with Freudian interpretations of authoritarianism such as Adorno and his co-workers' is that they suffer from the theoretical and conceptual weaknesses to which reference has already been made (page 36). Eysenck[14] voices a common criticism to the effect that an *a priori* assumption of a relationship between attitudes and personality prevents a valid, empirical exploration of the concept. Instead, he proposes a *social-learning theory* of prejudice which hinges upon his well-known two-factor theory of personality (extraversion-introversion; neuroticism-stability) and his contention that extraverts (social, impulsive individuals) are more resistant to socialisation than introverts (quiet, reflective persons).

Using a conservatism scale,[15] which is claimed to be an adequate measure of the dimensions of authoritarianism tapped by Adorno and his co-workers' F-Scale, the social-learning theory of prejudice has been explored by Bagley and his associates[16] with students in colleges of education and polytechnics. They hypothesised as follows:

1. The dominant value system in Britain is that of conventional observance of religious, moralistic and racialist-punitive values.
2. Extraverts socialise less well than introverts.
3. Thus, extraverts will tend to have internalised to a lesser degree the dominant value system and will therefore be less conservative and racialist than introverts.
4. There will thus be a significant negative correlation between extraversion and attitudes such as conservatism and racialism.

Bagley and his fellow researchers tested these hypotheses by selecting individuals who were both *neurotic and introvert* (based on the 20 per cent of extreme scorers in either direction) *stable and introvert, neurotic and extravert* and *stable and extravert* from a sample of over 200 subjects.

In support of their predictions, they found that stable extraverts had significantly *lower* scores than the other three groups on *conservatism* and *racialism*. By contrast, neurotic introverts scored highest on these two measures.

On balance, the evidence suggests that there is a recognisable pattern of personality consisting of tendencies to prejudice and authoritarianism which is rooted in a rigid regime of childhood socialisation. Furthermore, it may well be, as Hartmann and Husband[17] observe, that the extreme and apparently pathological bigotry of certain individuals is best explained by reference to psycho-analytical accounts of personality dynamics. But it is possible, is it not, that both authoritarianism and prejudice seemingly 'go together' because both are independently associated with, say, poor education or low socio-economic status? From this perspective, 'prejudice and authoritarianism are psychologically unrelated products of particular kinds of childhood experiences and social circumstances, and prejudice serves no greater psychological need than conformity to any other group norm'.[18] And what, we must ask, of the findings[19] that many authoritarians do not display higher levels of prejudice than the 'normal' population nor do highly-prejudiced individuals necessarily have authoritarian personalities? The problem with psychological explanations of prejudice is simply that they do not go far enough, for in addition to the question, 'What personality functions are served by prejudice?' one must surely ask, 'What are the social functions of intolerance, bigotry and discrimination in the wider society?' This is a question for the sociologist which we deal with later in the chapter. For the moment we look at research into stereotyping and prejudice.

Stereotypes and Prejudice

Psychologists have long been fascinated by the ways in which we form impressions and feelings about one another. Because it is quite impossible to respond to all aspects of other people, each and every one of us resorts to a process of categorisation. *Stereotyping* is just such a process. It has three characteristics:[20]

1. A categorisation of persons.
2. A concensus on the traits that we attribute to them.
3. A discrepancy between our attributions and their actual traits.

Stereotyping is the process of attributing traits to a person or a group solely on the basis of the category to which that person or group belongs. What this means in everyday terms has been demonstrated in an oft-quoted series of studies[21] of American university students. Briefly, three generations of Princeton undergraduates (the classes of 1932, 1951 and 1969) were encouraged to characterise various national, racial and ethnic groups using a list of 84 traits and attributes. Comparisons between the three sets of data showed that although there was a decline in the definitiveness of certain stereotypes over the years (on the third repetition of the study, for example, Negroes were less often characterised as 'lazy') nevertheless, stereotyping was still very much in evidence. The 1969 students' stereotypes reflect the more liberal norms on the Princeton campus. On this occasion, Negroes were typified as 'pleasure loving' and 'musical' rather than 'lazy' and 'superstitious', clear evidence of the continuing existence of stereotyping.

Psychologists regard stereotyping as a basic process of perceptual organisation, essential if we are to function effectively in an on-going, ever-changing series of new experiences. It is a process, moreover, in which people, objects and events are identified and labelled in such a way that attention is focused on some characteristics rather than others. The process of stereotyping can best be illustrated by the example shown in Box 2.3.

Box 2.3: The Process of Categorisation in Stereotyping

If we define a liquid as medicine our attention becomes focussed on its curative properties rather than on its taste, appearance or texture. If on the other hand it is called a beverage then its health-giving characteristics become largely irrelevant while its taste, appearance and texture assume major importance.

The mere process of labelling something structures our perceptions of it — makes them *biased*, if you like. More than this, however, labelling tends to result in an exaggeration of the similarity of objects within the same category, and of the differences between objects in different categories. This exaggeration is not random but occurs only for those characteristics put into focus by the labelling process. Thus people tend to exaggerate the extent to which beverages are palatable and to exaggerate the difference in palatability between beverages as a class and medicines as a class. This of course is a distortion, for many medicines, in fact, taste better than beverages.

Source: Adapted from Hartmann and Husband.[22]

This propensity to exaggerate differences between categories and similarities within categories which we illustrate in Box 2.3 was demonstrated by Tajfel and Wilkes[23] in an experiment involving university students.

Three groups of subjects were presented with a series of lines which differed in length by a constant ratio. In *Group 1*, the four shorter lines were labelled A and the four longer lines were labelled B. In *Group 2*, the eight lines were randomly labelled A or B. In *Group 3*, the eight lines were not labelled.

Subjects were required to estimate the length of each line in turn. The results showed that Group 1 undertook the estimation task *on the basis of the labelled categories A and B*, despite the fact that they were not asked to categorise but merely to estimate line length. Compared with Groups 2 and 3, Group 1 *exaggerated both the differences between the lines marked A and B and the similarities between the lines within each of the two categories.*

The experiment aptly demonstrates the process of stereotyping. Extrapolating from the artificiality of the laboratory-type experiment to the complexity of everyday events, Tajfel[24] comments as follows:

> There is an obvious and essential difference between the
> judgement of lines in . . . experiments . . . and stereotyped
> judgements of human beings when these are associated with
> prejudice.
>   In the case of lines, it would have been enough to present
> some form of reward to the subjects for accurate judgement
> and to penalise them for inaccurate ones in order to eliminate
> quite rapidly the biases that were obtained. *This is certainly
> not the case when hostile stereotypes are used* [our emphasis].
> Their rigidity and resistance to information which contradicts
> them is undoubtedly one of their most salient features . . .
> [Furthermore] the consequences of a mistake in judgement are
> radically different in the two situations. If a man is prejudiced
> he has an emotional investment in preserving the differentia-
> tions between his own group and the 'others' . . . the existence
> of prejudice . . . not only provides additional support and
> rewards for hostile judgements; it also removes the possibility
> of a 'reality check' for those judgements which then feed upon
> each other and become more and more strongly entrenched in
> the form of powerful social myths.

What Tajfel seems to be suggesting here is that when
prejudiced people have recourse to stereotyping, then a variety of
perceptual-defence mechanisms may be called into operation
which enable them to avoid seeing things in their environment
that are threatening, anxiety-provoking or dissonant with their
beliefs and opinion about certain others. There is a wealth of
experimental evidence on the selectivity of social perception[25]
that supports this assertion.

But have stereotypes no basis whatsoever in *fact*, the reader
may well ask? The answer must be that although the degree of
consensus on any particular stereotype can only ever be partial,
there is evidence that certain commonly-held stereotypes may at
least have some partial substantiation in fact. It is at this
juncture that psychologists introduce the concept of *modal
personality*.

Because each of us is shaped by the social events surrounding
us in our particular cultural setting it is to be expected that there
will be a degree of homogeneity in our social learning which is
reflected in a degree of consistency in our adult behaviour. The
concept of modal personality is used to describe the typical

behaviour of a member of a particular group or society. It is useful for general descriptive purposes; it is not intended to apply to every individual in a society, nor does it enable specific predictions to be made about the behaviour of particular individuals. Nevertheless, as McDavid and Harari[26] observe, to the extent that the cultural context does contribute to the personality structure and typical behaviour of an individual, then the concept of modal personality is the seed of truth in every stereotype.

Social Psychological Explanations of Prejudice

Until this point in the chapter explanations of prejudice have focused on the irrational side of human nature. Psycho-analytical accounts, as we have seen, search the unconscious for sources of motivation said to lie hidden there, frustration-aggression theory concerns itself with pent-up anger generated by perceived deprivation and personality theory explains negative stereotyping as a defensive distortion of the prejudiced mind. It is clear that in accounting for prejudice, psychologists are largely concerned with individual pathologies in cognising and feeling.

Social psychologists, by contrast, choose to work on a broader canvas. A social psychological explanation of prejudice, they insist, is essentially a social psychology of intergroup relations, and intergroup relations cannot be explained by personality disorders or individual frustrations. Social psychologists focus on the relationships that exist within and between groups. They employ concepts such as *in-group* and *out-group* to explain the phenomena of *group conflict* and *group co-operation*. *In-group* refers to persons who share a like identity and a sense of belonging. From the point of view of in-group members, *out-group* refers to persons who possess some distinctive characteristics that set them apart from the in-group.

Armed with these concepts, social psychologists approach the study of prejudice with three basic questions in mind:

1. Under what conditions do unfavourable attitudes towards groups arise?
2. What principles explain the continuation of unfavourable attitudes?

3. What factors contribute to changing attitudes in a favourable direction?

To illustrate the social psychological perspective, we discuss the work of Sherif and his associates[28] and outline a theory of intergroup relations that has been developed as a direct consequence of their experimental findings.

Over several years Sherif and his co-workers undertook a series of controlled experiments in intergroup relations among pre-adolescent boys in the real-life settings of American summer school camps. Their intention was to test a theory of intergroup relations which can be summarised as follows:[29]

1. When individuals seek to achieve some goal through *independent* action they become a group and develop a social hierarchy and specific norms.
2. When two groups are required to achieve incompatible goals and one group can only succeed if the other fails, an unfavourable perception develops between the groups such that members of one group can only think of and engage in hostile contacts with members of the other group.
3. There is an increase in the solidarity within the groups and, of necessity, their social structures adjust to the conflict situation.
4. The only thing which can reduce the hostility between the groups is the realisation of *superordinate* goals which require a common effort on the part of all the members of both groups.
5. The effect of such an endeavour is to make the perception of the other group more favourable and to permit the establishment of comradeship among the members of the two groups.

These rather formal statements of Sherif and his co-workers' theory contrast sharply with their graphic account of the rivalry, hostility and (eventually) the friendship and co-operation that occurred between groups, rejoicing under such exotic names as the Red Devils, Bulldogs, Rattlers and Eagles!

Typically, the experiments involved two groups of twelve-year-old boys, all reportedly 'psychologically well-adjusted and homogeneous with respect to their general backgrounds'. During

Stage 1 of the experiments when *neither group knew of the other's existence*, camping, cooking, swimming and playing games soon created recognisable group structures consisting of stable hierarchies of social ranks and roles together with norms over such matters as 'toughness', 'swearing', etc.

In Stage 2 of the experiments the two groups were brought together for five days of competitive games and contests in which prizes were awarded on the basis of an individual's contribution within his own group, but during which time, referees' decisions were purposely slanted to favour one particular group. In the course of tug-of-war competitions, treasure hunts, football and baseball games intense rivalry and strong hostility developed:

> On the very first day of the contest, the group which lost captured the victor's flag and burned it. During the following days there were raids on each side to disrupt the sleeping quarters of the other group. [Indirect measures taken by means of candid cameras and hidden microphones] showed that competition strongly influenced the perceptions, representations and attitudes of the antagonists.
>
> Thus, the image of the out-group became very unfavourable compared with the image of the in-group. The performance of team-mates was overestimated compared with others. The structure of the groups also changed and solidarity increased in both.[30]

Sociometric tests and interpersonal rating scales were used to measure the degree of unfavourability accorded to each other by the two groups during this intergroup competition stage of the experiments. Box 2.4 shows the extent of unfavourable stereotyping that occurred in each group.

An initial attempt to resolve the conflict generated during Stage 2 of the experiments involved bringing the two groups into contact again in non-competitive activities such as watching a film, visiting a fireworks display and eating together. It failed miserably. If anything, the level of aggression grew worse. It was clear to Sherif and his team that two groups can pursue similar and compatible goals without any reduction occurring in their mutual hatred and hostility.

It was only when both groups of boys were brought together and confronted with urgent *superordinate* goals that could only

Box 2.4: Stereotyping Ratings of Out-groups at the End of Stage 2 of the Experiments

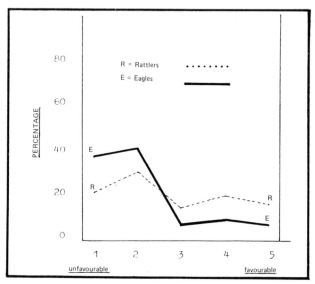

Source: Adapted from Sherif *et al.*[31]

be attained by their united efforts that a relaxation in hostilities was gradually brought about. The tasks they were faced with included inspecting pipes and tanks to trace the loss of vital water supplies, towing back to camp a broken down lorry loaded with food stores and clubbing together in order to hire a highly-desirable film. The results of their co-operative efforts were not immediately discernible. Only after pursuing several superordinate goals did intergroup friction begin to abate. By the end of Stage 3 of the experiments, as Box 2.5 illustrates, the stereotype ratings of out-groups increased in favourablility and friendship choices occurred between members of different groups.

We have been able to illustrate only one example from a vast and growing social-psychological literature of intergroup relationships, much of which reports the finding of experiments and quasi-experiments in laboratory settings rather than boys' summer camps! And yet as we have shown, a social psychological explanation of prejudice is essentially concerned with the character of the relationships that exist between in-groups and out-groups and the ways in which their on-going activities generate beliefs, attitudes and behaviours that are consonant with these relationships.

Box 2.5: Stereotype Ratings of Out-groups at the End of Stage 3 of the Experiments

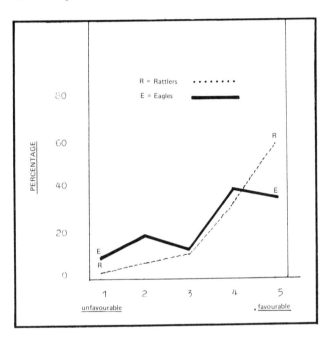

Source: Adapted from Sherif *et al.*[32]

Sociologists' perspectives on prejudice are complementary to, yet typically broader than, those of social psychologists. Their principal concern is with the origins of majority/minority-group relations in society at large and the factors in the social structure that maintain prejudice and discrimination.

Sociological Explanations of Prejudice

A distinctive feature of many sociological accounts of prejudice and discrimination is that they are concerned to identify underlying causes of minority-group differentiation both in historical and comparative contexts.

The term *minority group* is used to describe 'any group of people that is defined by a power elite as different and/or inferior on the basis of certain perceived characteristics and is consequently treated in a negative fashion'.[33] Thus, minority groups may consist of blacks, women, Catholics, the mentally-ill or the working class.

Why is it, sociologists ask, that such groups become the subject of control and discrimination? Why are they defined as different and inferior to majority groups? What keeps such groups in their inferior positions? How do they relate to each other and to majority elites? Finally, how and why do these relations change over a period of time?

To answer these questions, sociologists employ several approaches,[34] for example:

1. The *Historical Approach:* How do minority groups emerge and develop in societies?
2. The *Demographic Approach:* What demographic and socio-economic conditions characterise minority as compared with majority groups?
3. The *Institutional Approach:* What political, economic and social institutions in society reinforce control of minority groups?
4. The *Attitudinal Approach:* What attitudes and stereotypes are there concerning minority groups both among their own members and among majority elites?
5. The *Social-Movement Approach:* What are the reactions of minority groups (as manifested in the form of social movements) to majority-group control?
6. *Major Types of Group Relations:* What are the resultant group relations in respect of majority-minority interaction?

It is clear that among social scientists, sociologists choose to work on the broadest canvas in accounting for prejudice and discrimination in society.

To illustrate the use of several of the sociological approaches outlined above, we summarise part of Rex's[35] explanation of racism in contemporary Britain.

Rex insists that to understand present day race relations in

Britain we need to look far beyond the immediacies of the contemporary economic situation and, indeed, beyond the British Isles. The economic and political basis of our present day existence lies in the social system of the British Empire including its Indian, African and West Indian dominions stretching back over a period of four hundred years. The whole development of British industrial capitalism, Rex argues, was dependent upon a process of capital accumulation in India and the West Indies. Moreover, the capacity of British capitalism in later times to support the costs of the Welfare state rested, in part at least, upon the unequal trade that Britain was able to carry on with her dependencies. A serious sociological analysis of race relations must, therefore, rest upon the concept of the *social structure* of the British Empire and of the *class formations* which occurred within it.

Rex goes on to show how the various forms of colonial-social structure came into being, each with its own system of classes, estates and castes. Complementary to the roles of ultimate slave, coolie, or peasant were the roles of overseer, manager and administrator — that is the capitalist entrepreneurs who actually ran the British Empire. Central to Rex's account of present racism is his observation that it was *'the individual and cumulative experience of these roles* [that] *helped shape the basic British belief system about colonial men and women'*. In a word, that black colonials were *inferior*.

Built in to our competitive metropolitan culture, Rex argues, was the notion that a caste barrier of some sort must be preserved if whites were not to be de-statused. Indians and West Indians were good enough people in their place, but their place was not Britain. The relatively recent granting of political independence to former colonial territories did little to ameliorate the sense of threat and competition with which white British faced the people of the Empire. It was more than likely then, says Rex, that the British people would regard the arrival of New Commonwealth and Caribbean immigrants in the late '50s and early '60s with fears and anxieties arising out of deeply-entrenched belief systems. Moreover, because those anxieties and beliefs were not brought out into the open, indigenous whites responded with hostility and aggression and then went on to justify their behaviour by new beliefs built upon the obvious physical and cultural differences of the new arrivals. The existence of racist beliefs, once established, leads to discrimination and this discrimination, Rex insists, produces conditions which further justify the beliefs:

> Thus the British image of the West Indian, Indian or Pakistani is not now simply that of a colonial savage, but additionally of a man in the ghetto, or a young man in trouble with the police.

To this point in his thesis, Rex has already had recourse to *historical, demographic, institutional* and *attitudinal* factors in accounting for present day racism in Britain. His explanation becomes particularly interesting when he advances reasons for the different social and political organisations that have arisen in Asian and West Indian communities as reactions to institutional, collective and individual racism on the part of members of the host society. Why, for example, have certain Asian groups become far more active in trade unionism than West Indians? Why, on the other hand, have some Asian minorities been content to put up with discrimination and lack of political rights? And why has a revolutionary black consciousness arisen among sections of West Indian youth? Rex's analysis of social movements among coloured minorities in Britain bears close and careful reading.

Let us conclude with a statement about prejudice that, *par excellence*, epitomises the sociological perspective:

> Prejudice is a product of *situations*, historical situations, economic situations, political situations, it is not a little demon that emerges in people simply because they are depraved.[36]

Notes

1. J. Dollard, L. Doob, N. E. Miller, D. H. Mowrer and R. R. Sears (1939) *Frustration and Aggression*, New Haven: Yale University Press.

2. C. Bagley and G. K. Verma (1975) 'Inter-ethnic Attitudes and Behaviour in British Multiracial Schools' in G. K. Verma and C. Bagley (eds), *Race and Education Across Cultures*, London: Heinemann.

3. G. D. Wilson (1973) 'Projective Aggression and Social Attitudes', *Psychological Reports*, **32**, 1015–18.

4. C. Bagley (1970) *Social Structures and Prejudice in Five English Boroughs*, London: Institute of Race Relations.

5. C. Bagley and G. K. Verma (1979) *Racial Prejudice, the Individual and Society*, London: Saxon House.

6. C. Bagley, G. K. Verma, K. Mallick and L. Young (1979) *Personality, Self-esteem and Prejudice*, London: Saxon House.

7. P. Kline (1981) 'Personality' in D. Fontana (ed.), Psychology For Teachers, London: The British Psychological Society and the MacMillan Press Ltd.

8. M. Jahoda (1975) 'The Roots of Prejudice', *New Community*, **4**, 179 –87.

9. Our account draws on the exposition in Bagley, Verma, Mallick and Young, *Personality, Self-esteem and Prejudice*.

10. The Open University (1976) *Personality Theories and Dimensions*, Educational Studies: Personality and Learning E201 Block 2, Milton Keynes: Open University Press.

11. Ibid.

12. T. W. Adorno, E. Frenkel-Brunswick, D. J. Levinson and R. N. Sanford (1950) *The Authoritarian Personality*, New York: Harper. For an up-to-date selection of readings in the area of authoritarianism, conservatism and dogmatism see: H. J. Eysenck and G. D. Wilson (eds) (1978) *The Psychological Basis of Ideology*, Lancaster: MTP Press.

13. Ibid.

14. H. J. Eysenck (1972) *The Psychology of Politics*, London: Methuen.

15. G. Wilson (1973) 'The Need for a New Approach to Attitude Measurement' in G. Wilson (ed.), *The Psychology of Conservatism*, London: Academic Press.

16. Bagley, Verma, Mallick and Young, *Personality, Self-esteem and Prejudice*.

17. P. Hartmann and C. Husband (1974) *Racism and Mass Media*, London: Davis-Poynter.

18. Ibid.

19. Ibid. Refer to the study by: M. Abrams (1969) in E. J. B. Rose and N. Deakin (eds), *Colour and Citizenship*, London: OUR/IRR, which showed that as many as 20 per cent of those scoring very low on authoritarianism were rated as prejudiced or prejudiced-inclined. See also: R. F. Pettigrew (1958) 'Personality and Sociocultural Factors in Intergroup Attitudes: A Cross National Comparison, *Journal of Conflict Resolution*, **2**, 29–42, who showed that highly-prejudiced white Afrikaner students had no higher authoritarianism levels than Anglo-Saxon white students. He suggested that the extreme levels of prejudice were associated with the political structure and prevailing norms of the country.

20. H. Tajfel and A. L. Wilkes (1963) 'Classification and Quantitative Judgement', *British Journal of Psychology*, **54**, 101–14. Bruner defines stereotyping as involving the grouping of people, objects and events around us into classes and responding to them in terms of their class membership rather than their uniqueness. See: J. Bruner, J. Goodnow and G. Austin (1956) *A Study of Thinking*, New York: John Wiley.

21. D. Katz and K. W. Braly (1933) 'Racial Stereotypes of 100 College Students', *Journal of Abnormal and Social Psychology*, **28**, 280–90; C. M. Gilbert (1951) 'Stereotype Persistence and Change Among College Students', *Journal of Abnormal and Social Psychology*, **46**, 245–54; M. Karling, T. L. Coffman and G. Walters (1969) 'On the Fading of Social Stereotypes: Studies in Three Generations of College Students', *Journal of Personality and Social Psychology*, **13**, 1–16.

22. Hartmann and Husband, *Racism and Mass Media*.

23. Tajfel and Wilkes, 'Classification and Quantitative Judgement'.

24. H. Tajfel (1969) 'Cognitive Aspects of Prejudice', *Journal of Social Issues*, **25** (4), 79–97.

25. See, for example, P. F. Secord and C. W. Backman (1964) 'Social Factors in Perceptual-cognitive Processes' (Part One), *Social Psychology*, New York: McGraw-Hill Book Company.

26. J. W. McDavid and H. Harari (1974) *Psychology and Social Behaviour*, New York: Harper and Row.

27. P. F. Secord and C. W. Backman (1964) *Social Psychology*, New York: McGraw-Hill Book Company.

28. See, particularly: M. Sherif, O. J. Harvey, B. J. White, W. R. Hood and C. Sherif (1961) *Intergroup Conflict and Cooperation. The Robber's Cave Experiment*, Norman, Okl.: University of Oklahoma; M. Sherif (1966) *Group Conflict and Cooperation: Their Social Psychology*, London: Routledge and Kegan Paul.

29. W. Doise (1978) *Groups and Individuals: Explanations in Social Psychology*, Cambridge: Cambridge University Press.

30. Ibid.

31. Sherif *et al., Intergroup Conflict and Cooperation*.

32. Ibid.

33. G. C. Kinloch (1979) *The Sociology of Minority Group Relations*, NJ Englewood Cliffs: Prentice Hall Inc, pp. 4–6.

34. Ibid.

35. J. Rex and S. Tomlinson (1979) *Colonial Immigrants in a British City: A Class Analysis*, London: Routledge and Kegan Paul. See also: J. Rex (1970) *Race Relations in Sociological Theory*, London: Weidenfeld and Nicolson.

36. R. A. Schermerhorn (1970) *Comparative Ethnic Relations*, New York: Random House.

3 UNDERACHIEVEMENT: SOME DIFFERING PERSPECTIVES

Introduction

During the late '60s, early '70s several studies[1] of academic achievement in different ethnic groups predicted that given equal conditions immigrant pupils would do as well as their English classmates. Others,[2] however, pointed to the underachievement of coloured children, particularly pupils of West Indian origin. Little,[3] for example, concluded that underprivileged white pupils performed at a higher level than children of West Indian origin and suggested that the needs of these latter pupils should be given the highest priority. Yule et al.'s[4] large scale survey also showed the extent to which children of West Indian origin born in Britain were performing below the average scores of an indigenous sample of pupils. The latest information on West Indian underachievement comes in the interim report of the so-called Rampton Committee.[5,6] This survey of school leavers in six English towns where the majority of West Indians live showed how badly black children fared in 'O', 'A' and CSE examinations compared to white and to children of Asian origin. In all CSE and O-level exams only 3 per cent of pupils of West Indian origin obtained five or more grades. The comparative figures for children of Asian origin were 18 per cent and for other school leavers 16 per cent. The Rampton Committee Interim Report further revealed that only 1 per cent of West Indians went on to full time degree courses compared with 5 per cent of Asians and 4 per cent of other leavers.

Our task in this chapter is to examine some psychological and sociological explanations of underachievement (in particular, West Indian underachievement) in multicultural classrooms. Specifically, we look at research to do with:

1. Coloured children's intellectual ability.
2. Teachers' attitudes towards these children.
3. The over-representation of certain coloured pupils in schools for the educationally subnormal.
4. The home circumstances of coloured pupils.

The issue of language and underachievement is taken up in Chapter 9.

Race and Intelligence

In 1969 Arthur Jensen,[7] an American psychologist, published a paper in which he proposed that the differences in intelligence-test scores within the white populations in Great Britain and the United States of America are caused 80 per cent by genetic factors (called the *heritability estimate*) and 20 per cent by environmental factors (the *environmental estimate*). Jensen went on to show that Negroes in the United States of America score, on average, 15 points lower on IQ tests than whites. Since the heritability estimate for whites is 80 per cent, Jensen argued, it follows that 80 per cent of the 15 IQ points difference between blacks and whites is caused by genetic factors. It should come as no surprise that Jensen's assertions have generated considerable and continuing debate! One of the most readable rebuttals of Jensen's arguments has been made by Hebb.[8] It is summarised in Box 3.1.

In choosing to avoid the fruitless debate on how much of the difference in intelligence is due to genes or environment, we follow Ryan[9] who argues that the idea of genetically-determined potential ability 'involves the notion of ability that is charac-teristic of an individual *prior to any interaction* with the environ-ment and thus independent of any social or specific educational influences'. Clearly, however, potential ability is necessarily expressed in actual behaviour. As Ryan observes, the notion of potential ability both as something abstracted from all inter-actions with the environment and at the same time as something measurable in a person's behaviour simply does not make sense'. Nevertheless, we need to examine the proposals of those who assert that the difference between 'black' and 'white' intelligence is biological in origin rather than due to social constraints on achievement or differences in motivation. We need also to identify the counter-arguments that have been raised in response to these assertions.

Jensen[10] proposes that there are two different types of learning ability which he identifies as Level I and Level II. These two levels correspond roughly to rote learning and conceptual

Box 3.1: A Critique of Jensen's Theory of the Relationship of Race and IQ

Just suppose that all baby boys are kept in barrels from birth and fed through bung-holes until they are mature. If their I.Qs are then tested and compared with the I.Qs of girls who have been brought up normally, it will most probably be found that the girls' I.Qs are considerably higher than the boys'.

Since all the boys have been reared in identical environments any differences in their I.Qs can be attributed to *genetic factors*. Are we then able to say that boys are less intelligent than girls and therefore that because the differences among the boys' I.Qs are largely created by genetic factors, the differences between boys and girls are also attributable to genetics? Certainly not! In the first place we cannot compare the part played by heredity in determining intelligence unless both boys and girls have been brought up in identical environments. Secondly, our comparison of boys' and girls' I.Q. scores will not tell us about the nature of intelligence as a whole.

Now apply this analogy, says Hebb, to the debate about race and I.Q. How can we compare the effects of genetics in determining blacks' and whites' I.Qs unless we can be sure that they have been reared in identical environments?

Jensen claims that because he has compared *middle-class* blacks with *middle-class* whites, and *working-class* blacks with *working-class* whites, he has successfully controlled for the environment! How sufficient is such a crude control and is it of the right kind?

Source: Adapted from Hebb.[11]

learning, respectively. While Level I is distributed *similarly* in different populations, Jensen asserts, Level II is distributed *differently*. Children with white faces according to Jensen have the monopoly of Level II ability. That is to say, blacks are good at rote learning alone; whites are good at both rote and conceptual learning. Both British and American studies,[12] however, have shown that when groups of black and white children are given the opportunity to learn fairly complex concepts from scratch the different racial groups achieve similarly.

Jensen's ideas in America and those of his counterpart Eysenck[13] in Britain have provoked acrimonious debate. Eysenck asserts, for example, that blacks in America are inherently stupid since it was the more stupid Africans who allowed themselves to be caught and enslaved. Moreover this black stupidity has been genetically transmitted. Imagine, comments Bagley,[14] blacks are responsible for their own slavery!

What humanity, what scientific insight, what profound genius has inspired such an observation.

Jensen's most recent publication[15] is directed at those of his numerous critics who decry the bias in the design of mental tests which favours the performance of white middle-class children:

> If we take bias to mean that the same test for blacks and whites is actually measuring different things, then it is impossible to show that such bias exists. In other words, the differences between blacks and whites in whatever the tests measure are genuine.

Jensen's critics respond to this assertion as follows:

> The fact that differences exist between black and white pupils requires serious study by educationalists because it brings to light certain disadvantages among some groups with respect to basic cognitive skills on which the very process of education depends. Such differences, however, prove nothing about their supposedly genetic origins.

Bynner[16] summarises the basic objections to Jensen's thesis as follows. First, there is the biological argument. Jensen defines intelligence in two distinct ways which he then proceeds to equate. The first is biological: the capacity to adapt behaviour. The second is psychological: the capacity for abstract reasoning and problem solving involving the use of language and symbols.

The biological argument can be used to distinguish between species in terms of their intelligence: thus chimpanzees are more intelligent than rabbits. Clearly, these differences in intelligence have a genetic origin. But to go on from this to say that differences within a species with regard to problem-solving and abstract reasoning must have a genetic base is far more difficult to justify. Language, that distinctive feature of humans that sets them apart from any other species, is a remarkably complex skill that is mastered with relative ease by virtually every member of the species. The application of this skill in the development of those activities with which mental tests are concerned need not have any genetic origins at all.

Second, Jensen's case depends upon amassing evidence for 'isolating' from mental-test performances what amounts to a quality of pure reasoning, 'g'. This quality is thought to reside in people independently of any environmental influences to which they are subjected and to correlate only with physical, that is genetically-determined, attributes. Bynner is critical of Jensen's out-of-date research methods and his attempts to isolate 'g'. Jensen ignores more recent techniques, says Bynner,[17] enabling the researcher to test *any* model of the structure of a set of abilities.

Finally, given that differences in test scores between races exist, there are two equally plausible theories to account for them: the *hereditary* and *environmental* with a range of positions between them. In the absence of total experimental control over human mating, reproduction and development, there is no entirely satisfactory test that can adjudicate between them. Jensen believes in the importance of an inherited component in intellectual capacity. He directs his energies to determining the boundaries it sets on intellectual growth and bases his educational prescriptions on the use of tests to select individuals for appropriate educational environments. In contrast, a psychologist like Hunt, believing in the modifiability of human potential in response to the environment from conception onwards, devotes his research to isolating those features in the environment that restrict intellectual growth and devises educational experiences that will enhance it. Ultimately, says Bynner, it comes down to a distinction between the pessimists and the optimists about human potential.

Contrast Bynner's critique with that of Leon Kamin.[18] In his book, *The Science and Politics of IQ,* Kamin argues that intelligence testing has been fostered by people committed to a particular view of society, a view that includes the belief that those on the bottom are genetically inferior victims of their own immutable defects. In consequence, intelligence testing has served as an instrument of oppression. 'There are few more soothing messages', Kamin asserts, 'than those historically delivered by IQ testers. The poor, the foreign-born and racial minorities were shown to be stupid. They were shown to have been born that way. The underprivileged today are demonstrated to be ineducable, a message as soothing to the public purse as to the public conscience.'

In this part of the chapter we have tried to show a range of views that psychologists and sociologists hold with respect to intelligence and race. We end with some observations that are particularly appropriate for teachers to consider.

In his book, *The Myth of The Deprived Child*, Ginsburg[19] argues that by the very nature of their construction, standardised IQ tests seek to *maximise differences* between subjects. But those very differences, Ginsburg says, may obscure certain factors that many children share in their intelligent behaviour and which they possess at much more equal levels than intelligence test scores imply. He suggests that we should concentrate instead on *cognitive universals*, that is the achievement of important cognitive stages in intellectual growth which the vast majority of children, black or white, have in common at similar ages.

Teacher Attitudes and Pupil Underachievement

One sentence in particular in the Rampton Committee's Interim Report[20] raised many eyebrows especially among teachers.

> A profession of half a million must reflect the attitudes of society at large and contain some with racist views . . .

Thankfully, the Report goes on, racist teachers are in a minority; it is *unintentional racism*, says Rampton, that is a major concern in the teaching profession, and it cites the following example. Teachers see West Indian pupils as problems or, at best, deserving sympathy. They expect that these children are unlikely to do well academically although it is commonly believed that they can excel in sport, drama and art. And teacher expectations, the Rampton Committee warns, frequently turn into self-fulfilling prophecies.[21]

Little and Willey's[22] extensive survey of provision for multi-ethnic education in England and Wales comes to somewhat similar conclusions about teacher attitudes as those expressed by Rampton:

> Many authorities and schools emphasize [the need to convince] teachers that they should consider the implications of a multi-ethnic society for their teaching.

> the first priority is to persuade teachers that relevant

curriculum development is necessary.

we need to help teachers develop positive attitudes towards cultures other than their own and to develop realistic expectations towards children's academic performance.

the major difficulty is intransigent attitudes from unawareness to outright prejudice.

These undisguised criticisms of teachers come at a time of economic cutbacks in education and widespread redundancies in the profession; a time when morale is low and the feeling among teachers is that the public at large is all too ready to criticise their efforts without due regard to the difficulties they have to contend with.

One can understand and, indeed, have some sympathy with the teacher quoted in the Rampton Report[23] as saying, 'We've had mixed ability; we've gone Community; and now it's bloody multi-cultural.' Sympathy notwithstanding, our task is to examine what Rampton calls *unintentional racism* among teachers as it relates to the underachievement of coloured pupils.

Let us begin with perhaps the best example of unintentional racism[24] that we have come across as it relates to children of West Indian origin. In 1978 the report[25] of a study undertaken by the Local Community Relations Council of the London Borough of Redbridge confirmed the underachievement of black pupils that earlier studies had identified from the late 1960s onwards. Part of the comment of the Chairman of Redbridge Education Committee on that report went as follows:

In general terms, and I mean this in the nicest possible way, the West Indian children are more interested in the creative activities, in sports . . . Do you want a hard-working, high-achieving young man or woman, or do you want to develop their present happy approach and make things up in due course?

The Chairman's words exactly illustrate the negative stereotypes of the West Indians which the Report suggests are associated with their underachievement! Recall that in Chapter 2 in our discussion of *stereotyping* we drew upon a definition of Bruner's[26] to the effect that stereotyping involves grouping people, objects and events around us into classes and responding to them in terms of their class membership rather than their uniqueness. Tajfel,[27] for example, has shown how individuals tend to categorise racial and ethnic groups on the basis of beliefs about the attributes of members of those groups rather than on a more objective appraisal of the characteristics and behaviour of individual members.

Applying the idea of stereotyping and categorising to class-rooms, there is evidence[28] that teachers may have in mind stereo-types of the *sort-of-children-who-do-well-at-school*. Two studies (Nash, 1973; Blease, 1978) employing repertory grid techniques[29] have shown how *ability* and *achievement* in classroom settings are closely associated with an affectual dimension of teacher behaviour; put simply, whether or not teachers like the children in question.

What of teachers in multicultural classrooms? Tomlinson's[30] research demonstrates the results of stereotyping and ethnic categorisation in a group of teachers in the Handsworth district of Birmingham (see Box 3.2).

Box 3.2: Teachers' Views of Asian and West Indian Pupils

There were distinct differences in the ways heads and teachers viewed West Indian and Asian children in their schools . . . On the whole, Asian families were felt to be supportive of schools, keen on education, and their children were viewed as likely to persevere in acquiring some kind of school or work qualifications.

By contrast, children of West Indian origin and their parents were viewed as more problematic. Pupils were considered to be 'less keen on education', 'lacked ability to concentrate', and were more likely to need remedial teaching . . . The learning problems of children of West Indian origin were thought to be more acute than white or Asian children . . . The behaviour of pupils of West Indian origin was also viewed as a serious problem. At primary school level the children were thought to be more 'boisterous, disruptive and aggressive', than white or Asian children, and by secondary level the defiance and hostility of some pupils was felt to seriously disrupt the normal school processes.

Source: Adapted from Tomlinson.[31]

Both Rex and Tomlinson's[32] study of teachers' perceptions of Asian and West Indian children and Brittan's[33] large-scale survey of teacher attitudes towards children of immigrant groups suggest that school staff may tend to operate within a framework of stereotypes which are reinforced rather than negated by the responses of the pupils themselves.

On the other hand, as Giles[34] discovered in his study of West Indian boys and girls in London schools, teachers may deliberately ignore questions of race and ethnicity and by insisting on treating all children alike deny the existence of real differences and difficulties arising in multicultural classrooms.

'What then is to be done?' readers may well ask. We suggest the following. Making accurate and up-to-date information readily available about children from different ethnic backgrounds offers teachers opportunities to examine assumptions about race and ethnicity as they affect their teaching in multicultural classrooms. Such information also enables teachers to understand *where* and *how* the educational process is affected by the existence of real and/or significant ethnic or social class characteristics among pupils born in Britain from ethnic-minority backgrounds.[35] Accurate and up-to-date information about ethnic-minority groups, we suggest, should be an integral part of initial and in-service teacher education programmes irrespective of the multicultural composition of the classrooms in which teachers are placed.

We turn now to the question of *overt racism* among teachers. What do we know of its incidence and effects in multicultural classrooms? Let us start with a concrete example of overt racism. Jeffcoate[36] recounts an incident that occurred in a school where he was responsible for a small group of West Indian children (see Box 3.3).

Box 3.3: An Example of Overt Teacher Racism

I was teaching . . . a group of West Indian children in a secondary school one morning. The room I used has a glass door which meant that anyone passing had a clear view of whoever was inside. On this occasion a senior member of staff passed, paused and looked in. He opened the door, grinned at me and said in a voice loud enough for all to hear, 'Excuse me, is this Dudley Zoo?'

Source: Adapted from Jeffcoate.[37]

Like Jeffcoate we can see no place in teaching for anyone guilty of this kind of professional misconduct. Hopefully, incidents such as this are rare. Recall however that in defining racism (page 13), we suggested that it manifested itself in the inferior or unequal treatment accorded to certain groups of people. Applying this criterion to classrooms we might ask whether it has been demonstrated that prejudiced teachers do, in fact, treat coloured pupils in an unequal (i.e. inferior) way? The answer is *yes*, although systematic, observational evidence is hard to come by. Such evidence, however, has been provided by a recent study of 1814 children and their teachers in four middle schools. The 28 male and 42 female teachers were all white British nationals. The pupil sample consisted of 940 white, 449 Asian and 425 West Indian children between the ages of 8 and 13.

Teacher-pupil interaction data were collected by means of the well-known Flanders' ten-category classification of verbal communication. The Flanders' schedule is a relatively simple categorisation of the teacher's professional behaviour in the classroom and pupils' reactions to it. From the interactional analysis Green,[38] the researcher, calculated the amount of time each teacher engaged in interaction with the class as a whole and with individual boys and girls of European, Asian and West Indian origin. Furthermore, he calculated the amount of time in which each of his 70 teachers was engaged in using different types of interaction as revealed by the Flanders' schedule.

From the data it was possible to deduce the emphasis given to various categories of interaction with various ethnic groups by each class teacher. Over 3000 observations of teacher-pupil inter-actions were recorded *in each classroom*. Green then invited the 70 participating teachers to complete an attitude inventory in which a 25-item prejudice scale had been 'buried'. The prejudice scale was scored and 24 teachers were identified, 12 of whom were highly-prejudiced and 12 of whom scored lowest on prejudice. Only then did the researcher return to examine the teacher-pupil interaction data, asking, 'Do highly-prejudiced teachers behave differently towards coloured pupils when compared with teachers who score low on prejudice?' Some of Green's results are summarised in Box 3.4.

Green's study usefully maps out broad areas of differential treatment towards certain ethnic-minority pupils. What is now required by way of complementing his quantitative approach is qualitative data on teacher-pupil interactions in multicultural classrooms, in particular the interpretations that each party places on the on-going dialogue or, as Green has shown, the lack

Box 3.4: Differences in the Behaviour of Ethnically Highly Tolerant and Ethnically Highly Intolerant Teachers

1. Highly intolerant teachers gave significantly less time to *accepting the feelings* of children of West Indian origin.

2. Highly intolerant teachers gave only *minimal praise* to children of West Indian origin.

3. Highly intolerant teachers gave significantly *less attention to the ideas contributed* by children of West Indian origin.

4. Highly intolerant teachers used *direct teaching of individual* children significantly less with pupils of West Indian origin.

5. Highly intolerant teachers gave significantly more *authoritative directions* to children of West Indian origin.

6. Highly intolerant teachers gave significantly less time to children of West Indian origin to *initiate contribution to class discussions*.

Source: Adapted from Green.[39]

of it in the case of certain ethnic-minority pupils and their teachers.

Educational Subnormality and Coloured Pupils

In a recent study of the ways in which professional people make decisions placing children in the category mild educational subnormality (ESN-M), Tomlinson[40] explores the accounts and explanations given by heads of referring schools, educational psychologists, medical officers and special school headteachers. She concludes that their judgements and decisions are constituted by *their own beliefs about 'what is' an ESN-M child* rather than on any agreed objective criteria. The extensive interviews undertaken by Tomlinson reveal that the criteria upon which professionals come to their decisions are 'complex, sometimes unformulated and unclarified, based upon qualities within the child and his family other than educational qualities, and closely connected to the vested interests of the professionals although overlain by an ideology of humanitarianism'.

Tomlinson identifies ten possible accounts or 'understandings' to which professionals have recourse in describing and explaining what they consider an ESN-M child to be.

Thus, a *functional* account might contain the observation that

Box 3.5: Professionals' Accounts of Mild Educationally-Subnormal Children

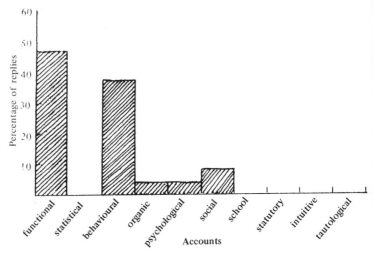

Referring heads' accounts of ESN-M children

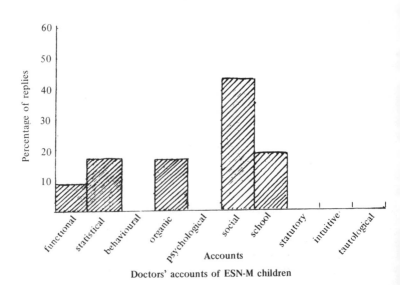

Doctors' accounts of ESN-M children

Box 3.5: *Cont'd.*

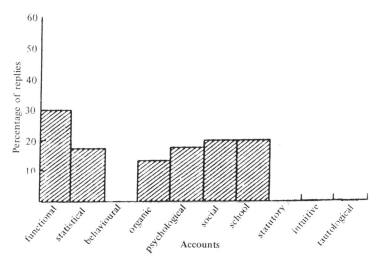

Educational psychologists' accounts of ESN-M children

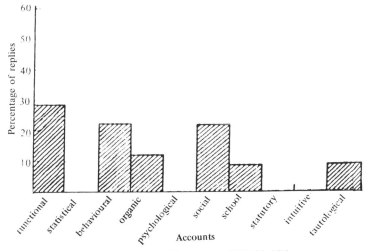

Special schools heads' accounts of ESN-M children

Source: Tomlinson.[41]

'the child cannot communicate adequately'. Similarly, a *statistical* account can be illustrated by the statement, 'the child has a low IQ'. The remainder of Tomlinson's ten categories are as follows: *behavioural* ('child is disruptive'); *organic* ('child has innate incapacity'); *psychological* ('child is emotionally disturbed'); *social* ('family is disorganised'); *school* ('child rejects school'); *statutory* ('child may be certified as in need of special education'); *intuitive* ('child has something wrong with him'); and *tautological* ('child is in need of special education treatment').

Using these ten broad generalisations, Tomlinson then goes on to classify the frequencies of the various 'explanations' of educational subnormality gathered in her interviews with headteachers, psychologists and medical officers. The variety of beliefs about what an ESN-M child 'is' is well demonstrated in the strikingly-different profiles shown in Box 3.5.

Having shown that professionals referring and assessing children as ESN-M act upon criteria that are unformulated, unclarified and largely noneducational, Tomlinson then asks the more fundamental question as to the purpose that a sub-normality categorisation serves in complex industrialised societies such as Britain.

She proposes the following sociological explanation of the increasing numbers of ESN-M children who over the past 30 years or so have been excluded from 'normal' education:

> Professionals such as psychologists, medical officers and headteachers have socially-constructed a category of people who are denied a 'normal' education and instead, receive a stigmatised 'special' or non-education but who are subsequently employed as part of the lowest strata of a productive work-force. In effect, professionals legitimate the reproduction of a part of the lower social class, the category ESN being a form of social control for a potentially troublesome section of the population . . . a major social function of the category of mild educational subnormality and the 'special' education for those in this category — may be to permit the relatively smooth development of the 'normal' education system. From a structural point of view . . . the special education system can be regarded as institutionalising the exclusion of a section of the population from chances of social mobility, from the

acquisition of cultural and economic capital and as a mechanism for ensuring their placement in the lowest social class.

Educational Subnormality and Pupils of West Indian Origin

The issue of educational subnormality in respect of coloured pupils is almost solely concerned with children of West Indian origin. The disproportionate number of pupils of West Indian origin who were being assessed as educationally subnormal and despatched to special schools began to concern the West Indian community in the mid 1960s. The 'overplacement' of this ethnic minority group in ESN schools is documented in the statistics shown in Box 3.6.

What do the figures in Box 3.6 show? Taking 1972 as our example, they reveal that 4.9 per cent of all children in ESN schools were of West Indian origin whereas they constituted 1.1 per cent of the total school population. In effect, there were four times as many of these children in special schools as there 'ought' to have been.[43] Chief Education Officers' explanations of this state of affairs in response to a DES inquiry in 1973 mentioned difficulties with discipline, dialect and teachers' assessments as factors in the over-representation of children of West Indian origin.

An alternative explanation of West Indian children's disproportionate presence in ESN schools is given by Coard in a document entitled *How the West Indian is Made Educationally Subnormal in the British Schools System.* Coard,[44] a West Indian, and for some time a teacher in ESN schools, argues that the organisation and the curriculum activities of ESN schools are geared to pupils of below normal academic ability and that West Indian pupils who are misclassified and assigned to such schools are not encouraged to perform to the best of their ability. Misclassification, he says, arises out of differences in culture and social class and low expectations of West Indian pupils on the part of their teachers. The very process of being assessed for possible placement in a special school, Coard asserts, makes the black pupil 'feel deeply that racial discrimination and rejection have been practised towards him by the authorities.' Once there, his refusal to co-operate and take part in the school's programme

Box 3.6: a. Total Number of Children in Maintained Primary and Secondary Schools and Total Number of Children in ESN Schools/Classes; b. Total Numbers of Children of West Indian Origin in Maintained Primary and Secondary Schools and Total Number placed in ESN Schools/Classes

a.

Year	Column 1 'Normal' school	Column 2 ESN school/classes	Column 2 as a percentage of Column 1
1968	8,190,745	49,818	.59
1969	8,391,756	49,931	.59
1970	8,597,451	51,768	.60
1971	8,800,843	52,843	.60
1972	9,032,999	60,045	.66
1974	9,560,060	53,353	.55
1975	9,617,474	52,744	.54
1976	9,669,000	53,772	.55

b.

Year	Column 1 'Normal' school	Column 2 ESN school/classes	Column 2 as a percentage of Column 1
1968	89,988	—	—
1969	106,126	—	—
1970	109,963	2,551	2.3
1971	107,136	2,896	2.7
1972	101,898	2,972	2.9

Source: Adapted from Tomlinson.[42]

of activities not only makes him appear retarded, but in the course of time, results in him becoming retarded through lack of mental activity.

The Home Circumstances of Coloured Pupils

Large-scale longitudinal studies[45] show a close association between the material circumstances of the home and the intellectual ability and academic achievement of the child, none perhaps more clearly than the report of the National Child Development Study entitled *From Birth To Seven*.[45] In that account, bar graphs are used to illustrate differences in IQ, arithmetic and reading achievement that are associated with variations in social class background, home circumstances and geographical location.

Consistently throughout the analyses in the National Child Development Study, *social class* (identified by *occupational status*) is shown to be the variable most strongly associated with children's intellectual ability and academic attainment. It comes as no surprise to learn that offspring of professionals, employers and managers do best at school, and that children from semi-skilled and unskilled manual backgrounds do worst. Occupational status is widely used as an index of social class in educational research despite scope for argument about the crudity of such a measure. We use it here to find out whether members of coloured ethnic-minority groups are distributed across socio-economic categories in similar fashion to the general population of Britain. Any marked dissimilarity in distribution, we suggest, may help illuminate the central theme of the present chapter — the underachievement of certain coloured pupil groups.

Box 3.7 shows the percentage socio-economic distribution of economically-active males and females in Great Britain.[47] It reveals significant differences between ethnic-minority groups and indigenous whites. In particular, West Indians and Pakistanis are under-represented in higher socio-economic groups and West Indians and Asians generally are over-represented in lower socio-economic categories, a trend that persists throughout the years under consideration. *Social class*, that is to say *occupational status*, is not of course a single factor; it is best viewed as an amalgam of factors that operate in different ways. Broadly speaking we can say that in comparison with members of lower socio-economic groups, people in higher socio-economic categories 'enjoy better health; live longer; live in superior homes with more amenities; have more money to spend; work shorter hours; receive different and longer education and are educationally more successful . . . to mention only a few examples'.[49]

The statistics in Box 3.7 show that coloured ethnic-minority groups are relatively disadvantaged as a result of their social class distribution. Using data from the Home Office Research Study No. 68 (1981) and the Runnymede Trust/Radical Statistics Race Group (1980) let us now look briefly at one aspect[50] of socio-economic circumstances as it bears upon the underachievement of certain coloured pupils. We deal with *housing*.

Box 3.7: Percentage Socio-economic Distribution of Economically-active Males and Females in 1966, 1971 and 1977

Socio-economic grouping		Country of birth			
		West Indies	India	Pakistan	Gt Britain
Professionals,	1966	1.8	15.1	6.0	11.6
employers and	1971	1.9	13.4	7.2	13.7
managers	1977	2.5	14.5	8.7	16.1
Semi-skilled	1966	53.1	32.2	64.3	30.5
and unskilled	1971	47.1	37.7	60.7	28.3
manual workers	1977	43.3	36.6	53.2	25.3

Source: Adapted from Home Office Research Study No. 68.[48]

Housing

On any measure of housing quality (age of fabric, location, amenities such as bath, plumbed hot water, inside WC, etc.) the dwellings occupied by coloured immigrants coming to Britain after the Second World War were substantially worse than those of the general 'white' population. Quality of housing is, of course, related to the position a person occupies in society. Because coloured ethnic-minority groups were (and still are) disproportionately located in 'lower' socio-economic categories their overall representation in poor quality housing can, in part, be accounted for. But this is not the whole story as we shall see.

Since the Second World War there has been a general rise in housing standards in Britain, though it is not easy to ascertain the extent to which coloured immigrants have fully shared in these improvements or have 'caught up' with the rest of the population. Coloured groups tend to be concentrated in certain large cities in major industrial areas. Within these cities, they tend to be concentrated in particular boroughs or even particular wards. Using Office of Population Censuses and Surveys measures of overcrowding (1.5 persons per room) we can see from the figures in Box 3.8 that there appears to be an increasing degree of convergence between the conditions enjoyed by coloured groups and the general population at large. Many, however, would judge one person per room per household as indicative of overcrowding. If the official measure of overcrowding (1.5 persons per room) were to be redefined downwards, says the 1981 Home Office Research Study report, then the relevant

Box 3.8: Home Circumstances of Coloured Groups and the General Population

Percentage of households in shared
dwellings

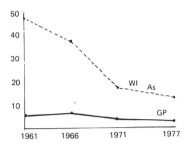

Average household size

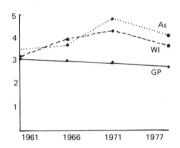

Percentage of households living at
more than 1.5 persons per room

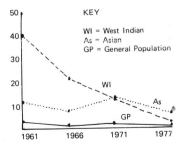

Source: Adapted from the Home Office Research Study No. 68.[51]

figures would appear as follows:

Living at more than 1 person per room
General population =   3 per cent of households
West Indians   = 12 per cent of households
and Asians   = 24 per cent of households.

Briefly let us look at the picture[52] in one Inner London Borough
and the disadvantageous home circumstances experienced by its
West Indian residents. Research showed that only 4 per cent of
the main breadwinners in West Indian families had non-manual
jobs compared with 20 per cent of the indigeneous population.
Fifty per cent of the West Indian families lived in overcrowded
conditions, 43 per cent did not have sole use of the kitchen,
bathroom, toilet or plumbed hot water. (The comparative figures
for the indigeneous population were 20 per cent and 16 per cent
respectively).

There is, too, the difficult problem of identifying racial
discrimination in respect of housing whether practised by those
selling properties, or financing their purchase, or allocating
council dwellings or approving improvement-grant applications
to owner-occupiers. Despite the fact that *direct* discrimination in
housing became an offence under the Race Relations Act (1968)
and *indirect* discrimination was deemed unlawful by the Race
Relations Act (1976), there is evidence[53] of the operation of a so-
called *colour-tax* causing coloured groups difficulty in obtaining
finance for house purchase, a result of which is that they pay
more when they do obtain it. In addition, there is evidence that
coloured groups pay more for rented unfurnished accommodation and that they are less successful than whites in obtaining
improvement grants in respect of the properties they occupy.

Coloured ethnic minority groups, as Deakin[54] observes, still
face difficult housing problems, a result 'not so much . . . of
overt discrimination as of a subtle and complex sifting process,
which race relations legislation has not so far proved effective in
combating'.

From our discussion so far we may conclude that coloured
ethnic-minority groups in general are over-represented in lower
socio-economic categories, in bad housing conditions and,
though space precludes discussion of the evidence, they are also
over-represented both in lower-paid uncongenial employment and

in unemployment statistics. These are crucial facts to be borne in mind in connection with the discussion of the home circumstances and achievement of coloured pupils.

Recall that at the beginning of this section we referred to the ongoing research of the National Children's Bureau, a cohort study of some 16,000 children (now young adults) that began in 1958. As part of that large-scale study, achievement data to do with first- and second-generation immigrants[55] were extracted, analysed and reported in several publications.[56] Two important conclusions have been drawn from these data:

> Firstly, immigrants tend to have relatively poor attainment overall, but *when children of similar financial and other material circumstances are compared most immigrant groups do as well as non-immigrants,* [our emphasis] the main exception to this being West Indians.
> Secondly, the poor school performance is generally only found among first-generation immigrants, not second-generation immigrants, and to some extent is relatively short-term and language specific.[57]

Notes

1. B. Ashby, A. Morrison and H. Butcher (1970) 'The Abilities and Attainments of Immigrant Children', *Research in Education*, 4, 73–80; J. McFie and J. Thompson (1970) 'Intellectual Abilities of Immigrant Children', *British Journal of Educational Psychology*, 40, 348–51. One recent study (Driver, 1980) argues that underachievement among West Indian pupils is simply not true. Driver's research has become something of a *cause célèbre*. See: G. Driver (1980) 'How West Indians Do Better at School (Especially the Girls)', *New Society*, 27 January, 111–14; and G. Driver (1980) *Beyond Underachievement: Case Studies of English, West Indian and Asian School Leavers at Sixteen Plus*, London: Commission For Racial Equality. For the most detailed critique of Driver's study to date, see: M. J. Taylor (1981) *Caught Between: A Review of Research into the Education of Pupils of West Indian Origin*, Windsor: NFER—Nelson, pp. 113–22. See also critics of his findings in: *New Society* (1980), 24 January, Letters; *New Society* (1980), 11 February, Letters; J. H. Taylor (1973) 'Newcastle-Upon-Tyne: Asian Pupils Do Better than Whites', *British Journal of Sociology*, 24, 431–47.
2. J. Payne (1969) 'A Comparative Study of the Mental Ability of Seven and Eight Year Old British and West Indian Children in a West Midlands Town', *British Journal of Educational Psychology*, 39(3), 326–7; C. Bagley (1971) 'A Comparative Study of Social Environment and Intelligence in West Indian and English Children', *Social and Economic Studies*, 20, 4.
3. A. Little (1975) 'Performance of Children from Ethnic Minority Backgrounds in Primary Schools', *Oxford Review of Education*, 1(2), 117–35.

4. W. Yule, M. Berger, M. Rutter and B. Yule (1975) 'Children of West Indian Immigrants II: Intellectual Performance and Reading Attainment', *Journal of Child Psychology and Psychiatry and Allied Disciplines*, **16**, 1–17.

5. The Rampton Committee Report (1981) *West Indian Children in Our Schools: Interim Report*, London: HMSO.

6. Now the Swann Committee.

7. A. R. Jensen (1969) 'How Much Can We Boost IQ and Scholastic Achievement?', *Harvard Educational Review*, **39**, 1–123.

8. D. O. Hebb quoted in M. Hardy and S. Heyes (1979) *Beginning Psychology*, London: Weidenfeld and Nicolson.

9. J. Ryan (1972) 'I.Q. — The Illusion of Objectivity' in K. Richardson and D. Spears (eds), *Race, Culture and Intelligence*, Harmondsworth: Penguin Books.

10. A.R. Jensen (1973) *Educational Differences*, London: Methuen; A. R. Jensen (1973) *Educability and Group Differences*, London: Methuen.

11. D. O. Hebb quoted in M. Hardy and S. Heyes (1979) *Beginning Psychology*, London: Weidenfeld and Nicolson.

12. E. Stones (1979) 'The Colour of Conceptual Learning' in G. Verma and C. Bagley (eds), *Race, Education and Identity*, London: Macmillan; P. Scrofani, A. Suziedelis and M. Shore (1973) 'Conceptual Ability in Black and White Children of Different Social Classes', *American Journal of Orthopsychiatry*, **43**, 541–53.

13. H. Eysenck (1971) *Race, Intelligence and Education*, London: Temple Smith; E. Eysenck (1973) *The Inequality of Man*, London: Temple Smith.

14. C. Bagley (1975) 'On the Intellectual Equality of Races' in G. K. Verma and C. Bagley (eds), *Race and Education Across Cultures*, London: Heinemann Educational Books Ltd.

15. A. R. Jensen (1980) *Bias in Mental Testing*, London: Methuen.

16. J. Bynner (1980) 'Black and White Arguments', *Guardian*, 18 March.

17. Note the differences here between Bynner's objection and the more fundamental point of Ryan about the idea of genetically-determined potential ability.

18. L. Kamin (1975) *The Science and Politics of I.Q.*, New York: John Wiley. The latest account of the on-going debate between the nature/nurture protagonists is: H. J. Eysenck (1981) *Intelligence: The Battle for The Mind. H. J. Eysenck v Leon Kamin*, London: Pan and Macmillan Press.

19. H. Ginsburg (1972) *The Myth of the Deprived Child*, New Jersey: Prentice-Hall.

20. Rampton Committee, *West Indian Children*.

21. We discuss empirical studies of teacher expectations in Chapter 7.

22. A. Little and R. Willey (1981) *Multi-ethnic Education: The Way Forward*, Schools Council Pamphlet 18, London: Schools Council, 160 Great Portland Street.

23. Rampton Committee, *West Indian Children*.

24. The example is taken from R. Jeffcoate (1979) *Positive Image: Towards a Multicultural Curriculum*, London: Chameleon. Jeffcoate is at pains to point out that the Chairman of the Education Committee intended no racism or malice towards black children in the remarks that he made. Rather, suggests Jeffcoate, the Chairman's attitudes usefully illustrate *institutional racism*, that is 'legacies of socialization into the dominant norms of a racist society'.

25. Redbridge Community Relations Council and Black Peoples Progressive Association (1978) *Cause For Concern: West Indian Pupils in Redbridge*, London: Redbridge CRC.

26. J. Bruner, J. Goodnow and G. Austin (1956) *A Study of Thinking*, New York: John Wiley.

27. H. Tajfel, A. Sheikh and R. Gardner (1964) 'Content of Stereotypes and the Inference of Similarity Between Members of Stereotyped Groups', *Acta Psychologica*, **22**, 191–201; J. Tajfel and G. Jahoda (1966) 'Development in Children of Concepts and Attitudes About Their Own And Other Countries', *Proceedings of the VXIII International Congress of Psychology*, **36**, 17–33; H. Tajfel (1969) 'Cognitive Aspects of Prejudice', *Journal of Social Issues*, **25**, 79–97; H. Tajfel (1970) 'Aspects of National and Ethnic Loyalty', *Social Science Information*, **9**, 119–44.

28. See: R. Nash (1973) *Classrooms Observed*, London: Routledge and Kegan Paul; D. Blease (1978) 'Teachers' Perceptions of Slow-learning Children: An Ethnographic Study', *Research Intelligence*, **4**(1), 39–42.

29. *Repertory grid techniques* involve presenting teachers (in this case) with the names of three pupils and asking them to specify in what ways one child differs from the other two. In this way, the researcher elicits pupil attributes that are important to teachers. For fuller details see, L. Cohen and L. Manion (1980) *Research Methods in Education*, London: Croom Helm, Chapter 14.

30. S. Tomlinson (1981) 'Multi-racial Schooling: Parents' and Teachers' Views', *Education 3–13*, **9**(1), 16–21.

31. Ibid.

32. J. Rex and S. Tomlinson (1979) *Colonial Immigrants in a British City: A Class Analysis*, London: Routledge and Kegan Paul.

33. E. M. Brittan (1976) 'Multi-racial Education 2: Teacher Opinion on Aspects of School Life. Part 2: Pupils and Teachers', *Educational Research*, **18**, 182–91.

34. R. Giles (1977) *The West Indian Experience in British Schools: Multi-racial Education and Social Disadvantage in London*, London: Heinemann.

35. Ibid.

36. R. Jeffcoate (1979) *Positive Image: Towards a Multicultural Curriculum*, London: Chameleon.

37. Ibid.

38. P. A. Green (1982) 'Teachers' Influence on the Self Concept of Ethnic Minority Pupils', Unpublished PhD thesis, University of Durham.

39. Ibid.

40. S. Tomlinson (1981) *Educational Subnormality: A Study in Decision Making*, London: Routledge and Kegan Paul.

41. Ibid.

42. Ibid.

43. In the absence of up-to-date figures we can only speculate about the current numbers of children of West Indian origin in ESN-M schools and classes.

44. B. Coard (1971) *How the West Indian Child is Made Educationally-Subnormal in the British School: The Scandal of the Black Child in Schools in Britain*, London: New Beacon Books.

45. See, for example: J. W. B. Douglas and J. M. Blomfield (1958) *Children Under Five*, London: Allen and Unwin; J. W. B. Douglas (1964) *The Home and The School*, London: MacGibbon and Kee; J. W. B. Douglas, J. M. Ross and H. R. Simpson (1968) *All Our Future*, London: P. Davies; 'Newsom Report', The Report of the Central Advisory Council For Education (England) (1963) *Half Our Future*, London: HMSO.

46. R. Davie, W. Butler and H. Goldstein (1972) *From Birth To Seven*, Slough, NFER.

47. These data were obtained in 1966 and 1971 censuses and from the National Dwelling and Housing Survey of 1977.

48. See the *Home Office Research Study No. 68 (1981)*, references to researches by: D. Smith (1976) *The Fact of Racial Disadvantage*, London: PEP;

M. Fenton and D. Collard (1977) *Do Coloured Tenants Pay More? Some Evidence*, Bristol: SSRC Research Unit on Ethnic Relations; V. Kahn (1977–8) 'The Financing of Owner-occupation and its Impact on Ethnic Minorities', *New Community*, **6**(1 and 2), 49–63; Rex and Tomlinson, *Colonial Immigrants in a British City*.

49. See I. Reid (1981) *Social Class Differences in Britain*, 2nd edition, London: Grant McIntyre Limited, for a key source book of facts on social class.

50. See The Runnymede Trust/Radical Statistics Race Group (1980) *Britain's Black Population* for discussions of *employment* and *health and social services* in relation to the disadvantages experienced by coloured groups.

51. *Home Office Research Study No. 68 (1981)*.

52. S. Field, G. Mair, T. Rees and P. Stevens (1981) *Ethnic Minorities in Britain: A Study of Trends in Their Position since 1961*, London: HMSO.

53. N. Deakin (1977–8) 'Housing and Ethnic Minorities — An Overview', *New Community*, **6**(182), 4–7, cited in the *Home Office Research Study No. 68 (1981)*, p. 20. For further elaboration of Deakin's point see Chapter 4 'Housing and Race' in P. Ratcliffe (1981) *Racism and Reaction*, London: Routledge and Kegan Paul.

54. Ibid.

55. A *first-generation* immigrant was defined as a 'child born abroad with at least one parent born abroad'. A *second-generation* immigrant was defined as a 'child born in Britain with at least one parent born abroad'.

56. P. J. Wedge (1969) 'The Second Follow-up of the National Child Development Study, *Concern*, **3**, 34–9; K. R. Fogelman (ed.) (1976) *Britain's Sixteen Year Olds*, London: National Children's Bureau; J. Essen and M. Ghodsian (1979) 'The Children of Immigrants : School Performance', *New Community*, **7**(3), 422–9; M. Ghodsian and J. Essen (1980) 'Children of Immigrants: Social and Home Circumstances', *New Community*, **8**(3), 195–205.

57. D. Pilling (1980) 'The Attainment of Immigrant Children: A Review of Research', *Highlight No. 40*, London: National Children's Bureau.

Introduction

It was well before the turn of the present century that William James first perceived our dependence upon others for our understanding of *who we are* and *what we are worth* in society.

> A man's *social self* . . . is the recognition which he gets from his mates . . . Properly speaking, a man has as many social selves as there are individuals who recognize him and carry an image of him in their minds. To wound any of these images is to wound him.[1]

The central concern of this chapter is with the social selves of pupils. How, we ask, do children develop ideas and feelings about themselves and others? How and when does ethnic awareness and ethnic differentiation occur? And what exactly is ethnic identity and so-called ethnic-identity confusion? We deal first with the concept of self.

Self-concept

Self-concept can be thought of as the image we have of ourselves as a result of our interactions with important people in our lives. That image consists of all the attitudes, abilities and assumptions that we hold concerning ourselves. It serves as a guide to our behaviour affecting the ways in which we approach tasks and the level at which we perform them. *Self-esteem* is simply the evaluation aspect of self-concept. When we enjoy high self-esteem, we have self-respect and consider ourselves worthy, loved, appreciated, capable and significant.

It is not appropriate here to explore theoretical notions of the self in any depth,[2] nor to attempt a detailed clarification of its close affinity with the concept of identity. The literature suggests that there are almost as many definitions of self-concept as there are theorists engaged in self-concept research. *Psycho-analytical* accounts, for example, propose that self-concept depends upon the nature of the inner image against which we measure ourselves and upon the ways that are available to us to live up to that image. *Social psychological* approaches stress a view of the self as a reflection of what we think others' judgements are of us. *Phenomenological* theory lays emphasis on our conscious feelings and perceptions as the central core of our self-concepts. *Existentialism's* chief concern is with our need to develop a sense of personal identity and to build meaningful links with the world. *Reference-group* theory focuses attention on social comparison processes in the formation and maintenance of the self, the term 'reference group' indicating those with whom we compare ourselves. *Self-consistency* theory proposes that our receptivity to information from others is strongly affected by our need to create and maintain a consistent state in our self-evaluations. Finally, *self-esteem* theory postulates that we have a need for positive feelings of self-worth which is satisfied when we receive others' approval and frustrated when we earn their disdain.

Whatever theory of self takes our fancy, there is a fair measure of agreement among theorists about the early development of the self. It is to this that we now turn.

Children's self-concepts

This crayon is brown. I'll take pink because I like pink. It's a lighter colour and it's better than all the rest. Myself's not pink.
Gregory, 5 year old black[3]

It is during the first five years of life that the most rapid growth of self-concept occurs. Initially, the child's most important developmental task is to grasp that he is distinct and separate from others. In a word, he must learn to distinguish *self* from *non-self*. As Piaget[4] points out, the infant's gradual distinction of himself from the external world is a major achievement at the sensori-motor stage of development. It is at the moment when this separation-individuation process is complete that the child's self-concept is born. Explanations of the early development of the self-concept commonly refer to the paramount importance of a loving mother in the child's acquisition of that basic trust which is the cornerstone of his sense of identity. The child's self-awareness accelerates and expands as he acquires the use of language. According to Mead, language is the connecting link between the self and others:

> Children can verbalize the attitudes of others towards them-selves, their vocal behaviours can be observed by themselves and other people. As children use language in many situations, a concept of 'generalized other' develops . . . Others' attitudes become organized and children can become their own object and think in terms of both the 'I' and the 'me', that is, they see themselves as others see them.[5]

For the pre-school child, the most important others in his life are, of course, his parents. Snygg and Combs affirm the crucial effects that parental concern and attention have on the child's emerging self concept:

> As he is loved or rejected, praised or punished, fails or is able to compete, he comes gradually to regard himself as important or unimportant, adequate or inadequate, handsome or ugly, honest or dishonest . . . or even to describe himself in the terms of those who surround him.[6]

School brings to the child an extension of his environment and a variety of new social contexts in which he can compare himself with others and perceive their evaluation of him. Two British studies[7] have shown that among younger school children physical characteristics loom large in their self-descriptions. As they grow older, children's self-reports give less emphasis to appearance, possessions, family and friends and greater significance to personal beliefs, attitudes and values. At adolescence, self-reports show that young people are extremely socially aware and concerned with how others perceive and evaluate them.

Identity

Mead's concepts of the *I*, the *me* and the *generalised other* to which reference was made earlier remind us that child development is at one and the same time a process of socialisation and internalisation. What initially the child experiences as external injunctions to behave in this way or that,

he eventually takes into his own consciousness. As Berger and
Berger put it:

> In a complicated process of reciprocity and reflection, a
> certain symmetry is established between the inner world of the
> individual and the other social world within which he is being
> socialised.[8]

The *I* and the *me* become 'partners in an on-going conversation',
the *I* representing the awareness of self that we all possess, the
me representing that part of our selves that has been fashioned
and shaped by society. Berger and Berger refer to the *socialized
part of the self* as *identity*. For them, all societies can be viewed
as holding a repertoire of identities — little boy, little girl,
father, mother, policeman, professor and so on. By a kind of
invisible lottery, they say, these identities are assigned to
different individuals. Some are assigned from birth (colour for
instance); others are assigned later in life (clever girl, stupid
boy); still others are put up, as it were, for subscription so that
individuals may gain them by deliberate effort (policeman or
professor perhaps). In learning the repertoire of identities on
offer, children are faced by three inter-related tasks.[9]

First, they must be able to perceive differences between major
groupings of identities in their immediate communities and
recognise those to which they themselves belong. Second, they
must learn the cues by which individuals are classified as identity
holders or non-identity holders. Third, they must learn the
appropriate attitudinal and behavioural responses towards
individuals who have achieved or have been assigned particular
identities. We may rephrase these broad statements of identity-
learning tasks by asking the direct question, 'How do children
categorize themselves and others and what cues do they use?'[10]
We focus our attention solely on ethnic identity and ethnic
awareness.

Ethnic Awareness and Ethnic Identification: I

In the literature on children's ethnic awareness it is scarcely
possible to read a research report that *does not* refer to the
pioneering work of the Clarks[11] in the United States in the 1940s.
The husband and wife team used doll-choice techniques to elicit
children's ideas about themselves. They concluded that black

children have identity problems arising out of difficulties in coming to terms with their colour.

Doll choice and the complementary technique of selecting photographs or drawings remain popular ways of researching into children's self-identities. A spate of studies[12] in the 1950s, '60s and early '70s produced findings on samples of coloured children as far afield as the USA, South Africa, Hong Kong, the West Indies, Great Britain and New Zealand. Broadly, what they had to say can be paraphrased by Coopersmith's[13] observations on the self-concept and self-esteem of black children in the United States of America. Black children, Coopersmith observed, are members of minority groups that have internalised the negative stereotypes imposed upon them by majority communities. Black self-hate and self-rejection arises out of lack of status, economic insecurity, social isolation, public disrespect and limited horizons, all of which lead to personal feelings of powerlessness, rejection and isolation. If ever conditions existed that would produce low self-esteem, Coopersmith opined, they presumably occur in the life of American blacks. In similar vein, Vaughan[14] explained Maori children's devaluation of their ethnic origins, Gregor and McPherson[15] accounted for Bantu children's self-rejection and Milner[16] interpreted the out-group preferences of Asian and West Indian children in British schools.

Milner's study involved 100 white, 100 West Indian and 100 Asian children, all between five and eight years of age, and all drawn from multicultural infant and junior schools in London.

Adapting the Clarks' doll choice technique, Milner asked of his subjects, 'Which doll looks most like you?' (*identity*); 'Which one do you like the best?' (*preference*); and 'Which one (picture) of these two men is the bad man?' (*stereotype*). Milner's results are set out in Box 4.1 on page 82.

How can these findings be explained? Did the coloured children in Milner's study really think that they were white? That is to say, were they *cognitively-confused* as a result of their minority group status in an overwhelmingly white culture? Or did coloured children's choices of white dolls result from self-rejection and own group devaluation? Milner plumped for the latter explanation by insisting that black British children showed strong preference for the dominant white group and an equally strong tendency to devalue their own group.

A study of a similar age range of children in multicultural

Box 4.1: Self-identities and Group Preferences in White, West Indian and Asian Children Aged Five to Eight Years

---

(identity)   Which doll looks most like you?
100% of the white children chose the white doll
 45% of the West Indian children chose the white doll
 24% of the Asian children chose the white doll

(preference)   Which doll do you like best?
100% of the white children chose the white doll
 82% of the West Indian children chose the white doll
 65% of the Asian children chose the white doll

(stereotype)   Which one of these two men is the bad man?
 0% of the white children had negative sterotypes about their own group
72% of the West Indian children had negative stereotypes about their own group
65% of the Asian children had negative stereotypes about their own group

---

Source: Adapted from Milner.[17]

London schools, but using a different approach, drew similar conclusions to Milner's. Bagley and Coard's[18] subjects were 73 white children and 43 children of West Indian origin of three schools. The primary interest of the researchers was in the children's body imagery. With the sensitivity of such an inquiry in mind, three pertinent questions were 'buried' in a lengthy oral questionnaire and introduced with 'dummy' prompts such as, if you could be born again, how tall would you like to be? The questions about body imagery were: *What colour hair would you choose to have? What colour skin? What colour eyes?*

Inter alia, Bagley and Coard found that 60 per cent of the children of West Indian origin expressed the desire to change the colour of their skin, the colour of their eyes, the colour or texture of their hair, or all three conditions. Such a level of self-rejection, they reported, did not occur among the white children in the study.

The result of both Milner's and Bagley and Coard's studies confirm evidence on the evolution of children's racial attitudes. *In societies which accord inferior status to racial minorities, children learn from a very early age the relative worth of being a black or white person.* As Jeffcoate[19] points out, the dawning of racial awareness around the age of three is generally accompanied or quickly followed by signs of racial preference and rejection. Even five-year-olds, Jeffcoate concedes, are capable

of commenting on the different social and economic roles
fulfilled by different racial groups.

Two British studies,[20] however, show that in *situations where
different racial groups are accorded equal status, the emergence
of racial awareness in young children is NOT accompanied by
negative evaluation of coloured groups.* The *situations* in
question were:

1. The foster homes in which the children of West African
   academics studying in Britain were left with white foster
   parents and their offspring for considerable lengths of time.

2. Two London nursery schools composed of a large number
   of white children and a small number of boys and girls of
   African and Asian origin.

In situation (1) Marsh[21] used colour photographs (Who looks
like you? Who do you like best?) to study the *cognitive
awareness of race* and the *values associated with race* among
some 77 white and West African children aged between two
years seven months and six years five months. He concluded:

Whilst the development of 'race values' in children is logically
contingent upon knowledge of racial differences, the obverse is
not necessarily true. That is to say, children can *know* all
about racial differences but do not *necessarily* attach value
judgements to them, especially those leading to the formation
of racial stereotypes, *unless* they are exposed to socializing
forces characterized by overt racial consciousness and/or
hostility. In the setting of this study such socializing forces
were absent . . . *hence* overt race values beyond those affective
bonds formed in personal relationships were also absent in the
children here tested and observed.

In situation (2), Laishley's[22] two nursery-school samples consisted of 68 children aged between three to five years in school 1
and 122 children aged between three and five years in school 2.
Doll choice was the technique employed to explore children's
awareness of differences in skin colour, their preferences for skin
colour and their interaction with children of different racial
groups. The form of Laishley's inquiry can be ascertained from

the description of her materials and questioning set out in Box 4.2. Laishley' conclusions echo those of Marsh:

> In this sample of London children, awareness of differences in skin colour, where they exist, are little more than the awareness of differences in colour. The differences between white and black and brown does not seem likely to be perceived as qualitatively different from the distinction between any other colours. Skin colour does not appear to be a very salient factor in these children's interaction with other children . . . Furthermore, none of the white subjects of this study showed the disturbance and self-rejection reported by so many [other] studies . . .

Box 4.2: A Doll-choice Study of Young Children's Racial Awareness and Racial Preferences

Dolls Used	Wording of Question	Type of Question
1. One brown and one white doll of the subject's own sex	'Which doll looks most like you?' 'Why do you say this one?'	
2. One white boy, one brown boy, one white girl	'Which doll is the different one?' Why do you say this one?'	Questions on awareness of differences in skin colour
3. One brown girl, one white girl, one brown boy	'Which doll is the different one?' 'Why do you say this one?'	
4. One white girl	'Let's pretend it's this little girl's birthday and her mummy says she can have six children to her party. Show me the six children she is going to choose.'	Questions on preference for one skin colour
5. One brown boy	'Let's pretend it's a rainy day and this little boy is playing in his house. He can have six other children to play with him. Show me the six children he is going to choose.'	
6. All dolls	'Give me the three dolls that you think are the nicest.'	
7. One brown boy and one brown girl	'Have you seen any brown boys and girls?' 'Do you play with any brown boys and girls?'	Racial contact questions

Source: Adapted from Laishley.[23]

The absence of overt negative evaluations of coloured pupils on the part of the white nursery-school children studied by Laishley by no means implies that such a youthful age group is incapable of prejudiced thinking. As Laishley observes, 'where prejudiced attitudes and behaviour exist in the adult population, young children, even those of nursery age, will repeat this prejudice, although they may not fully comprehend the words and actions'. This latter point was well demonstrated by Jeffcoate[24] in an experiment in an all white nursery school whose headteacher firmly believed young children to be 'innocent of racial sentiments'.

Two separate intakes (a morning and an afternoon session) of nursery-school children were shown 14 photographs presenting black people in a variety of situations and in a respectful and unstereotyped way. However, the headteacher was encouraged to employ the photographs differently with the two groups. In the morning session, the head stimulated discussion in her usual manner, asking questions about the photographs (race and ethnicity, of course, excepted). In the afternoon session, the head simply drew the children's attention to the photographs without asking any questions at all. The dramatic differences in the responses of the two groups shown in Box 4.3 refuted her hypothesis that neither group of children would make disparaging or derisory remarks about skin colour.

Box 4.3: An Experiment in Racial Ideas and Feelings in an all White Nursery School

In the *morning session*, the children had a lively, interested discussion. At no time did any child refer to a racial or a cultural difference in connection with the photographs.

In the *afternoon session*, the children made such negative comments about the photographs, punctuated by cries of 'Ugh! Blackies', that within a few minutes the head felt obliged to intervene and terminate the session.

Source: Adapted from Jeffcoate.[25]

How can these strikingly different reactions of the two groups of nursery-school children be explained, particularly in light of the headteacher's insistence that there were no differences between the morning and afternoon intakes to her school?

Jeffcoate points to the importance of the attitude to race that the head implicitly encouraged in her school. Along with her teaching staff, she believed that nursery/infant children were unaware of race. Moreover, she felt it wrong to promote awareness of racial or cultural differences. In effect, says Jeffcoate, the head instituted a *taboo* on race and the children clearly demonstrated that they had learned and internalised that *taboo* in so far as it operated at school. Pupils in the morning session behaved as they were expected to behave under the conventional pedagogic regime of question and answer. They avoided the *taboo* area, taking the headteacher's lead and talking warmly and interestingly about the photographs.

It was the headteacher's atypical behaviour with the afternoon group that signified 'a moral as well as a pedagogic withdrawal', leaving the children free to respond in a relatively uninhibited fashion. In effect, it seems that they were allowed free rein to express their 'out-of-school-learning' about coloured minorities.

Ethnic Awareness and Ethnic Identification: II

Since the mid 1970s, American studies[26] of ethnic awareness and ethnic identification have shown that the widely-held conclusion of earlier research, to the effect that coloured groups are self-rejecting in respect of their ethnic identities, needs considerable qualification. What these more recent studies demonstrate is a significant decline in own-group rejection among coloured minorities. To no small extent these changes are a consequence of the vigorous and sustained efforts of Civil Rights and Black Power movements to remove the stigma of skin colour, and the increasing involvement and representation of coloured people in all aspects of the social, economic and political fabric of American society at local and at national level. Not surprisingly, more recent studies of coloured pupils also report a greater degree of self-acceptance and pride in ethnic identity. The theme 'black is beautiful', which accompanied demands that American schools and colleges should include courses on African culture and African history, reflects the increasing self-pride and self-acceptance among coloured students that is reported in the American research literature from mid 1970s onwards.

What of the situation in Britain? Of the few recent empirical studies of ethnic awareness and ethnic indentification that have been carried out in this country, two deserve special mention. Davey and Mullin[27] employed a factorial[28] design in their investigation of the development of racial attitudes in primary-school children.

Photographs were used with seven, eight, nine and ten year old boys and girls of white, West Indian and Asian origin to discover their *ethnic awareness*, (Which one looks most like you?) and *ethnic preferences* (If you could choose, which one would you most like to be?).

In contrast to the findings of coloured children's self-rejection reported in studies by Milner[29] and by Bagley and Coard,[30] the pooled results from West Indian and Asian groups in Davey and Mullin's study show that statistically, there is no greater likelihood of coloured pupils saying that they are white than there is of white pupils saying that they are coloured. That is to say, these findings confirm the trend towards own-group acceptance reported in more recent American studies.

Davey and Mullin's analysis of their ethnic-preference data, however, tells a very different story (see Box 4.4). Whereas white

Box 4.4: Percentaged Own-group Preferences Among White, West Indian and Asian Origin Primary-School Children

Group	Age				Average
	7	8	9	10	
White	85%	83%	87%	90%	86%
West Indian	38%	50%	44%	66%	50%
Asian	39%	46%	46%	50%	45%

Source: Adapted from Davey and Mullin.[31]

children's preferences are largely for their own group, West Indian and Asian children's clearly are not. Nor is it the case that the two coloured minorities prefer each other. Only 4 per cent of the Asian children chose a West Indian photograph; only 5 per cent of the West Indian children would have preferred to have been an Asian child. Overwhelmingly, both minority groups chose the photograph of a white boy or girl.

Taking their group identification and group preference data together, Davey and Mullin found that 40 per cent of the coloured children identified with their own race group but expressed a preference to belong to another racial group (i.e. white):

> Minority group children . . . have little doubt as to who has the favoured place in the social pecking order . . . The discrepancy between the results from the identification and preference tests [suggest] that *it is in this crevice between the heightened sense of personal worth and the sharpened perception of relative status that the seeds of inter-group hostility will germinate.*

A second study recently carried out in Britain raises questions about some of the methods employed by researchers into children's ethnic awareness and identification.

Two-choice doll or photograph test situations, its author Wilson[32] argues, confront children with a ready-built model of society in which the racial structure is strictly dichotomous. She queries whether or not students of race relations are justified in applying the dichotomous black/white American model to the study of ethnic identity in coloured British children. 'Do children actually see their immediate everyday racial identity in terms of the two distinct categories, "black" and "white"?' Wilson ingenuously asks. Her study of 51 racially-mixed children aged between six and nine suggests that when the rigidity of a two-fold identity test is relaxed and young children are encouraged to give *their definitions* of the situations in which they find themselves, they employ complex criteria in constructing their ethnic identities:

> What was striking about the children's responses was . . . the taken-for-granted quality the judgements seemed to have for the children. The complexity of their assessments are impressive: some children took fine gradations of colour as their main criteria . . . others used the racial combination of the parents as the deciding factor . . . some [used] only culture, ignoring mixture and colour; 'Indian', 'Jamaican', and 'English' . . . some children managed to combine all or several of these elements into a set . . . many children were

not only able to isolate *their* racial categories but . . . they had
their own ideas about how 'coloured' related to 'black',
whether or not being 'Indian' corresponded to being 'half-
black', where 'brown' fitted in to 'coloured'.[33]

In effect, Wilson argues, these children were conforming to
what the 'real-life' situation is in contemporary Britain, namely
that most people use a variety of criteria to construct numerous
(not *two*) racial categories to express their own and others'
positions in the racial structure. Her study, moreover, is a timely
warning that a child's developing ethnic awareness and ethnic
identity is a subtle and complex process that draws upon factors
often overlooked by social scientists as potentially significant
categories of racial identification. As Wilson observes, '. . . in
the street, the home and the playground it is often necessary for
a child to recognise and juggle with all the different characteristics that go to make up *race* — how I look, speak, dress,
dance, do my hair; what music and food I like, what stereotypes
I hold about my own and other groups'. She concludes, 'in
future research on ethnic identity, we need to soil our neat
theoretical hands with the real life vagueness, imprecision and
confusion of racial categorisation in Britain'.

Ethnic-identity Confusion

The concept of *personal identity* and *identity-development* are
closely linked with the work of Eric Erikson.[34]
   Erikson proposes that one of the major 'tasks' of adolescence
is to 're-synthesise all childhood identifications in some unique
way and yet in concordance with the roles offered by some wider
section of society'. Successful *identity-formation* is contrasted
with what Erikson terms *identity-diffusion*, the symptoms of
which are said to include time-confusion, bi-sexual confusion,
authority-confusion, confusion over values and role fixation.
According to Erikson, where adolescents are unable to establish
a consistent style of organisation of their experiences, a state of
identity-confusion may arise. Where society's characterisations of
adolescents can be brought into accord with their emerging self-
definitions, then the 'task' of identity-formation is likely to be
successful. Successful identity-development requires sufficient
time for experimentation during adolescence. Bringing

adolescence to an end too early, Erikson asserts, results in *identity-foreclosure* rather than the *final identity* that makes the completion of adolescence and the emergence of adulthood.

Erikson's insight and compelling ideas have had wide appeal despite the vagueness of his concepts and the difficulty of putting them to empirical test. On the face of it, his theory seems particularly well-suited to accounting for the predicament of adolescent offspring of coloured immigrants in Britain. As Kitwood observes (speaking specifically of contemporary British-Asian youth in Bradford):

> As adolescents, (Erikson's theory suggests) they would be likely to find it extremely hard to develop a consistent style of life and a unity in ordering their experience. They are required to act within two very contrasting cultural frameworks. They might be supposed to have a particularly strong tendency to reject identifications with parents and others in the Asian community, while perhaps having insufficient contact with the kind of people with whom they could realistically identify else-where . . . If any group could be held to exemplify Erikson's theory in its negative aspect — the probability of failure to complete the 'task' of adolescence — it is this group (of Muslim adolescents).[35]

We return to Kitwood's test of Erikson's theory shortly. First, however, we illustrate some of Erikson's concepts and ideas as they are employed by Weinreich[36] in a case study of John, a 16-year-old West Indian whose identity confusion is said to arise out of his 'identification with a group (white) other than his own (black)'.

Weinreich elicits from John those groups of people who have been important sources of positive reference for him (*his past identifications*) and those who currently serve as salient parts of his self-image (*his current identifications*). The strengths of these past and present identifications are measured along a continuum ranging from 0.00 (absence of identification) to 1.00 (maximum identification). Box 4.5 below purports to reveal the 'heart' of John's problem, that is the changes that have occurred between his past and his current identifications with West Indian and English people.

Box 4.5 shows a dramatic shift in John's identifications

Box 4.5: Changes between John's Past and Current Identifications

Reference groups	Past identification (a)	Current identification (b)	Direction of change
West Indian people	.27	.08	away from this group
West Indian boys	.40	.38	away from this group
West Indian girls	.20	.15	away from this group
Black Power	.27	.15	away from this group
That little group of blacks	.53	.08	away from this group
English people	.27	.46	towards this group
White boys	.20	.31	towards this group
White girls	.40	.27	away from this group
Friendly whites	.33	.62	towards this group

Source: Adapted from Weinreich.[37]

across ethnic boundaries. John's identity crisis resolution, Weinreich observes, has resulted in his hostile appraisal of certain blacks and his identification generally with whites. Interview data are presented in support of this interpretation:

> John *(describing Jamaicans)*. I don't like their temper and how they goes around in their little groups.
> John *(talking of West Indian girls)*. I don't like them. They haven't got nothing to them. No looks, nothing. Don't take any notice.
> John *(talking about his skin colour)*. I don't like my own colour. I must admit that.
> John *(explaining why people respect him)*. I goes around with whites, 'cos not many kids do that.

Weinreich's explanation of John's predicament is both perceptive and persuasive. However, in light of our earlier remarks (page 36) on the inability of falsifying Freudian theory, we leave readers to make up their own minds about his psycho-analytical interpretation of the boy's identity confusion and turn instead to Kitwood's[38] study of British-Asian adolescents in Bradford.

Basically what Kitwood has to say is this. He questions the widely-held belief that adolescents of Asian origin living in this country are liable to so-called identity-confusion. It is not Asian adolescents who are confused, says Kitwood, but (indigenous white) observers! The former have no problems with identity; it's the latter who have problems of identification. Kitwood argues his case[39] on the basis of intensive observations and discussions with groups of British-Asian adolescents. He traces the development of personal identities among these young Muslims within a framework of three basic social psychological processes — *social feedback, social comparison* and *self-attribution.*

The first element, *social feedback*, refers to the making of inferences from the reactions of others. Muslim adolescents, Kitwood observes, gain information about themselves from a wider variety of others' reactions than is available to their white indigenous counterparts for, whereas many of the latter 'move out' from home, psychologically speaking, from adolescence onwards, the typical Muslim adolescent remains firmly integrated into the Asian community despite the fact that many Muslim boys may also enjoy considerable personal liberty during their early teens to stay out fairly late, visit amusement arcades, cinemas and discos, to go into pubs and to try their success with a 'British' girlfriend. *Social comparison*, the second element in the process of self-conception, requires the individual to relate his or her performance to that of others. Muslim adolescents, Kitwood notes, make their most significant social comparisons with others from the same kind of cultural background, that is to say, other Muslim youth who are known through the 'community', the extended family and the school. In addition to such general criteria of social comparison as appearance, temperament and achievement, Muslim adolescents have recourse to a number of unique perspectives that are especially relevant to their situation. Kitwood identifies these as being 'traditional' rather than 'modern'; 'devout' as opposed to 'irreligious'; 'aware of Asian culture' rather than 'unaware'; 'allowed freedom' as opposed to 'restricted'; and 'taking a stand on racist issues' as compared with 'remaining silent'.

Frequently, too, social comparison processes arise out of visits to Pakistan where the culture shock commonly experienced by many British-Asian adolescents soon becomes part of the stock of common knowledge of Muslim youth back home in the North of England.

The final element in the process of self-conception, *self-attribution*, refers to the drawing of direct inferences without reference to others; in a word, by *self-assessment.* Because they have generally enjoyed a more sheltered childhood than their white counterparts, Muslim adolescents face many more occasions during which they experience events that are funda- mentally new. In the absence of clear evidence through social feedback and social comparison, Kitwood argues, they are obliged to fall back upon direct inferences from actions and inner states when reactions such as, 'I didn't know that I would feel like that,' or 'I didn't know that I had it in me to behave like that,' may well occur following a first challenge to parental authority or a first opportunity to act on feelings of sexual attraction. Whilst young Muslims no doubt engage in such reflections either privately or in discussion with friends it is very questionable whether this aspect of self-assessment challenges their sense of who they are which is so firmly and socially grounded.

All in all, Kitwood concludes, it is not British-Asian adolescents who are confused but *us.* Most of us meet these young people only superficially. When we do, we are presented with two conflicting sets of data:

> On the one hand, some aspects of their presence are definitely foreign, even mysterious or exotic: notably their physical appearance and their use, on occasions, of unintelligible tongues. On the other hand they often adopt interactional styles virtually indistinguishable from those of their British contemporaries, including speaking English with impeccable regional accents.

Most British people, says Kitwood, have no clear basis either in theory or experience by which to reconcile these two sets of data. One solution that is quite illogical in light of the evidence is to attribute to these boys and girls *a problem of personal identity,* the ground having been prepared by the incorporation of Erikson's ideas into commonsense psychology. Nor is this commonly-made attribution falsified, Kitwood notes, since for most of us interaction with these young people remains at a superficial level.

Like Wilson's study of racial identities, Kitwood's timely research calls into question widely-held oversimplifications and inaccuracies that continue to feed majority views about racial and ethnic minorities in Great Britain.

Children's Racial Attitudes and Behaviour

Recall that earlier in the chapter (page 80) we talked of three interrelated tasks facing children in the development of their social selves. The first two of these — (1) perceiving differences between major groupings of identities, and (2) learning cues by which identity and non-identity holders are categorised — we have dealt with at some length in our discussion of self-concepts, ethnic awareness and ethnic identification. We turn now, albeit briefly, to the third and final task, namely, the learning of appropriate attitudes and behaviours towards individuals who have achieved or have been assigned particular identities. We outline the findings of three British studies that bear upon this question.

Laishley's[40] study of ethnic attitudes among some two hundred or more white, comprehensive school pupils is based upon a model of attitude formation and development that closely parallels the one we employ in Chapter 2 in our discussion of categorisation and stereotyping. Laishley's model is set out in Box 4.6. It shows a sequence of developing attitudes that continues throughout childhood as the individual's cognitive growth allows for the comprehension of concepts necessary for additional processes. By adolescence, the essential structuring shown in Box 4.6 will generally have been developed.

Box 4.6: The Development of Ethnic Attitudes

Recognition of differences between people
↓
Belief in the importance of these differences
↓
Categorization system for differentiating and labelling people
↓
Like/dislike, preference, approach/avoidance
↓
Attribution of traits, the stereotyping process
↓
Perceptions of social situations, interpretations of the positions of ethnic groups in society

Source: Adapted from Laishley.[41]

Laishley used a questionnaire to obtain her data. It consisted of five scales, each of which related to a distinct aspect of the structuring of ethnic attitudes shown in Box 4.6. Thus, a *Social Comparison* scale tapped white pupils' needs for positive self-images when they compared themselves with their fellow coloured pupils; a *Group Images* scale measured white pupils' attributions of traits to coloured groups; a *Homogenous Thinking* scale elicited the extent to which white pupils saw all members of a particular coloured group as 'alike'; an *Intrinsic Thinking* scale revealed how white pupils attributed responsibility for various social conditions experienced by coloured-minority groups. Was it, for example, 'their own fault' or was it, perhaps, due to circumstances beyond their control? Finally, a *General Beliefs* scale exposed racial attitudes to do with such matters as 'coloured immigration to Britain', 'mixed-marriages' and so on.

By exploring associations between pupils' scores on each of the five scales, Laishley was able to tease out a description of prejudiced white adolescents and, incidentally, to substantiate the proposed patterning of racist attitudes set out in Box 4.6. We summarise Laishley's conclusions in Box 4.7 below.

Box 4.7: A Profile of Prejudiced White Secondary School Students

Prejudiced white adolescents, Laishley reports, have high needs for positive self images when comparing themselves with their fellow coloured students, the latter serving as semipermanent comparison groups which prejudiced whites use to their own advantage in self-enhancement. Prejudiced white students are further distinguished by their negative stereotyping of coloured pupils and their beliefs that coloured groups are themselves responsible for the social conditions they experience rather than agencies outside their control, views incidentally, Laishley notes, which allow person-to-person comparisons to the advantage of prejudiced whites. Finally, prejudiced white students hold negative attitudes towards coloured groups and these again can be construed as serving to support the use of coloured ethnic minorities to the advantage of *self* and the detriment of *other*.

Source: Adapted from Laishley.[42]

Bagley and Verma's[43] research with white British adolescents largely confirmed the stepwise nature of attitude development set out in Box 4.6 above. But, whereas Laishley's study focused specifically on cognitive aspects of ethnic attitudes, Bagley and Verma went a step further by asking the question, 'Do prejudiced white students carry their racist attitudes through into actual behaviour towards their coloured fellow-pupils?' What Bagley and Verma did was this.

First they identified highly prejudiced white pupils by means of a *beliefs measure* (e.g. West Indians are peaceful/aggressive clean/dirty; kind/unkind, etc.); a *feelings measure* (e.g. acceptance or rejection of black doctors, West Indians, black immigration, etc.); and a *behavioural readiness measure* (e.g. having a black boy/girlfriend; letting a room to a coloured person; employing a Pakistani, etc.).

They then observed the classrooms in which highly-prejudiced, neutral and least-prejudiced white students went about their studies alongside coloured fellow-pupils, scoring 'inter-ethnic contacts' as they termed them as follows:

negative contact (abuse, hostility)   − 1
neutral contact   + 1
positive contact, (warmth, friendship) + 2

Bagley and Verma found that 66 per cent of the interactions made by highly-prejudiced white students with coloured pupils were classified as *negative contacts* (there were numerous *no contacts* too). By contrast, 75 per cent of the interactions between least-prejudiced whites with coloured boys and girls were *positive contacts* and only 8 per cent were *negative*, thus confirming the hypothesised connection between racist attitudes and hostile behaviour in school.

We turn now to the third and final British study. Whereas the Laishley and the Bagley and Verma studies specifically set out to identify racially-prejudiced white students, Simmons and Wade's research had other intentions. Nevertheless, their findings allow us to conclude this chapter on a more hopeful note.

Simmons and Wade[44] used sentence-completion techniques in a recent large scale study of adolescent values to elicit boys' and girls' views on a range of issues and experiences directly relevant to young people in contemporary society.

Eight-hundred-and-twenty pupils in six Midlands secondary schools (one of which has a substantial racial-minority population) completed an open-ended questionnaire, one sentence-stem of which asked for their view on: *The sort of person I would least like to be* . . . Out of 820 responses only five referred to race or to ethnicity. Of the five responses (four boys and one girl) only one was overtly racist: '. . . is someone who has got something wrong with them, a tramp, a nigger, and a chink and a paki'. The others were either 'neutral': '. . . would be a black man', or 'sympathetic': '. . . is a negro or a coloured man because even nowadays they are treated as animals in some parts of the world and groups such as the NF and the Klu-Klux-Klan'.

The paucity of racial responses to *the-sort-of-person-I-would-least-like-to-be* stem prompted an analysis of every sentence completion task in the questionnaire in a search for any comment that could be construed as referring to colour or ethnicity. Only five more responses were found, all elicited from the prompt sentence: *The worst thing about life is . . .* Of the five responses (two boys and three girls), three were overtly racist:

'. . . Niggers who think they are big' (M), '. . . Too many foreign people ruining the country. I'm a nazi. I'm proud of it too' (F), '. . . having blacks in the country' (M). One was 'sympathetic': '. . . no matter what colour you may be you have a right to be happy and should be able to live without thinking about being safe' (F), and one had to do with personal relationships: '. . . my mum and dad. they don't like my boyfriend because he is black and I am white and they did every thing to make me pack him in but I would not. I am a very stubbon girl' (F).

We share the view of the researchers that the extremely small degree of racially-hostile comment in the anonymous, open-ended situations of this large-scale survey is very encouraging indeed.

Notes

1. W. James (1890) *Principles of Psychology*, New York: Holt, Rinehart and Winston.
2. For a useful review of the theoretical foundations of self-theory, see: S. C. Samuels (1977) *Enhancing Self-concept in Early Childhood*, New York: Human Sciences Press. We draw upon Samuels' account in our brief commentary on theories of self. See also: J. B. Thomas (1979) *The Self In Education*, Windsor: NFER; R. Burns (1979) *Self-Concept: Theory, Methodology and Research*, London: Longman.
3. L. Y. Young (1978) 'A Comparative Study of the Evaluative Meaning of Colour: Implications for Identity and the Development of Self-esteem in Young Black Children', unpublished MPhil dissertation, University of Surrey.

4. J. Piaget (1926) *The Language and Thought of the Child*, New York: Harcourt, Brace and World.

5. The theorist we refer to is Mead and his concept of the 'generalized other'. Our account follows Samuels, *Enhancing Self-concept*, p. 71. See G. H. Mead (1956) *Mind, Self and Society from the Standpoint of a Social Behaviourist*, Chicago: University of Chicago Press.

6. D. Snygg and A. W. Combs (1949) *Individual Behaviour: A New Frame of Reference For Psychology*, New York: Harper.

7. J. B. Thomas (1974) 'Self Pictures of Children', *Froebel Journal,* **30**, 31–6; W. J. Livesley and D. B. Bromley (1973) *Person Perception in Childhood and Adolescence*, London: Wiley.

8. P. L. Berger and B. Berger (1975) *Sociology: A Biographical Approach*, New York: Basic Books.

9. A. G. Davey and M. V. Norburn (1980) 'Ethnic Awareness and Ethnic Differentiation Among Primary School Children', *New Community,* **8**, 51–60.

10. Ibid.

11. K. Clark and M. Clark (1947) 'Racial Identification and Preference in Negro Children' in T. M. Newcomb and E. L. Hartley (eds), *Readings in Social Psychology*, New York: Holt, Rinehart and Winston; K. Clark and M. Clark (1950) 'Emotional Factors in Racial Identification and Preference in Negro Children', *Journal of Negro Education,* **19**, 341–50.

12. See, for example: A. J. Gregor and D. A. McPherson (1966) 'Racial Preference and Ego-identity Among White and Bantu Children in the Republic of South Africa', *Genetic Psychological Monographs,* **73**, 217–54; D. Milner (1972) 'Racial Identification and Preference in Black British Children', *European Journal of Social Psychology,* **3**, 281–95; L. Young and C. Bagley (1979) 'Identity, Self-esteem and Evaluation of Colour and Ethnicity in Young Children in Jamaica and London', *New Community,* **7**(2), 154–69; A. Marsh (1970) 'Awareness of Racial Differences in West African and British Children', *Race,* **11**(3), 289–302; G. M. Vaughan (1964) 'The Development of Ethnic Attitudes in New Zealand School Children', *Genetic Psychological Monographs,* **70**, 135–75; J. Morland (1966) 'A Comparison of Race Awareness in Northern and Southern Children', *American Journal of Orthopsychiatry,* **36**, 22–31; J. Morland (1969) 'Race Awareness Among American and Hong Kong Chinese Children', *American Journal of Sociology,* **75**, 360–74.

13. S. Coopersmith (1975) 'Self-concept, Race and Class' in G. K. Verma and C. Bagley (eds), *Race and Education Across Cultures*, London: Heinemann.

14. Vaughan, 'The Development of Ethnic Attitudes'.

15. Gregor and McPherson, 'Racial Preference and Ego-identity'.

16. Milner, 'Racial Identification and Preference'.

17. D. Milner (1975) *Children and Race*, Harmondsworth: Penguin.

18. C. Bagley and B. Coard (1975) 'Cultural Knowledge and Rejection of Ethnic Identity in West Indian Children in London' in G. Verma and C. Bagley (eds), *Race and Education Across Cultures*, London: Heinemann.

19. R. Jeffcoate (1977) 'Children's Racial Ideas and Feelings', *English in Education,* **11**(1), 32–46.

20. A. Marsh (1970) 'Awareness of Racial Differences in West African and British Children', *Race,* **11**(3), 289–302; J. Laishley (1971) 'Skin Colour Awareness and Preferences in London Nursery School Children', *Race,* **13**(3), 47–64.

21. Ibid.

22. Ibid.

23. Ibid.

24. Jeffcoate, 'Children's Racial Ideas'.

25. Ibid.

26. J. Hraba and G. Grant (1970) 'Black is Beautiful: A Re-examination of Racial Preference and Indentification', *Journal of Personality and Social Psychology*, **16**, 398–402; S. H. Ward and J. Braun (1972) 'Self-esteem and Racial Preference in Black Children', *American Journal of Orthopsychiatry*, **42**, 644–7; D. J. Fox and V. B. Jordan (1973) 'Racial Preference and Identification of Black, American, Chinese and White Children', *Genetic Psychological Monographs*, **88**, 229–86; P. L. Bunton and T. A. Weissbach (1974) 'Attitudes Towards Blackness of Black Pre-school Children Attending Community Controlled or Public Schools, *Journal of Social Psychology*, **92**, 53–9; C. L. Moore (1976) 'The Racial Preference and Attitude of Pre-school Black Children', *Journal of Genetic Psychology*, **129**, 37–44; Y. M. Epstein, E. Krupat and C. Obudho (1976) 'Clean is Beautiful: The Effects of Race and Cleanliness on Children's Preferences', *Journal of Social Issues*, **39**, 109–18.

27. A. G. Davey and P. N. Mullin (1980) 'Ethnic Identification and Preference of British Primary School Children', *Journal of Child Psychology and Psychiatry*, **21**, 241–51.

28. Factorial designs enable investigators to study the effects of a number of variables within the scope of one inquiry. In Davey and Mullin's study, *race, sex, age, region of the country* and *density of immigrant population* were all included in the design of the research.

29. Milner, *Children and Race*.

30. Bagley and Coard, 'Cultural Knowledge'.

31. Davey and Mullin, 'Ethnic Identification and Preference'.

32. A. Wilson (1981) 'Mixed Race Children: An Exploratory Study of Racial Categorisation and Identity', *New Community*, **9**, 36–43.

33. Ibid.

34. E. Erikson (1965) *Childhood and Society*, New York: Norton; E. Erikson (1968) *Identity: Youth and Crisis*, London: Faber and Faber.

35. T. Kitwood (1982) 'Self-conception Among Young British-Asian Muslims: Confutation of a Stereotype' in G. Breakwell (ed.), *Threatened Identities,*, London: John Wiley.

36. P. Weinreich (1979) 'Cross-ethnic Identification and Self-rejection in a Black Adolescent' in G. K. Verma and C. Bagley (eds), *Race, Education and Identity*, London: Macmillan.

37. Ibid.

38. Kitwood, 'Self-conception'.

39. Kitwood's explanation is in line with Ballard's account of the adeptness of young Asians at dealing with their existence in two parallel worlds (see page 27).

40. J. Laishley (1975) 'Cognitive Processes in Adolescent Ethnic Attitudes' in G. K. Verma and C. Bagley (eds), *Race and Education Across Cultures*, London: Heinemann.

41. Ibid.

42. Ibid.

43. C. Bagley and G. K. Verma (1975) 'Inter-ethnic Attitudes and Behaviour in British Multi-racial Schools' in C. Bagley and G. K. Verma (eds), *Race and Education Across Cultures*, London: Heinemann.

44. C. Simmons and W. Wade (forthcoming) *I Like To Say What I Think*. London: Kogan Page.

5 FRIENDSHIP AND SOCIAL RELATIONS IN MULTICULTURAL CLASSROOMS

Introduction

As many of our schools, particularly those in urban conurbations, have become increasingly ethnically mixed, research suggests that racial homogeneity has become a salient characteristic of the composition of peer groups within these institutions. This tendency towards ethnocentricity, evident from work done in both the United States and Britain, appears to assume a decisive influence on pupils' careers, educationally, economically and socially, often in undesirable ways. What is called for, therefore, is an exploration of strategies for restructuring group relations in ways which will make the differences among individuals less invidious and less likely to be a source of conflict, tension and frustration.[1] Before this can be done, however, the degree to which ethnic-minority pupils interact with each other and their white school mates needs to be studied carefully and one way of doing this is to examine pupils' friendship choices, for the evidence to date, manifested in the large number of in-group choices and nominations, clearly indicates that race is a crucial factor operating in the peer group selection process amongst both white indigenous and ethnic-minority pupils.

Children's racial attitudes have traditionally interested social scientists and have increasingly come under the scrutiny of educational researchers. Some of the interest has been theoretically motivated: the study of racial attitudes, for example, throws light on the broader topic of socialisation practices and outcomes. Interest in more recent times, however, stems from a desire to use social science and educational research in the pursuit of racial equality and racial integration. The generally unattractive picture presented in this connection by research so far would seem to indicate that the enterprise is fully justified and that an even greater concentration of effort is called for.

The summary findings of the research literature on children's awareness of, and response to, colour differences and the consequences of these for friendship choice and social relations in multicultural classrooms[2] indicates that: (1) children very early recognise colour differences and correctly identify their own skin colour; (2) recognition and identification are soon followed by the development of racial attitudes, perhaps as early as the pre-school years, the attitudes strengthening with age; and (3) behavioural discrimination, measured in the main by friendship choice, develops rather later, during the primary-school years.

Given this context, and having examined the factors of ethnic awareness, identification and attitude in the preceding chapter, it is our intention in the present chapter to take the third conclusion just noted and use this as a point of departure, that is behavioural discrimination as measured by friendship choice. We shall look at two aspects of this, first, ethnic preference and second, some, at least, of the factors that appear to influence sociometric choice.

Such an undertaking requires that three points be borne in mind. First, friendship choice is characterised by considerable lability even within intra-group contexts; this point applies with even greater force where inter-group relationships are concerned. Thus, the findings we present will be suggestive rather than a final statement of truth. Second, we shall be looking at representative samples of both British and American research. The problems of race relations in the United States, however, cannot be wholly equated with the emerging situation in Britain. The historical, social and economic background of ethnic-minority groups in Britain, for example, is different from that of the blacks in the United States. Furthermore, the educational systems of the two countries are different. Perhaps such distinctions are less important where inter- and intra-ethnic friendship choice is concerned than with, say, the etiology of prejudice, but the facts need to be acknowledged. And finally, as Taylor[3] has pointed out, many studies in this area have concentrated on children of primary age at the expense of adolescence, a period in young people's development when friendship might be considered to be particularly important. She suggests that this might well be the case because of the difficulty of obtaining suitable materials and, in particular, devising appropriate discriminatory questions which could be used to effect with older pupils.

Before considering these two aspects, ethnic preference and factors influencing it, we shall describe some methodological approaches to the study of friendship and related issues.

Approaches to the Study of Inter-personal Relations and Related Issues in the Multicultural Classroom

Two kinds of sociometric techniques have been used for the study of peer group friendships and preferences in the classroom: the *peer-nomination method*, which is used in many sociometric studies, and the *roster-and-rating scale questionnaire*. The latter is particularly favoured by researchers in the United States. In the case of the peer-nomination method, a child is asked to name or identify a given number of peers with whom he or she would, or would not, choose to be associated in certain specified contexts or situations (play with, work with, sit with, etc.). In most studies of this nature, children are asked to record their preferences or otherwise on a printed questionnaire. A particularly good example of this technique may be found in Box 5.1, the questions being divided equally between preferences and rejections and between academic and social settings. A variation of this approach is the *sociometric interview* in which, as its name indicates, the child is *asked* about his or her preferences and the interviewer records the responses.

In the roster-and-rating scale method, the child gives a rating on a numerical scale to *all members of the class*. Singleton and Asher[5] remind us of the advantages of this method over the peer-nomination approach: (1) the class roster (register) decreases the likelihood of a person not being chosen by a child because he was momentarily forgotten; (2) the scale allows each child to indicate a rating for each classmate rather than just a few; and (3) since each child is rated by all his or her classmates, the technique provides an indication of the child's acceptance by all of the group members. This, the authors suggest, produces more reliable scores than are obtained from a peer-nomination measure. Another advantage is that there is less race bias because there are no forced choices.

Some researchers are careful to distinguish *two types of sociometric study*: first, and perhaps most typical, the kind assessing the extent to which children choose class members *as friends*; and second, the one that assesses *the degree of liking or acceptance*. The difference is that acceptance as a criterion yields a more positive and realistic picture than the criterion of friendship. This appears particularly to be the case in multicultural contexts.

Box 5.1: Sociometric Questions

Positive intellectual questions:

1. If you were having a problem with reading or arithmetic, which pupil in this room would you go to for help?
2. Which child in this room do you think should get first prize in their school work?
3. Who do you think is the smartest child in this room?
4. Which child in this room would you most like to sit with when you're reading or doing work in a workbook?

Positive social questions:

1. If you were captain of a team, who would you choose to be on your team?
2. Whose team would you like to play on in a game with the children in this room?
3. Who in this room would choose you to be on his or her team?
4. Of the children in this room, who would be the best captain of a team?

Negative intellectual questions:

1. If you were having trouble in reading or maths which pupil in this room would you surely not go to for help?
2. Which child in this room do you think would never get a first prize for good school work?
3. Which child in this room would you least like to sit with when you're doing reading or doing work in a workbook?
4. Of the children in this room, who do you think has the most trouble learning things?

Negative social questions:

1. If you were captain of a team, who is the person you would not want on your team?
2. Whose team would you not want to play on?
3. Who in this room would not choose you to be on his or her team?
4. Who in this room would be the worst team captain?

Source: Adapted from Bartel *et al.*[4]

One of the chief criticisms of the sociometric method is that it may yield only measures of perceived, imagined, or hoped-for choices that may not be reciprocated. One way of overcoming this problem where one wants to discover what is actually the case is to employ *classroom observation procedures* in addition to the sociometric techniques. These will provide two types of information about children's classroom interaction: (1) the frequency with which children are alone or with their peers; and

(2) an index of the quality of their peer interactions, that is the proportion of their interactions that are positive or negative. Conversely, the limitation of the observational approach when used on its own is that it does not tell you how children would *like* to behave or with whom they would *like* to associate.

A method commonly used to gather behavioural-observation data is that of *time-sampling*. The principle of this approach is illustrated in Box 5.2 where Singleton and Asher's use of it is described.[6]

It is not uncommon for researchers to use more than one contextual criterion for sociometric choice in their studies. In the investigation by Bartel and his colleagues,[7] for instance, the researchers were interested in both *academic* and *social* situations. They found that the mean number of black children chosen by both blacks and whites for academic situations decreased significantly from first to fourth grade. When asked about social situations, however, both black and white children showed increased preference for their own race from kindergarten through the fourth grade. It can be inferred that children may choose different peers for work and play situations.

Most sociometric studies of multicultural classrooms have tended to use the peer-nomination method, one of the earliest studies to use it being that of Moreno.[9] Then it was found that children's preferences for their own sex were much stronger than own-race preferences in the early elementary years. Preference for own-race groups appeared in about the third and fourth grades and continued to increase through the eighth grade.

Insofar as a trend can be discerned in recent years, then it is in the increasing use made of sociometric techniques in preference to doll choices and other projective techniques. The reason for this is not difficult to understand: in the case of the latter, the only basis of choice for a pupil is race; in sociometric tests, however, children may choose from those they actually know and associate with. Thus, personalities, abilities and interaction histories provide alternative bases of choice, and for these reasons the outcomes will be more realistic in that they will more accurately reflect what is likely to be the case.

Some American studies

We have seen that ethnic preference has been a subject of study

Box 5.2: Time-sampling

Beginning one week after the administration of the sociometric test, an observer visited each of the nine classrooms. Two visits separated by from two to five days, were made to each room. A sequential time-sampling method was used. The first child on the list was observed for 6 seconds. During the next 4 seconds, the child's behaviour was coded. For the next 6 seconds, the next child on the list was observed and so on. Twenty five observations were made per child during each visit. The observer recorded whether the child was alone, interacting positively, or interacting negatively. The observer also recorded the race and sex of any child or children with whom the subject was interacting. A positive interaction was one in which a child was being overtly positive (e.g., sharing, smiling) or engaging in what might be called maintenance activity (e.g., quietly talking, working on a task with another child). A negative interaction was one in which a child behaved aggressively or expressed hostility toward another child (e.g., physical or verbal abuse, taking another child's materials). In 2.9% of the intervals, more than one category of behaviour occurred. Here the observer recorded both behaviours.

Source: Singleton and Asher.[8]

for researchers in America since Moreno's work in the 1930s. It is fitting, therefore, that we look briefly at some of the studies conducted more recently there before turning to this country. We need to sound a note of caution first, however. As we have already indicated, the history of the relations between blacks and whites in the United States is vastly different from a comparable history of native white and ethnic-minority groups in this country, particularly in the case of the latter those of West Indian and Asian origin. For one thing, the problems arising from race relations in the States are of a long-standing kind, whereas in this country they are a relatively recent issue. Then there are etiological factors that differ in the two countries, especially those of an institutional, social and economic kind. But perhaps the most important factor distinguishing the two traditions as far as schools are concerned is that of segregation — the legal insistence that blacks and whites shall be educated separately. Prior to the passing of Federal legislation in the 1950s, racial segregation was the official policy in American schools. Since then, American schools and the American educational system generally have experienced a period of transition during which all concerned have attempted to adjust to the newer policies of desegregation. Of course, not all factors to do with race can be directly interpreted as the effects of segregation and integration, but studies of ethnic preference certainly need to be viewed against this backdrop and the growth of black consciousness. It needs to be appreciated, for example, that data presenting a negative picture of integration were often gathered from schools with only recently integrated classrooms, whereas studies conducted in schools having a longer history of integration offer a more optimistic picture.

The findings of American studies on ethnic preference have demonstrated that ethnic self-preference occurs at an early age — whites prefer whites and blacks prefer blacks, though there is some evidence that some blacks prefer whites. It has also been shown that own-race preference increases with age. To give something of the flavour of the work that has been done in this connection, we have chosen three studies by groups of American researchers that seem to us to be of particular interest for one reason or another. The investigation by Bartel and his colleagues,[10] for instance, is noteworthy for the fact that, unlike many other sociometric studies of classrooms, it was undertaken in several integrated *open* classrooms, thereby permitting an analysis of inter-personal attraction and cross-racial interaction in a setting in which not only was the opportunity for inter-personal interaction relatively maximised but was also one in which the nature of the interaction might more closely approximate some of the conditions for equal status inter-racial association. As the authors say:

> The interracial balance, although not equal, was clearly more proportionate than has been reported in many other studies. Furthermore, the open classroom conditions and the non-graded treatment of pupils from kindergarten through grade four produced a relatively less competitive and less anxious atmosphere than has been observed in regular classrooms.

A 16-item sociometric test was administered to 160 children in which four items covered each of the following areas; Positive Intellectual (PI), Positive Social (PS), Negative Intellectual (NI) and Negative Social (NS) (see Box 5.1 for details).

The results indicated that black children selected *more* black children overall; white children selected more black children on NS and NI items; more white on PS and PI items. On both PS and PI, both groups tended to select members of their own race; and on NS and NI items, both tended to select black children. In their concluding discussion of the results, the authors note that

> Race is an important factor in determining sociometric choices
> in elementary school children even if their classrooms are
> integrated in relatively equal proportions and open in the sense
> of the British Infant School. More specifically, it appears that
> blacks and whites respond differently to the factor of race.
> Black children chose more black than white children for each
> of the four types of question. On the other hand, although
> white children chose approximately the same number of blacks
> as white overall, they sharply discriminated in their choices
> between positive versus negative evaluative situations. Whites
> chose more whites than blacks for both Positive Intellectual
> and Positive Social question types, but they chose more blacks
> than whites for both Negative Intellectual and Negative Social
> type questions.

Their general conclusion is that race is an important factor in
determining sociometric choices in elementary school children,
even if their classrooms are integrated.

Another study focusing on integrated classrooms was the one
by Singleton and Asher[11] in which the researchers sought to
assess sociometric status and social interaction among third-grade
children. The study was designed in response to a school
district's interest in the social effects of 'bussing' in their
schools. A combination of roster-and-rating scale sociometric
technique and classroom observation was used (see earlier section
and Box 5.2). As far as the roster-and-rating scale was
concerned, two criteria were used — the children were asked how
much they liked *to work* and *to play* with their classmates. Four
issues were examined: (1) the relative influence of race and sex
on children's sociometric choices; (2) the difference in race and
sex effects on the play and work scales; (3) the importance of
achievement level to sociometric status; and (4) the extent to
which social-interaction patterns in the classroom paralleled the
sociometric findings. We are mainly concerned here with the first
issue; the others will be considered later in the chapter.

The results indicated that, as far as the criterion of play was
concerned, own-race ratings were generally higher than cross-race
ratings for both blacks and whites. Black children gave higher
scores to everyone than white children. As far as work was

concerned, own-race ratings were again higher than cross-race ratings but the differences were not as large as those for the sex factor. In general terms, however, the results of the study present, in the words of the investigators, a rather positive picture of inter-racial association in the integrated third-grade classroom. The influence of race on sociometric choice, though significant, was small and a considerably less important influence than sex.

In considering why race effects in the study, although they had been found to be significant, were smaller than those reported in earlier American studies, the researchers suggest that it may be due to the possibility that the children in the study showed positive effects of being in racially-integrated classrooms throughout their school experience. Another reason may be the choice of roster-and-rating techniques which enabled the children to rate each of their classmates. Because forced choices were not required, less race bias may have been the result.

An interesting, and in some ways more realistic, approach to the issue of friendship choice in multicultural classrooms was adopted by Asher and Singleton[12] who set out to compare the results from two types of sociometric study. The first and more typical study assessed the extent to which children chose members of another race *as friends*. For this, they drew on the findings of previous studies. The second and more novel type of study set out to assess the degree of cross-race *liking or acceptance*, rather than cross-race friendship. For this they conducted their own study.

The reasons for using the second type of sociometric study arose in part from a dissatisfaction with the perceived short-comings of the former, the standard sociometric test. As they put it:

> Evaluations which use this measure implicitly assume that the social goal of desegregation is the development of cross-race friendships. Given the social climate in which desegregation often takes place, few desegregated schools can pass this test. For one thing, many parents themselves are prejudiced and do little to encourage cross-race friendships.

If, however, the social objective of desegregation was not just the long-range objective of cross-race friendship, they argue, but included the more easily achievable objective of cross-race acceptance, a fairer and more realistic test would be whether children come to like or accept one another. 'Liking or acceptance', they observe, 'although a prerequisite to friendship, can occur without close friendships actually developing.'

The results of this study by Asher and Singleton using *acceptance* as a criterion were encouraging. Children gave fairly high ratings to both own-race and cross-race classmates. Although some degree of bias was evident, being also statistically significant, the amount was small compared with the 'best friendship' findings of earlier studies. The authors concluded that the children in the study expressed essentially positive sentiments about members of another race when the measures used to assess general acceptance, rather than more intimate relationships such as friendships, and added that the data were particularly encouraging since many of the black children were 'bussed' to school and had minimal opportunities for before-school and after-school contact.

For further information on American research on friendship choice in multicultural classrooms, we refer the reader to the review by Carter and his colleagues.[13]

British Research on Friendship Choice in Multicultural Classrooms

Studies of friendship preference in Britain are conspicuously fewer in number than those of the United States. Much of the work in this county has been done with small samples in single schools or day nurseries. Moreover, with some exceptions, much of the work has been with West Indian children. Given these limitations, however, and also the differing histories of race relations in Britain and the United States, British studies have tended to disclose a similar ethnic cleavage to that revealed in American research, as the following selection will show.

Rowley[14] studied 1,747 children in primary and secondary schools in the West Midlands of whom 63.5 per cent were white, 20.5 per cent Asian and 14 per cent West Indian. Among other features of the study, Rowley questioned them on friendship choice in the contexts of 'play', 'sitting in a class' and 'tea at home'. He found that the majority of the children selected friends from their own ethnic group. There were proportional differences, however, in that 90 per cent of the white children chose white friends, while only 60 per cent of West Indian pupils chose friends of their own ethnic group, the remainder preferring mainly white friends.

Working about the same time as Rowley, Kawwa[15] tended to endorse Rowley's findings. He was interested in the friendship patterns of pupils in three types of school — a junior school, a boys' secondary modern school and a comprehensive school. The numbers of black pupils in each school were small. Nevertheless, he found that they tended to be more ethnocentric than others. This was particularly the case in the junior and secondary modern schools. They also revealed a greater expectation than any other immigrant group of being ignored by white British children.

A study restricted wholly to junior pupils was Durojaiye's.[16] The purpose of it was to investigate the distribution of choice of friends among the three ethnic groups in the school and among boys and girls; and to examine the differences in the patterns of choice of children at different age levels. The subjects were 310 children, the whole population of a junior school in a multi-cultural area in Manchester. Ages ranged from eight to eleven. Three empirically-defined ethnic groups were identified in the school — white English children, children of mixed parentage with white English mothers and West Indian fathers and coloured children. Thus there were 202 white children, 33 children of mixed parentage and 75 coloured children (West Indian and Asian).

The study disclosed that the pattern of friendship choices was largely ethnic in character. Ethnic self-preference occurred in every age-group and in every form for both sexes. Generally, children aged nine in each of the two groups showed slightly *less* ethnic self-preference than did the eight-year-olds. Those at ten showed a further decrease in the size of the ethnic self-preference index. The study also revealed that the in-group preference of the majority of white children was markedly stronger than in the in-group preferences in the minority-coloured group.

In order to investigate the degree of integration of Pakistani immigrant children in their school classes, Henderson[17] gave a sociometric questionnaire to three complete classes aged 5 +, 8 + and 11 +, respectively, in a Bradford school. These totalled 86 pupils. Each class contained both boys and girls, a minority of Pakistani children and the majority native British. The questions were designed to discover both positive and negative friendship choices, the results being analysed by various statistical procedures in terms of three variables — sex, ethnic origin and age.

It was found that while ethnic origin was clearly a factor in determining both friendship and rejection patterns, there was no evidence of the 'complete colour cleavage' reported in some American studies of whites and Negroes. The attitude of native Bradford children to Pakistani children was frequently indifferent rather than hostile, and there was little evidence to suggest that Pakistani children were noticeably 'unpopular'. Indeed, some of the Pakistani children, it was found, appeared to have aspirations to associate with Bradford children. The study also disclosed that, unlike the Durojaiye study, comparisons of age groups did not reveal any clear progression, but suggested that the older Pakistanis achieved a higher degree of ethnic group self-preference.

A particularly important study in the field, because it utilised a large national sample, was that by Jelinek and Brittan.[18] They investigated friendship patterns among pupils from a number of ethnic groups when aged eight, ten, twelve and fourteen. Altogether thirteen primary schools and twelve secondary schools were involved. These had from 18 per cent to 84 per cent of pupils of ethnic-minority origin. The West Indians, for example, numbered 188 out of 677 at the age of eight, 152 out of 611 at ten, 244 out of 1507 at twelve and 234 out of 1505 at fourteen. All pupils were asked to name as many as three pupils they would like to 'play with at school', 'to have as friends' and 'to go about with at school'.

The findings revealed that by the age of eight race was already a strong factor in friendship choice, with the majority choosing friends from their own ethnic group. The West Indian primary children in particular showed greater own-group preferences in 'desired' friendships than did the Asian children, and the secondary school West Indians showed a greater own-group preference than did the British pupils. It was also found that the West Indian secondary pupils were much more likely actually to choose friends of their own colour than white indigenous children.

A study by Spooner[19] investigated the extent of the influence of the factors of school of origin, socioeconomic status, residential propinquity and ethnic origin on the sociometric choices of a sample of 244 children aged 7+ to 10+ within a primary school. The sample consisted of two subgroups of children, one of which was indigenous to the school having entered at 4+ years of age. The second subgroup, which consisted of a majority of white children and a minority of children of Asian origin, entered the junior department of the school at 7+ years from a different infant school. The factors under observation were investigated when the variables of sex, school class and age were controlled. A sociometric questionnaire was administered which was designed to discover the choices made by the children within the sample in terms of three preference criteria and one reality criterion. The results were analysed using chi-square and indices of subgroup structure. Among the findings, it was discovered that the incumbent children at 7+, 8+ and 10+ tended to exhibit subgroup self-preference, appearing to be indifferent to the children who had originally entered the school at 7+ years. At all ages the boys originally from the separate infant school gave many of their choices to the incumbent children. At 7+ and 8+ the girls from the separate infant school gave the majority of their choices to the incumbent girls but tended to own-group self-preference at 9+ and 10+. The white children, at all ages, gave few actual or preferred playtime choices to the Asian children. Finally, the Asian children, at all ages, preferred to play with the white children but in reality most of their play associates were Asian.

In their study of friendship choice in a mixed-race primary school, Braha and Rutter[20] set out to test the following hypotheses: (1) white children will choose white friends pre-dominantly, and non-white children will choose non-white friends; (2) the bias towards in-group choice will increase with age; and (3) friendship choice will be related to racial attitude in both white and non-white children. One-hundred-and-twenty children took part in the study, and all were pupils at a large primary school in Coventry. The intake was 20 per cent white and 80 per cent non-white, most of the children having been born in Britain.

It was found that the first prediction was strongly supported — whites chose whites; coloured chose coloured. This was found to be true even at four to five years of age. Neither of the other two hypotheses was supported.

Finally, we refer to a study by Wood[21] who investigated some aspects of social class and ethnic-group differentiation. He randomly sampled three groups of 30 children thus: (1) third and fourth year English boys in upper-academic streams; (2) third and fourth year English boys in lower-academic streams; and (3) all West Indian boys in the third and fourth years. Among the findings, it was discovered that (a) the upper-academic English boys stream was more hostile to West Indians than the lower-academic English boys stream, though there was no significant trend the other way, that is from the West Indian boys to the upper-academic English boys stream; and (b) school friendship preferences are a function of ethnic group membership with West Indian pupils showing greater in-group preferences than English pupils. Indeed, the West Indian in-group preferences were found to be 'extraordinarily high'.

Not all studies disclose this same pattern of ethnic self-preference, as the following brief selection illustrates.

Contradictory evidence

A study by Silberman and Spice[22] was carried out in a multicultural area of Liverpool. From the sociometric data obtained it was concluded that there was no racial discrimination evident in the choice of friends. And another study, the findings of which contrast with the general trend for ethnic-minority pupils to prefer their own race, is Milner's.[23] He sampled a group of 300 West Indian, Asian and English children aged five to eight in two English cities in 1970. The children were asked to indicate their preferences for one racial group over another using a selection of black and white dolls. Specifically, the children were asked which of the dolls they liked best, they would like to play with in the playground, sit next to in class, share their sweet with and which looked like their best friend. Milner found that 72 per cent of the West Indian children made a majority of choices favouring the white figures over the figures representing their own group. Indeed, they chose white figures more often than English children chose black figures. Such symbolic choices, however, did not faithfully represent what was actually the case.

What is of interest, however, is that black pupils would at least prefer to have, even if they did not in fact have, more white friends.

More recently, Ball[24] investigated friendship groups in a multicultural comprehensive school. Three classes were studied in the school (1x, 3x and 3y). One of them (1x) had 30 members — 17 British, seven non-British by race and six non-British by race and nationality. The second (3x) had 27 members only seven of whom were not British by race and/or nationality. The third (3y) had 29 members, 18 of whom were British by race and nationality, seven non-British by race and four non-British by nationality.

As the author says, the races and nationalities were not 'clearly marked off' from one another and neither race nor nationality emerges as having a decisive or divisive influence upon the organisation of groups of friends. Indeed, only two of the friendship groups in the classes directly observed were 'pure' by race or nationality.

From the interview material, however, it appeared that the existence of multicultural-friendship groupings and the larger number of cross-racial and cross-national friendship choices did not necessarily justify the suggestion that there was no prejudice or racial consciousness. The role of these factors, for some individuals and pupils in their interaction with their friends and classmates, was separated from their role in the individual pupil's perspective upon wider social processes. What is suggested by this and other material is that pupils of all races and national groups may carry racial stereotypes or prejudice that they may apply to other pupils in the school, while still having friends or classmates of different races and nationalities to whom they do not apply these stereotypes and in relation to whom their attitudes are not prejudiced.

In a study by Davey and Mullin,[25] the researchers set out to investigate ethnic identification and preference in British primary-school children. Equal numbers of children at ages seven, eight, nine and 10+ were drawn from 16 primary schools, eight in London and eight in Yorkshire. Two-hundred-and-fifty-six children were white, 128 were of West Indian parentage and 128 were of Asian parentage. For both the identification and preference test, full length photographs of primary-school children were used. The photoed children were identically dressed. For the preference test, three sociometric questions were asked the children — 'who are the two children you would most like to sit next to in class?', 'who are the two children in the school you would most like to play with in the playground?' and 'who are the two children in the school you would most like to invite home?' The authors concluded that in schools where the ethnic mix was such as to allow children a more or less equal opportunity of choosing own-race friends or other race-friends, only a minority wished to confine their friendships exclusively to members of their own group. Overall, 66.5 per cent preferred to have some other-group friends. This was most pronounced among the West Indian children (78.5 per cent) and least often expressed by the Asians (55.4 per cent), with the white children falling between the two (63.6 per cent). The authors add that the fact that some 34 per cent of the children appeared to be exclusive in their friendship patterns does not necessarily mean that they had no other-race friends. It may merely have meant that these friends were not ranked high enough to be named amongst the top two on any of the three criteria with which the children were presented.

Another study offering a positive picture is Smalley's.[26] It set out to examine the hypothesis that there was a relationship between acceptance of self and acceptance by others (peers and teachers) in a group of 115 children in a multicultural first school in Leeds. A sociometric test was used to measure the pupil's acceptance by others, and the Bledsoe self-concept rating scale was used to assess a pupil's acceptance of himself.

What is of particular interest to us is that the ethnic background of pupils was found to be *unrelated* to pupil's sociometric status, to the self-concept level, to teacher evaluations of pupil sociometric status and teachers' personal feelings towards their pupils.

Factors Influencing Friendship Choice in the Classroom

Having in the preceding three sections looked at studies to do with ethnic preference in the classroom and the extent to which own- or other-race pupils are chosen as friends, we propose here to review briefly studies that have attempted, *inter alia*, to identify factors influencing, positively or negatively, ethnic preference in the classroom. Because studies looking at individual factors are few in number, their findings need to be seen as indicative or suggestive rather than conclusive. For the same reason, we draw freely on both American and British research.

Inter-racial Contacts

Although some studies have found increased inter-racial contact to result in more positive attitudes, particularly on the part of whites towards blacks, there is little agreement about the effects of inter-racial contact on attitude change. As Carter *et al.*[27] point out, however, most researchers agree that the earlier the contact the better, and that frequency of contact is not as important as type of contact to stimulate inter-racial acceptance.

The 'natural experiment' provided by the contrasting policies of segregation and desegregation in the United States has yielded interesting conclusions. In their study of sociometric ratings and social interaction among third-grade children in an integrated-school district, for example, Singleton and Asher[28] asked why it was that the race effect in the study, though statistically significant, was smaller than that reported in previous research. One explanation was that children in their study were showing positive effects of being in racially-integrated classrooms throughout their school experience.

The importance of *informal* contacts in achieving favourable inter-racial attitudes is highlighted in the case study by Clement and Harding[29] of patterns of social-race relations in a desegregated elementary school in North Carolina. As the authors say:

> The lack of significant informal relationships between black and white students at Grandin mirrors and derives in part from the limited contact they have outside of school. Residential segregation and patterns of dual institutions along social-race lines mean that students are unlikely to encounter one another in the neighbourhood or in places like church.

Academic/Achievement Acceptance

Another factor deemed by some to be an important determinant of ethnic choice is academic and/or achievement acceptance. Some support for the view that academic/achievement acceptance inhibits cross-ethnic choice comes from Wood's study[30] in a mixed secondary modern school in Huddersfield. Two groups of English boys, designated 'upper academic' and 'lower academic', along with a third group of wholly West Indian boys were sampled. Wood found that the 'upper academic' group was more hostile to the 'lower academic' group than vice versa and, of greater significance, the 'upper academic' group was even more hostile to the West Indian group than to the 'lower academic' group. There was no significant trend the other way, that is from the West Indians to the 'upper academic' group. Overall, friendship choices were seen as a function of academic grouping.

In the study by Bartel *et al.*,[31] a 16-item sociometric device was administered to 160 children from integrated open classrooms. As we saw earlier, four items dealt with each of the following areas of evaluation: positive intellectual, positive social, negative intellectual and negative social. The results indicated that white children selected more black children on NS and NI items, more white on PS and PI. On PS and PI items, both groups tended to select members of their own race; on NS and NI items, however, both tended to select black children.

In a study of the role of music in the lives of West Indian youths in Britain, Troyna[32] found that pupils nominated peers who occupied structurally similar positions in the school's stream system. There appeared to be a relationship between stream position and the degree of in-group commitment: black pupils in the lower streams immersed themselves in peer groups which were racially exclusive. The author is reminded of a similar finding by Driver[33] who argued that 'top stream black pupils, pursuing "purposive, academic and socially prestigious activities" tended to de-emphasise their intra-group loyalties. Conversely, those black pupils in the lower streams formed relationships almost exclusively with their own ethnic set'.

In a study of the effects of sex, race and achievement on schoolchildren's friendships, Tuma and Hallinan[34] found that a child's friendship choices were positively associated with being the same sex and race as the other child *and with having a similar achievement level.*

In contrast to these findings, Durojaiye,[35] investigating patterns of friendship choice in an ethnically-mixed junior school, found that intelligence and school attainment were not significantly related to the friendship choices observed in the study.

Socio-economic/social acceptance

According to Carter and his colleagues,[36] socio-economic status has been found to be an influential variable in a number of studies. Hyman[37] summarised twelve studies and concluded that whites' increased acceptance of, and positive attitudes towards, blacks were related to social status. This was supported by St John and Lewis[38] who found that the social acceptance of blacks and whites by white children in Grade 6 was related to socio-economic status. Further support was provided by Glock and his associates[39] who found prejudice to be related to economic deprivation.

The earlier study in Britain by Silberman and Spice,[40] to which we have already referred, disclosed that economic factors as indicated by dress appeared to be responsible for *some* children discriminating against others.

Contrasting with these findings, however, St John and Lewis[41] found that socio-economic status was unrelated to social acceptance by black Grade 6 pupils, and Gerard *et al.*[42] did not find socio-economic status to be related to white acceptance of minority pupils (aged five to twelve) following integration. Again in this country, Durojaiye[43] found that factors which included socio-economic status were not significantly related to friendship choices.

Referring purely to social factors, the study by Bartel and his associates[44] found that white children selected more black children on 'negative social' items and more white on 'positive social'. On 'positive social' items both groups tended to select members of their own race and on 'negative social' items, both tended to select black children.

An interesting finding in Wood's study[45] disclosed that 'social acceptability' scores were significantly related to prowess at sport. Thus, high prowess among West Indian pupils meant high acceability scores, that is significantly higher than English pupils with low prowess at sport.

Sex

In their summary of trends in inter-racial acceptance, Carter and his colleagues[46] consider that a child's acceptance of others is more sex-linked than race-related: that is, sex is a more potent determinant of friendship choice than race. They quote numerous American studies to support this. The study by Tuma and Hallinan,[47] for instance, found that a child's friendship choices are positively related to being the same sex and race as the other child. And in Britain, Henderson[48] found that while ethnic origin was clearly a factor in determining both friendship and rejection patterns, sex appeared to be even more significant.

Self-concept/Self-acceptance

Carter *et al.*[49] note that a positive self-concept is frequently associated with peer acceptance; and it is generally predicted that popular children have more positive self-concepts than less popular ones. However, research evidence does not confirm this prediction consistently. Smalley,[50] for example, set out to examine the hypothesis that there was a relationship between the acceptance of self and acceptance by others in a group of 115 children in a multicultural first school in Leeds. The study indicated a weak relationship between a pupil's acceptance of self and acceptance by others within each of the five classes studied.

Black/White Ratios in the Classroom

Carter *et al.*[51] point out that black/white ratios in the classroom are more important variables influencing inter-racial peer acceptance. They note that when the proportion of blacks is less than 50 per cent, black pupils' achievement increases and social acceptance is enhanced. They found low correlations between racial composition below 53 per cent and peer acceptance. However, the black/white ratios contributed to the prediction of social and academic acceptance by black and white females, to academic acceptance by black males and to social acceptance by white males. Weinberg[52] concluded that the nature of white friendships with black children varied with the racial composition of the classroom. In a predominantly white classroom, white children have a larger element of choice as to whether or not they develop a friendship with a black classmate. Thus, they can choose more spontaneously and the result is a more intimate relationship. In predominantly black classrooms, however, the choice is a narrower one, and resulting relationships are less spontaneous and intimate. An earlier study by McPartland[53] of high school students aged 14 to 18 appears to have arrived at similar findings: 'As the proportion of students from other races increases in a student's class, the proportion of those who have close friends outside of their own race increases'. However, he also found that 'the highest percentage of teachers reporting racial tension was 13.9 per cent occurring among those who had between 50 per cent and 74 per cent whites in the class'. St John and Lewis[54] found that the ratio was unrelated to social acceptance among twelve-year-old whites, that black boys were more popular in majority-black classes and that black girls were more accepted by whites in majority-white classes. Although studies are not in total agreement concerning the ideal racial composition, it seems clear that racial compositions of the classroom are related to peer acceptance.

Teacher attitude

Teacher attitude has been found to be related to inter-racial acceptance in the classroom. Gerard *et al.*,[55] for instance, found that teacher bias was related to whites' acceptance of minority students as friends and St John and Lewis[56] discovered a significant relationship between whites' inter-racial acceptance and teachers' fairness. Weinberg[57] reviewed desegregation studies and concluded that the tone of leadership provided by teachers influenced the students' acceptance of integration.

In Smalley's study,[58] however, she found that the ethnic background of pupils was unrelated to teacher evaluations of pupil sociometric status and teachers' personal feelings towards their pupils.

Age

Age has quite frequently been associated with inter-racial acceptance, increasing racial separation being apparent as children grow older. Both Carter *et al.*[59] and Singleton[60] refer to studies which demonstrate marked racial cleavage among pupils in early and mid-teens. In Britain, Robertson and Kawwa[61] demonstrated increasing in-group preference with age. And Jelinek and Brittan[62] found a reliable increase in desired own-group friendship between the primary school sample (eight-year-olds combined with 10-year-olds) and a further significant increase between the 12+ and 14+ age groups. Some findings, however, conflict with these. In Henderson's study,[63] comparisons with age groups did not reveal any clear progression, but suggested that the older Pakistanis achieved a higher degree of ethnic group self-preference. And the study by Durojaiye[64] demonstrated a diminution of ethnic self-preference with age (eight to ten).

In Asher and Singleton's study,[65] there was a modest trend towards increased racial separation with age, the trend being more evident for black than white children. They proffer reasons why changes over age in children's cross-race acceptance might occur. First, there is the increasing discrepancy in academic performance between white and black children. Such discrepancies probably become more salient to the children due to increases in academic competitiveness in the upper grades. Second, in the particular sample studied, the black and white children differ in social class terms as well as race. As both grow older, it is feasible that their inter-personal styles and expectations become increasingly different. Finally, in this particular study (it was a longitudinal one) there was the possibility that the black children as they grew older were establishing stronger identities as blacks and, therefore, were identifying more strongly with their black peers.

Geographical Location

There may well be geographical differences according to whether there are large proportions of ethnic-minority groups in the community from which the children studied are drawn. In Kawwa's study, for instance,[66] it was found that whilst the majority of the London secondary school children sampled expressed negative attitudes to immigrants, only a small minority of adolescents in Lowestoft did so.

Language

We shall see in a subsequent chapter how language can be a barrier to communication and understanding between West Indian pupils, for example, and the teacher,[67] and as such a potential source of confusion for the latter. Here we briefly examine the problem as it manifests itself between children of different racial origins.

For example, in so far as language is a factor in inter-ethnic friendship choice, Clement and Harding[68] saw it as a barrier to desegregation. In their case study of the emerging patterns of social-race relations and the process producing them in a desegregated public elementary school in North Carolina, they found that the use of social-race terminology expressed social distance and hostile feelings between blacks and whites, although the terms were not obligatory.

In an exploratory study of interaction amongst British and immigrant primary children, Brown[69] discovered that the differences in verbal contacts within and between the groups indicated a language barrier. This was reinforced by the finding that immigrant children were more likely to make bodily contacts with British children than with each other.

Behavioural Style

Yet another factor inhibiting the establishment of inter-ethnic friendships is what has been termed by Clement and Harding[70] as 'behavioural style'. They write:

> . . . many black and white students make attempts to establish relationships with one another. The reasons they fail include differences in behavioural style. The case study of Grandin's fifth and sixth graders indicates that by this stage of their careers, students have learned identities and styles of acting and interacting that can serve to derail the development of cross-social-race friendships. The identities and styles of interacting with which black students tend to be familiar only partially overlap with the set of identities and behavioural routines with which white students are familiar. These differences, although they are not overwhelming and although they do not affect all students equally, frequently embroil and confuse black/white interaction, mitigating against the establishment of close relationships. Although students make attempts to engage one another in interaction or even to form friendships, cross-colour attempts are seldom successful for these reasons.

School Factors

An important set of factors that can influence inter-ethnic friendship patterns are clearly those rooted in the school system itself. Surprisingly, this appears to be an area neglected by researchers. However, the few studies that do touch on it show

how fruitful such research could be. Clement and Harding's study,[71] as we have seen, set out to examine the conditions influencing the emergence of patterns of informal segregation in a desegregated elementary school. It was found that, although not frequent, *direct intervention* on the part of teachers helped to establish relations between black and white students. As the authors say in this regard, 'Some teachers, despite the general norms which are limited to encouraging polite cooperation, try to help students make cross-colour friends. They also affect these relationships indirectly by the students groupings they create in class and in extracurricular activities.'

Asher and Singleton[72] refer to a number of studies which have recently examined whether curricula which encourage co-operation actually increase children's cross-race acceptances. Studies with fifth grade, junior high school and high school students, for example, do indicate that such curricula are quite effective in improving cross-race relations.

Athletic Ability

Athletic ability has been shown to be a relevant variable in inter-racial peer acceptance, particularly among boys. Wood,[73] for example, found that 'social acceptability' scores were signifi-cantly related to prowess at sport. Thus, high prowess among West Indian pupils meant higher acceptability scores, that is significantly higher than English pupils with low prowess at sport.

The study by De Vries *et al.*[74] investigated the effect of *Teams-Games-Tournament*, an instructional strategy employing biracial learning teams and instructional games, on cross-racial friendship in integrated classes. The results indicated that TGT was an effective means of increasing cross-racial friendship in integrated classes.

In a study of social interaction between blacks and whites in free play periods at the sixth grade, Polgar[75] used *play* as a model of social relations. She used two patterns of play: competition between black and white teams and play in mixed-colour teams. The differences in the process of play in these two contexts are discussed and their implications for cross-colour relationships are considered.

In conclusion, we ask the question, given the plethora of

information yielded by studies of friendship choice in multicultural classrooms, what does it disclose that is of particular
relevance to teachers? Perhaps the one overriding factor is that,
inspite of some evidence to the contrary, race is an important
determinant of friendship choice from as early as the pre-teenage
years. Given this fact of racial cleavage, then, what can be done
to promote greater inter-racial acceptance in multicultural classrooms? Clearly, the establishment of an effective multicultural
curriculum must figure high on any list of priorities in this
respect, as must appropriate inputs to courses concerned with the
pre-service and in-service preparation and training of teachers.
The real issue of integration, however, is simply *what goes on in
the classroom*, as Carter and his colleagues point out.[76] As they
explain:

> The mere physical placing of pupils in the classroom is not
> enough. Under the teacher's direction, successful participation
> of all pupils is essential. This involves complex social and
> psychological factors including self-image, achievement
> motivation, ethnic understanding, and social skills. Inter-
> vention techniques that promote peer acceptance should
> include opportunities for pupils to participate and feel
> successful in a variety of socially rewarding activities.

A teacher can make a start in this direction by making use of his
or her commonsense knowledge of classroom relationships and
any sociometric data he or she chooses to collect to bring isolates
or racially-homogeneous groups into working situations with
other members of the class, and at the same time develop
appropriate attitudes and sensitivities which in turn will dispose
others to respond in like fashion.

Notes

1. G. K. Verma (1975) 'Inter-group Prejudice and Race Relations' in G. K.
Verma and C. Bagley (eds), *Race and Education across Cultures*, London:
Heinemann.
2. V. Braha and D. R. Rutter (1980) 'Friendship Choice in a Mixed-Race
Primary School', *Educational Studies*, 6(3), 217–23.
3. M. J. Taylor (1981) *Caught Between: A Review of Research into the
Education of Pupils of West Indian Origin*, Windsor: NFER.
4. H. W. Bartel, N. R. Bartel and J. J. Grill (1973) 'A Sociometric View of
Some Integrated Open Classrooms', *Journal of Social Issues*, 29(4), 159–73.

5. L. C. Singleton and S. R. Asher (1976) 'Sociometric Ratings and Social Interaction Among Third Grade Children in and Integrated School District', *Journal of Classroom Interaction*, **12**(1), 71–82.

6. Ibid.

7. Bartel, Bartel and Grill, 'A Sociometric View'.

8. Singleton and Asher, 'Sociometric Ratings'.

9. J. L. Moreno (1934) *Who Shall Survive?: A New Approach to the Problems of Human Interrelations*, Washington, DC: Nervous and Mental Diseases Publishing Company.

10. Bartel, Bartel and Grill, 'A Sociometric View'.

11. Singleton and Asher, 'Sociometric Ratings'.

12. S. R. Asher and L. C. Singleton (1978) 'Cross-race Acceptance in Integrated Scools', *Integrated Education*, **16**(5), 17–20.

13. D. E. Carter, L. Detine-Carter and F. W. Benson (1980) 'Interracial Acceptance in the Classroom' in H. C. Foot, A. J. Chapman and J. R. Smith (eds), *Friendship and Social Relations in Children*, Chichester: John Wiley and Sons.

14. K. G. Rowley (1968) 'Social Relations Between British and Immigrant Children', *Educational Research*, **10**, 2145–8.

15. T. Kawwa (1968) 'Three Sociometric Studies of Ethnic Relations in London Schools', *Race*, **10**(2), 173–80.

16. M. O. A. Durojaiye (1970) 'Patterns of Friendship Choices in an Ethnically-mixed Junior School', *Race*, **12**, 189–201.

17. A. M. Henderson (1973) 'A Sociometric Study of Ethnic Integration and Choice of Friends in Some Bradford Schools', MSc. dissertation, University of Bradford.

18. M. M. Jelinek and E. M. Brittan (1975) 'Multiracial Education: 1. Inter-ethnic Friendship Patterns', *Educational Research*, **18**(1), 44–53.

19. L. R. Spooner (1977) 'Children's Preferences: A Sociometric Study of Peer-group Relationships Within a Primary School', MSc. dissertation, University of Bradford.

20. Braha and Rutter, 'Friendship Choice'.

21. E. R. Wood (1973) 'An Investigation of Some Aspects of Social Class and Ethnic Group Differentiation in a School-based Junior Activities Centre', MA thesis, University of Newcastle.

22. L. Silberman and B. Spice (1950) *Colour and Class in Six Liverpool Schools*, Liverpool: Liverpool University Press.

23. D. Milner (1975) *Children and Race*, Harmondsworth: Penguin.

24. S. Ball (1977) 'The Study of Friendship Groups in a Multiracial Comprehensive School: Research and Methodology', MA thesis (Social Studies), University of Sussex.

25. A. G. Davey and P. N. Mullin (1980) 'Ethnic Identification and Preference of British Primary Schoolchildren', *Journal of Child Psychology*, **21**, 241–53.

26. E. J. Smalley (1981) 'The Relationship Between Acceptance of Self and Acceptance by Others, Using Sociometric Techniques and Self-concept Rating Scales with a Group of Primary School Children', MSc. dissertation, University of Bradford.

27. Carter, Detine-Carter and Benson, 'Interracial Acceptance'.

28. Singleton and Asher, 'Sociometric Ratings'.

29. D. C. Clement and J. R. Harding (1978) 'Social Distinctions and Emergent Student Groups in a Desegregated School', *Anthropology and Education Quarterly*, **9**, 272–82.

30. Wood, 'Social Class and Ethnic Group Differentiation'.

31. Bartel, Bartel and Grill, 'A Sociometric View'.

32. B. S. Troyna (1978) 'Race and Streaming: A Case Study', *Educational Review*, **30**(1), 59–65.

33. G. Driver (1977) 'Cultural Competence, Social Power and School Achievement: A Case Study of West Indian Pupils Attending a Secondary School in the West Midlands', *New Community*, **5**, 353–9.

34. N. B. Tuma and M. T. Hallinan (1979) 'The Effects of Sex, Race and Achievement on Schoolchildren's Friendships', *Social Forces*, **57**(4), 1265–85.

35. Durojaiye, 'Patterns of Friendship'.

36. Carter, Detine-Carter and Benson, 'Interracial Acceptance'.

37. H. H. Hyman (1969) 'Social Psychology and Race Relations' in I. Katz and P. Gurin (eds), *Race and the Social Sciences*, New York: Basic Books.

38. N. H. St John and R. G. Lewis (1975) 'Race and the Social Structure of the Elementary Classroom', *Sociology of Education*, **48**, 340–68.

39. C. Glock, R. Wuthnow, J. Piliavin and M. Spencer (1975) *Adolescent Prejudice*, New York: Harper and Row.

40. Silberman and Spice, *Colour and Class*.

41. St John and Lewis, 'Race and the Social Structure'.

42. H. B. Gerard, T. D. Jackson and E. S. Conolley (1975) 'Social Contact in the Desegregated Classroom' in H. B. Gerard and N. Miller (eds), *School Desegregation*, New York: Plenum Press.

43. Durojaiye, 'Patterns of Friendship'.

44. Bartel, Bartel and Grill, 'A Sociometric View'.

45. Wood, 'Social Class and Ethnic Group Differentiation'.

46. Carter, Detine-Carter and Benson, 'Interracial Acceptance'.

47. Tuma and Hallinan, 'The Effects of Sex'.

48. Henderson. 'A Sociometric Study'.

49. Carter, Detine-Carter and Benson, 'Interracial Acceptance'.

50. Smalley, 'Acceptance of Self and Acceptance by Others'.

51. Carter, Detine-Carter and Benson, 'Interracial Acceptance'.

52. M. Weinberg (1968) *Desegregation Research: An Appraisal*, Bloomington, Indiana: Phi Delta Kappa.

53. J. McPartland (1968) *The Segregated Student in Desegregated Schools*, Final report to the Center for the study of social organisation of schools, Educational Resources Information Center, Document Number EDO21944.

54. St John and Lewis, 'Race and the Social Structure'.

55. Gerard, Jackson and Conolley, 'Social Contract'.

56. St John and Lewis, Race and the Social Structure'.

57. Weinberg, *Desegregation Research*.

58. Smalley, 'Acceptance of Self and Acceptance by Others'.

59. Carter, Detine-Carter and Benson, 'Interracial Acceptance'.

60. Asher and Singleton, 'Cross-race Acceptance'.

61. T. S. Robertson and T. Kawwa (1971) 'Ethnic Relations in a Girls' Comprehensive School', *Educational Research*, **13**, 214–17.

62. Jelinek and Brittan, 'Multiracial Education'.

63. Henderson, 'A Sociometric Study'.

64. Durojaiye, 'Patterns of Friendship'.

65. Asher and Singleton, 'Cross-race Acceptance'.

66. T. Kawwa (1968) 'A Survey of Ethnic Attitudes of Some British Secondary School Pupils', *British Journal of Social and Clinical Psychology*, **7**, 161–8.

67. Driver, 'Cultural Competence'.

68. Clement and Harding, 'Social Distinctions'.

69. G. A. Brown (1973) 'An Exploratory Study of Interaction Amongst British Immigrant Children', *British Journal of Social and Clinical Psychology*, **12**, 159–62.

70. Clement and Harding, 'Social Distinctions'.

71. Ibid.

72. Asher and Singleton, 'Cross-race Acceptance'.

73. Wood, 'Social Class and Ethnic Group Differentiation'.

74. D. L. De Vries, K. J. Edwards and R. E. Slavin (1978) 'Biracial Learning Teams and Race Relations in the Classroom: Four Field Experiments Using Teams-Games-Tournament', *Journal of Educational Psychology*, 7(3), 356–63.

75. S. K. Polgar (1978) 'Modeling Social Relations in Cross-colour play', *Anthropology and Education Quarterly*, **9**, 282–9.

76. Carter, Detine-Carter and Benson, 'Interracial Acceptance'.

6 HOME-SCHOOL RELATIONS: I. PARENTS AND PUPILS

Introduction

In a White Paper, the Government has said:

> The educational service has important contributions to make
> to the well-being of immigrant communities in this country,
> and to the promotion of harmony between the different ethnic
> groups of which our society is now composed. This is because
> first, the education service has some responsibility to assist
> citizens of all ages to develop their ability to the full, and
> within that responsibility, a special obligation to children who,
> for one reason or another, are most at risk of not achieving
> their true potential. And second, education can be a potent
> instrument for increasing understanding and good-will between
> the races.[1]

In identifying these crucial issues for education in our multicultural society — the realisation of pupils' true potential,
thereby combating the problem of underachievement, especially
among ethnic-minority pupils and the establishment of true
understanding and good-will between ethnic groups — the
Government has brought sharply into focus the enduring and
intractable problems confronting the teacher of ethnic-minority
children.

A key factor to be borne in mind when considering these
problems is that of *home-school relations*, for their resolution
can be aided by positive and constructive relations between
ethnic-minority children, their parents and their teachers. Yet the
establishment of such relations is far from easy: ignorance,
misunderstandings and prejudice — the root causes of poor
home-school relations — inevitably persist where there are few
opportunities for planned and meaningful dialogue. Elsewhere
we have examined the more obvious aspects of home background
insofar as they relate to ability and achievement. In this chapter
and the one following, we look at the less immediately obvious,
though equally important, relations between home and school as

revealed by the plexus of attitudes, opinions, expectations and meanings held by parents, pupils and teachers, respectively.

As far as the present chapter is concerned, we begin with a review of immigrant parents' attitudes to education and the aspirations they hold for their children. We then go on to consider successively the more general views held by parents of ethnic-minority pupils on multicultural education; the extent of parental involvement in school life; pupils' attitudes to school and their own career aspirations; the issues of pupil adjustment and maladjustment with regard to home and school; and, finally, the role of the community school in achieving better home-school relations.

Parental Attitudes to Education and Their Aspirations for Their Children

It is commonly believed that parents of ethnic-minority children value education highly. Hill, for example, says that Pakistani parents 'place considerable value upon their children's education, for they hope it will lead to an increase in the family's status, and they see themselves as instrumental in ensuring that their children apply themselves fully in their school work'.[2] This seems sensible enough, but as an impressionistic comment it could apply equally to any other ethnic-minority group, the Navaho Indians of North America just as well as the Pakistanis. But what do we really know about these matters with specific regard to ethnic-minority parents in Britain? Ideally, for good home-school relations, parental attitudes to education will be wholly favourable and parents will have realistic and attainable aspirations for their children based on a thorough acquaintance of the workings of the educational system and of what is possible for their children career-wise. But what is the position in real terms? What, for example, is the *meaning* of education for ethnic-minority parents in this country? Does it differ from the meaning placed on it in their country of origin? Precisely what aspirations do parents hold for their children? How realistic are these? Do all parents advise their children on what they should do on leaving school? What sort of advice is given? Is any distinction made between sons and daughters? What are the pitfalls for parents advising their children? Studies to date are

few in number and variable in reliability, yet it is possible to
piece together a tentative framework for a general picture.

In the Handsworth study of 1976, Rex and Tomlinson sought
information on the educational backgrounds of ethnic-minority
parents, their contacts with schools, their views on the schools
their children attended and their career aspirations for their
children.[3] The survey was directed at West Indian and Asian
parents, and also at a comparative group of British white
parents. It was found that enthusiasm for education abounded
among the ethnic-minority parents. As Tomlinson says, 'Overwhelmingly, ethnic-minority parents wanted their children to stay
on in education after the minimum leaving age, girls as well as
boys.'[4] The reasons for this appear to be largely instrumental —
the schools are a means of gaining educational qualifications
enabling their children to overcome the discrimination that they
will meet on seeking employment. Such findings would appear to
support the claims of Hill referred to earlier with respect to
Pakistani parents.

When the findings of the Handsworth study are set beside
Foner's earlier work,[5] an interesting new facet is revealed — how
social and cultural context can affect priorities. Investigating the
meaning of education to Jamaicans at home and Jamaican
migrants in London, she found that the former placed significantly greater emphasis on it than the latter. For Jamaicans at
home, education was the key to success; the gateway to a better
life. Parents cheerfully worked harder and went without so their
children could have the opportunities they were denied.
Education was a dominant topic of conversation in every-day life
and a persistent theme in the interviews conducted by Foner in
her research. On interviewing Jamaican migrants in this country
some years later, however, she found that education was no
longer the main focus of interest. This is not to say that
education was not seen as important. Certainly it was, but it no
longer had the status accorded it in Jamaica. Foner suggested
three reasons for this change of emphasis. First, education in
Jamaica was the primary means of achieving a better life; in this
country alternatives exist. Second, free secondary and college
education were available in England; in Jamaica such facilities
were scarce and, therefore, more highly prized. Third, there was
the factor of racial prejudice. As Foner herself says in this
respect, 'Among Jamaicans in England status distinctions based

on occupation and education were superceded by the overwhelming importance of colour.

Findings from studies of the aspirations of ethnic-minority
parents for their children appear to be conflicting: some show
that parental hopes in this connection are realistic, others reveal
a different picture. Foner, for example, felt that the Jamaican
migrant parents had fairly realistic views of the occupational
opportunities for their children. In hoping that their sons would
enter professional or white-collar jobs, some parents in the study
were aware that their aspirations might be pitched too high.[6] Rex
and Tomlinson similarly felt that the West Indian parents in
their Birmingham sample had realistic hopes for their children's
future occupations.[7] Twice as many West Indian parents as white
parents did not know what jobs their sons would do and left the
decision to them. Sixteen per cent hoped their sons would take
up professional careers and 65.6 per cent wanted them to stay on
at school.

In her review of research into the education of pupils of West
Indian origin, however, Taylor cites studies with contrasting
findings.[8] For example, a CRC study of differing perspectives on
the education of ethnic-minority children covering eight disadvantaged areas across the country found that West Indian
parents had greater expectations for their children than parents
of similarly disadvantaged white children.[9] Richmond, too,
found in Bristol that West Indian parents were more ambitious
for their children than English parents in the same working-class
district.[10] And Pollak in her study of nine-year-old children in
London claimed that mothers of West Indian children in her
sample were likely to have unrealistic aspirations for their
children and that the parents were less likely to leave their child's
choice of career to him.[11]

The Handsworth study throws interesting light on the extent of
parental direction in career choice. About one third of the three
groups of parents — West Indian, Asian and white British —
declined to choose a career for their children and left the choice
to them. This applied to girls as well as boys. Parents who did
specify a particular career for their children mentioned a wide
variety of jobs. For boys, professional occupations such as
medicine, law or engineering were mentioned slightly more by
Asian parents. All groups of parents wanted their children to
obtain jobs involving skills and having security and long-term

prospects. The following were identified in these respects:
technicians, draughtsmen, mechanics, computer operators,
clerical officers, builders, policemen, apprenticeships and the
armed forces. There was slightly less variety for girls, with
teaching, nursing, medicine, banking, accounting, commercial
and shop work, hairdressing and entertainment being
mentioned.[12]

Different aspirations for sons and daughters were also
disclosed in a study by Driver, though in this case greater
support was given to the daughters.[13] The investigator
interviewed parents of West Indian children chosen on the basis
of how well or how badly they were doing in the third year of
their secondary school. Without reference to their daughters'
academic performance, parents — and especially mothers —
wanted their daughters to be given as much support as possible
in order to achieve economic independence and social status.
They insisted on their daughters doing well at school and finding
secure and suitable work on leaving school. Although relations
with sons were more strained, parents — and particularly fathers
in this case — had high hopes for them, placing great faith in
the school's ability to give them the kind of education that
would lead to careers of varying pretentions.

In endeavouring to advise their children on what career to
follow and on the best route to take, ethnic-minority parents
face numerous difficulties. Ignorance of the educational system
is perhaps the chief obstacle, as Tomlinson notes:

> . . . any immigrant parent is disadvantaged in trying to
> understand the complex English educational system, with its
> stop-go policy of comprehensivisation, its curriculum innova-
> tions, and its mysterious streaming and setting processes.
> These things are difficult enough for indigenous parents, and
> doubly so for immigrant parents, some of whom are also
> handicapped by language difficulties.[14]

She also shows how such ignorance can in some cases lead to a
mild form of exploitation on the part of the school. For
example, pupils can be encouraged to stay on in the sixth form
without parents really knowing why they are staying on, or
without the nature of the courses their children are taking or
what they can lead to being explained to them. Another instance

cited by Tomlinson is that of parents not always being informed of the relative usefulness of, say, acquiring O-levels at 18 instead of 16. She suggests that one way of improving home-school relations with ethnic-minority parents would be:

> The introduction of much more structured links, both to inform parents about the education system in general, and thus help make discussions of their own children's education more meaningful, and also to encourage teachers to listen to the views of ethnic minority parents without preconceived stereotyping.

Parents' General Views on Multicultural Education

The one thing that literally anyone in our society can be expected to have opinions on is the school system and the parents of ethnic-minority children are no exception in this respect. Just how positive or negative, strong or weak, well-founded or ill-founded such opinions are will inevitably contribute to the quality of home-school relations. In the comparatively recent past, a number of studies into ethnic minorities have included the area of parents' views on multicultural education. One of the most important of these is the Handsworth study referred to above and reported by Tomlinson.[15] Within a wider survey of 1100 West Indian, Asian and a comparative group of British householders, parents, were asked among other matters about their satisfactions and dissatisfactions with the schools their children attended.

Box 6.1 illustrates reasons the parents gave for either their satisfaction or dissatisfaction. Four-hundred-and-forty parents said they were satisfied, compared with 105 who were dissatisfied, sometimes quite strongly so.

Tomlinson reports that if children get good reports, appear to be doing well and have 'good' teachers, all groups of parents view school with some satisfaction. However, she considered that the immigrant parents did perhaps place more faith in the phrase 'doing well' and on the comments of teachers. More British than immigrant parents expressed satisfaction because of 'good teachers', a phrase given interesting glosses by the parents themselves. All groups had in mind teachers who got down to

Box 6.1: Parental Satisfaction and Dissatisfaction with School

	West Indian %	Asian %	British %
Satisfied because:			
Children doing well/good reports	77	56	64
Good teachers	11	11	22
Regular schooling	5	16	6
Happy at school	4	8	—
Not held back by coloured children	—	—	4
Other	3	9	4
	100 (212)	100 (165)	100 (63)
Dissatisfied because:			
Held back by coloured children	4	14	48
Teachers no good	16	19	4
Low standards of education	22	14	19
Poor teaching methods	22	11	15
Poor discipline	4	18	7
No encouragement for slow learners	16	3	—
Didn't get school of choice	4	4	—
Other	12	17	7
	100 (50)	100 (28)	100 (27)

Source: Tomlinson.[16]

the business of teaching literacy and numeracy at primary level, and subjects leading to examinations at secondary level. The immigrant parents preferred teachers who were strict and who 'pushed' their children but who were at the same time kind. When referring to discipline, both West Indian and Asian parents defined it as a firm, controlled environment where it was possible to get on with the task of learning, rather than punishment. Immigrant parents also preferred teachers who were non-racist.

A minority of all groups, Tomlinson reports, were dissatisfied with their children's education and viewed schools with some dismay. The British parents were worried that their children were 'held back by coloured children' although there has never been evidence to support this. Oddly, a few West Indian and Asian

parents took this view as well. Some members of all groups were
critical of what they saw as a low standard of education compared with other schools they knew of, and also criticised
teaching methods, curriculum content and discipline. Interestingly, whereas some Asian parents were anxious that their
children kept in contact with their own culture by regular
instruction in mother tongue and religion, the West Indian
parents were ambivalent about the idea of promoting a West
Indian or 'black' culture. They viewed the introduction of 'black
studies' or cultural programmes in schools with some suspicion.
Some parents were influenced by their own educational
background which had stressed European history and achievements and wanted their children to 'learn about Britain'. Others
thought that time spent away from 'ordinary' subjects and
acquiring the qualifications needed to succeed in British society
was time wasted.

Two studies of 1977 reflect negative views of parents on the
whole and contrast with the findings of the Handsworth study.
The CRC investigation[17] referred to earlier found that West
Indian parents were least likely to like their children's school.
Those parents whose children were not taught by West Indian
teachers were almost equally divided on whether they would or
would not like their children to be taught by West Indians,
although 50 per cent said that their children were either taught
nothing or not enough about their own culture. The opinions of
such parents about the absence of black studies in school were
confirmed in a study by Mack.[18] She also found that many West
Indian parents were unhappy about discrimination and discipline
as well as teachers' attitudes to their children which they felt
affected their school work adversely.

More recently, Davey and Norburn[19] have collated more
positive evidence on ethnic-minority parents' views on their
children's education and on the influence they exert on their
children's perceptions of other ethnic groups. As part of a larger
study, nearly 500 West Indian, Asian and white parents of
children of primary age who lived in London and industrial
Yorkshire were interviewed by members of their own race. The
West Indian parents were very considerably in favour of pupils
of different ethnic groups being educated in the same schools.
Most of these parents were able to identify their own children's
friends and, as with the white parents, were anxious to show that

their children had friends of other races. Few of them wanted to
have a say in their children's choice of friends — unlike Asian
parents. When presented with three hypothetical racial incidents
that had been suggested by the researchers, 75 per cent of the
West Indian parents expected the teacher to be firm in handling
classroom behaviour and a third would support their child's
efforts to retaliate in a racial incident. Parents said that their
children were not particularly curious about differences in
colour, religion, customs or countries of origin and although
some said they would be willing to explain such matters to their
children, the researchers considered that they relied to a large
extent on the school performing the task. Indeed, a high
proportion of the parents thought that schools should have a
multicultural curriculum.

Davey and Norburn's work is of particular interest because it
is one of the very few studies throwing light on the relationship
between West Indian parents' views and those of their children.
Some of these connections are especially interesting, for example,
parents favouring multicultural education tended to have more
tolerant children. And parents advocating immediate action from
teachers in the face of pupil discrimination in the classroom had
fewer ethnocentric children. Only among the West Indians was
there an association between parental responsibility for their
children's attitudes and the way they handled their children's
racial problems and their children's ethnocentricity. Eighty-two
per cent of those West Indian children who expressed favourable
attitudes to other ethnic groups had parents who were prepared
to acknowledge their responsibility for inter-racial education.
The remaining West Indian parents placed the chief responsibility for multicultural education with the schools, even to a
greater extent than either the Asian or white parents.

Parental Involvement with their Children's Schooling

Nothing can be quite as effective in overcoming the problems
and difficulties standing in the way of effective home-school
relations as active and regular involvement by minority-group
parents with the schools in which their children are being taught.
Yet we may find a vicious circle operating here — the very
problems that can be resolved by greater involvement may

prevent such involvement occurring in the first place: ignorance of the system, for example, may make a parent hesitate before stepping inside the school building. We have seen how some parents of ethnic-minority children show great interest in their education. But how far and to what extent does it go as far as actual visits to the schools in question and discussions with heads and teachers about their children's work and intentions? Evidence appears to be somewhat conflicting in this respect. In a large ILEA investigation, for example, Mabey[20] found that only 50 per cent of West Indian parents had had discussions with their children's teachers compared with over 80 per cent of the white parents. And in a study of nine-year-old children in London, Pollak[21] found that the West Indian parents were less involved with their children's schooling: they visited the teachers less frequently, had been to school functions less often and were even less likely to take their children to school. Similarly, Payne,[22] investigating the views of nearly 400 parents in EPAs in London and Birmingham, found that the West Indian parents in the group were less likely to have had contact with their children's schools: 'to have seen the head, to have engaged in school activities, or to have gone to school on their own initiative'.[23] In contrast to these findings, Rex and Tomlinson[24] found in Birmingham that 79 per cent of the West Indian parents in their sample had visited school in the recent past. An example of the possible beneficial effects of parental involvement is illustrated by the Haringey Reading Project which involved close teacher-parent co-operation in encouraging children's reading.[25]

The Handsworth study[26] further disclosed how both the West Indian and Asian parents' visits to their children's schools reflected serious efforts to understand a complex and unfamiliar system of education. In this connection Tomlinson[27] writes:

We considered that actually visiting a school constituted a good measure of parental interest. Various reasons have been put forward for ethnic minority parents failing to visit schools — ''parental apathy'' being one of the most common. We found little evidence of apathy, even among parents who had not visited the schools. One Indian parent discussed the question seriously with us, but felt that teachers should be left to educate his children ''without my interference''. Other parents felt their command of the English language was not good enough to communicate meaningfully with teachers. Long working hours and shift work have also been offered as reasons for parents failing to visit schools, and indeed our study showed that West Indian and Asian parents, including mothers, worked longer, more "unsocial" hours, and did more shift work, than whites living in the same district.

Box 6.2 shows from the study that whilst the 'British' were the *most* likely to have visited their child's school in the preceding six months, the majority of West Indian and Asian parents had attended it; it was interesting, in the light of the view sometimes expressed that Asian parents are more interested in their children's education, to see that West Indian parents were rather more likely to have visited their children's school than Asians.

Box 6.2 also shows that just over half the parents had been to a parents' evening or Open Day which, as Tomlinson makes clear, is not the ideal time to discuss a child's progress, or for parents to get to know the options open within a school. Many of the West Indian and Asian parents, however, had made the effort to go to the school to talk to the head or teachers about their children's progress. Only six West Indian parents had visited the school about a discipline problem.

Finally, teachers in 70 per cent of the 525 secondary schools in a recent Schools Council Project Studies in the Multiethnic Curriculum said that ethnic-minority parents were less active in PTA groups and other forms of parental involvement.[29] Details of how one school encouraged ethnic-minority parents to visit school may be found in Brown.[30]

Pupils' Attitudes to School and Career

The influence that pupils can exert on home-school relations is very considerable indeed, if only for the obvious reason that they live and operate in both environments. It is, therefore, somewhat surprising that comparatively little research has been undertaken on ethnic-minority pupils' attitudes to school. Most of what is available is restricted to pupils of West Indian origin.[31] One of the earliest studies was by Hill[32] who questioned 400 pupils in their final year in six secondary modern schools. He found that the West Indians in general had favourable attitudes to education

Box 6.2: Parental Involvement in their Children's Schools

A. *Parental visit to school in last six months:*

	West Indian %	Asian %	British %
Haven't been	21	31	11
Saw teacher	47	50	48
Saw head	22	15	20
Saw both	9	4	20
Saw careers officer	1	—	1
	100 (285)	100 (202)	100 (92)

B. *Reason for school visit (those who had been)*

	West Indian %	Asian %	British %
Parents' evening/Open Day	54	56	53
See child's work	10	13	3
General progress	21	21	29
Academic problem	1	2	3
Discipline problem	6	—	4
Attendance/illness	2	1	2
Can't remember/other	6	6	6
	100 (225)	100 (140)	100 (92)

Source: Tomlinson.[28]

and that although the girls had favourable attitudes to school they did not feel similarly towards their teachers. The West Indian boys by contrast regarded their teachers as people to imitate.

In another study four years later,[33] a sample of West Indians aged 16 to 24 in Birmingham also expressed favourable attitudes towards their earlier school experience, although they had not done as well as they expected. John,[34] on the other hand, using a large sample of 16-year-old West Indians found only 40 per cent had positive attitudes to school. It appeared that the greater number of them were disillusioned with their school work and with the kinds of jobs they could expect to take up. Views on teachers were reflected in studies by Marvell[35] and Rex and Tomlinson.[36] In a study conducted in 1974 the former found that a small number of West Indian children in his participant observation study saw their headmaster as a distant figure. The latter, five years later, found that the majority of the 25 West

Indian 16 to 21-year-olds said that they did not consider that their teachers were interested in them and their work.

One of the most significant studies of West Indian pupils' attitudes to school is Jelinek's[37] which was part of a series of NFER researches on immigrant children that began in the early 1970s. Opinions of pupils from different ethnic groups on the ethos of the multicultural school, schoolwork and school life in general were sought by means of an attitude questionnaire. Although the West Indian pupils' attitudes to schoolwork and school in general were broadly consistent with those of the group as a whole, they tended to hold distinctive opinions on the multi-cultural school. They held the least favourable attitude towards the ethos of the multicultural school compared with other ethnic-minority groups, especially at 10 + . They did not appear to be very interested in school work, especially at 12 + , although they had positive attitudes towards school in general, this being particularly the case for the West Indian girls at 10 + and 12 + . It needs to be borne in mind that studies at this period were concerned with many pupils who were, strictly speaking, immigrants in that they had been born in the Caribbean and who may, therefore, have experienced some schooling there. Furthermore, as Taylor[38] reminds us, studies of pupil attitude at this time need to be seen in the context of secondary, rather than comprehensive, schooling.

In the year following Jelinek's study, Dawson[39] studied the attitudes of nearly 500 14-year-olds to school and parents and came to similar conclusions. The pupils in question came from schools in mainly working-class areas having a range of from nearly 10 per cent to more than 60 per cent black pupils. Dawson found that both black and white pupils had positive attitudes to school and were particularly favourable to it as a means of preparing them for the future. Most pupils, however, excepting those in the higher-ability groups, felt that the schools had too many rules and were too strict. The researcher also found that those who were positive towards school were also likely to be similarly disposed to their parents. Interestingly, the black pupils scored significantly higher than white pupils on all attitude scales and particularly on attitudes to school in general and on the value of further education. They also achieved higher scores for parental respect. The data further disclosed that pupils had a more favourable attitude to school and parents when they attended schools with roughly equal proportions of black and white pupils; and that the commitment of black pupils to further education is stronger in the school with a majority of white middle-class pupils.

In a small-scale study in 1975, Dove[40] investigated the views of pupils in their mid-teens at three London comprehensive schools. The sample, which included first and second generation 'immigrants', consisted of 545 boys and girls. Of these, 31 per cent were black (made up of West Indian and Asian) and the rest were white (British and Cypriot). The inquiry set out to examine pupils' views on their future in terms of schooling, further education, training and jobs. With regard to schooling, Dove found that, in general, pupils showed respect for their education and an awareness of the importance of paper qualifications. The large majority of the sample either liked school or were neutral about it. Cypriots and Asians more often stated that they positively enjoyed it than did West Indians and white British. Girls on the whole were more positive and British boys least so.

As regards relations with teachers, most thought that, on the whole, they got on well with their teachers. Girls tended to be more positive; West Indian boys got on least well of all. In general, most tolerated school, some enjoyed it and only a few found it unbearable.

Dove also looked at pupils' aspirations. In contrast to the white British pupils, only a small proportion of the minority groups wanted to leave school at the earliest opportunity. One of the surprising results was that the West Indians, especially the girls, were anxious to stay on notwithstanding the relatively negative attitudes they had to school. Dove conjectured that there was possibly a distinction between attitude to a particular school and the importance attached to gaining qualifications. The finding further casts doubt on the racial stereotype of the fun-loving, indolent West Indian, languishing at the bottom of the occupational ladder because he is unwilling to improve himself.

The spirit of these latter findings by Dove reflect those of the earlier study by Townsend and Brittan[41] who, in a national survey of nearly 100 multicultural secondary schools, found that twice as many West Indians and other immigrants stayed on for a fifth year compared with native pupils; and that proportionately more members of each immigrant group stayed on into the sixth form. The study also revealed that many of the immigrant pupils were still pursuing CSE and O-level courses in the sixth form, an indication of their desire to succeed.

More recent indications of the extent to which West Indians participate in further and higher education comes from a pilot study[42] which sampled nearly 3,000 fifth and sixth formers in all the secondary schools in one London borough in 1979. Of this number, 9 per cent were West Indian. It was found that although the West Indians did not do as well as their peers, they were none the less more likely to go on to further education, even when compared with middle-class pupils or the very able.

How do ethnic-minority pupils compare with native British pupils in terms of career aspirations and their fulfilment? Studies by Figueroa[43] of West Indian school leavers in a number of London secondary modern schools suggested that the prospects for them were not as good as those for their British counterparts from similarly deprived backgrounds and that they were much less likely to have jobs to go to on leaving school. Indeed, not only were the West Indians less successful in getting the jobs they wanted, but the choice open to them was more limited. The West Indian boys were more likely to acquire lower-grade jobs than British boys and, as was also the case with West Indian girls, were less well paid. Most pupils in the study — and this was particularly true of the British — thought that the West Indians were discriminated against in the job market. What was difficult to ascertain, however, was whether the job prospects for West Indians were associated more with having a disadvantaged background, cultural differences, or colour discrimination, although the author identifies British racism as being one of the important factors affecting the poor prospects for West Indian pupils. A later study, however, identified the following factors as obstacles to job-getting: lack of will-power on the part of applicants, no or poor qualifications, shortage of jobs and not being clever enough.[44]

The question inevitably arises, who or what influences ethnic-minority pupils' career aspirations? Beetham[45] found that West Indian pupils tended to have higher career aspirations than their English peers and that the main influence on their career hopes was their parents who were prepared to let them stay on at school. Yet another potent influence on ethnic-minority pupils' aspirations is the peer group and their expectations. A study by Hilton,[46] for example, reporting on the ambitions of fourth-form pupils in Manchester found that West Indian boys tended to have more limited occupational horizons and that these were more influenced by peer-group expectations than their fathers' jobs. There is some evidence, however, that suggests that ethnic-minority pupils are increasingly influenced by their careers officers.[47]

Attitudes to school constitute an important feature of ethnic-minority pupils' outlook, but what of their actual behaviour? How do such pupils adjust and relate to their school, and indeed home, environments? It would be useful at this point to examine studies attempting to correlate attitudes and behaviour among ethnic-minority pupils. Unfortunately, there are none to draw upon. There are, however, a growing number of studies examining adjustment, maladjustment and deviance among ethnic-minority pupils both at school and at home and it is to these that we now turn our attention.

Adjustment, Maladjustment and Deviance in Ethnic-minority Pupils

When considering home-school relations, the question how well do ethnic-minority children cope with life at home and at school is important in that answers to it could yield valuable insights, not only into the way behaviour in one situation compares with behaviour in the other, but also in that such a comparison could help to explain maladaptive behaviour either at home or school. A number of studies have been undertaken which seem to indicate that black West Indian children, for example, have higher rates of behavioural deviance than English children. The pattern of deviance also appears to be different in that black girls were much more likely than their white peers to manifest 'anti-social disorders'.[48] On the other hand, studies of juvenile delinquency have actually shown that black children were under-represented in the crime statistics.[49] No significant differences in deviant behaviour were found between black children born in Britain and those born in the Caribbean.[50]

A study by Bagley[51] set out, among other things, to establish the prevalence of deviant behaviour in West Indian and English children in a specified population and then to compare certain factors in the social and material background of families of deviant and non-deviant children in the West Indian group. Questionnaires and group tests were applied to the total population (approximately 2,000) of ten-year-old children attending LEA schools in one inner London borough who were on the point of starting their final year of junior school. On the basis of information from teachers about birthplace, a random sample consisting of 58 children from families in which both parents were born in the West Indies and 106 children from English families were chosen for intensive study. Two thirds of the West Indian families came from Jamaica. The parents were interviewed at home using a previously standardised interview of known reliability. Altogether 54 West Indian parents and 97 English parents were questioned. Wherever possible, the mother was seen on her own. Interviews were tape-recorded and were coded during and immediately after the interview. Two thirds of the West Indian families were seen by the same group of interviewers who interviewed the white families. The remaining third were seen by black West Indians who had lived in London several years.

According to the teachers' reports, black children were markedly more deviant than white children. But it seems there were some biases in teachers' descriptions of their black children, and a clinically-based interview with the teachers subsequently indicated a much lower prevalence of deviant behaviour in the black children. Nevertheless, a significant number of black children were deviant and rebellious in the school situation. By contrast, black children in their own homes were found to be as well adjusted as their white peers.

The evidence provided by the study suggested that there may be two separate sources of behavioural deviance in black children. The first kind is similar to the causes of such disorders in white children. The second kind of cause is presumably related to the fact of being black, and having to suffer in a racist society and racist educational system. In order to elucidate these hypotheses, the researcher compared the social circumstances of those children considered deviant following the clinical interview with the teacher with those thought to be non-deviant. Rather more of the deviant children were not living with both natural parents; in 4 per cent of the deviant cases and in 3 per cent of the non-deviant cases the child frequently confided in his or her father; and in 30 per cent of the deviant and in 7 per cent of the non-deviant cases there was lack of warmth between the child's parents. Since the amount of warmth between parents was the same when the white and the black parents interviewed were compared, this apparent cause of behaviour disorder pertains both to the West Indian and English samples. However, the first two probable causes — separation from one or both parents, and lack of interactions between father and child — have a higher prevalence in black parents compared with white, and are presumably the legacy of both the historical and contemporary circumstances of racial oppression.[52]

A study undertaken by Rutter and his colleagues[53] was designed to investigate the rates of behavioural deviance and psychiatric disorder also among West Indian children and to identify possible causative influences. A total population survey was made of all ten-year-old children in an inner London borough. Teachers' questionnaires were completed on all children and teachers and parents of a representative subsample were interviewed using standardised and previously tested methods. As part of the study, comparisons were made between children born to West Indian migrants and children from non-immigrant families, and within the West Indian group between children born abroad and those born in this country.

It was found that West Indian children showed rather more behavioural difficulties at school but they did not differ from other children in terms of disorder shown at home, nor did they differ in terms of emotional disturbance in·any setting. What is apparent from the study is that the home-school difference in terms of deviant behaviour was greater in the West Indian children and its direction different from that in other children. Whereas there were many West Indian children with disorders at school but not at home, there were few examples of the converse. Three possible reasons for the difference were identified by the researchers: first, a high proportion of West Indian children were considerably retarded in their educational attainments and it was known that reading retardation and disorders of conduct are strongly associated. It was probable that the West Indian children's greater educational difficulties led to behavioural disturbances at school which would not necessarily generalise to the home situation. Second, schools with a high proportion of children from immigrant families tended also to be schools with somewhat higher rates of pupil turnover. It was found that high rates of turnover are associated with behavioural deviance in white non-immigrant children and it is probable that school variables also influence the behaviour of West Indian children. Third, there is strong evidence of racial discrimination in this country. It is likely that the children's awareness of this discrimination will be greater at school than at home and consequently may influence behaviour more at school. In examining the causative influence for the deviance in the West Indian children, it was posited that children not living with their two natural parents, who had had at least one week in care of the local authority, whose mothers showed little warmth to their husbands and whose fathers failed to communicate with them were particularly at risk.

An absence of comparable studies among children of Asian origin prompted Kallarachal and Herbert[54] to undertake a study of maladjustment in Indian children in the schools of Leicester. They set out to compare rates of maladjustment in samples of Indian and English children. A total of 52 Indian boys and 52 Indian girls were randomly selected for study. The contrast group consisted of the same number of English boys and girls matched by age, sex and classroom. One hundred Indian families and 98 English families were interviewed. Among the Indian children a total of 11 per cent were classed as maladjusted by parents and/or teachers. Of the English children, a total of 31 per cent were so designated.

The difference in the amount of maladjustment between the Indian and English children was found to be statistically significant, that is the rate of maladjusted behaviour among the first generation of what were typically Indian immigrant children was lower than that in comparable populations of urban native non-immigrant children.

In endeavouring to interpret these findings, the researchers identified two broad areas that seemed to account for the presence or absence of problems in the children studied. First, there was the quality of family life, this clearly being superior in the case of the Indian children. For example, all the Indian children in the sample were living with both their natural parents; no serious disruptions in family relations were reported; parent-child relations were harmonious and warm; and the children were well disciplined. Second, there were environmental factors. The Indian families were better off financially than the English families in the same area and were better able to cope with the hardships having come from a country with lower standards and fewer amenities. Such strong points were more prevalent in the Indian families and helped to ward off the potentially high risk of emotional and behavioural problems in the children.

In the concluding section, we consider ways in which better home-school relations might be engineered.

The Role of the Community School

At the conclusion of her article on ethnic-minority parents and education, Tomlinson[55] suggests that one way of improving home-school relations with ethnic-minority parents would be:

> The introduction of much more structured links, both to inform parents about the education system in general, and thus help make discussions of their own children's education more meaningful, and also to encourage teachers to listen to the views of ethnic minority parents without preconcieved stereotyping.

In the course of this chapter a number of reasons have emerged why productive home-school relations should be the aim of all those interested in the education of ethnic-minority pupils. They can, for example, have a vital bridging role between different sections of the community; they can do something about racial attitudes formed in early childhood; and they can help lessen the tension existing in inner-city areas. More particularly, home-school relations will take on a more positive note where parental attitudes to the multicultural school and its work are favourable.

Singh[56] reminds us that some schools realised early on that if they were to have sufficient knowledge of their immigrant pupils they would have to create a constructive dialogue with parents. Such schools organised meetings with parents and arranged to have talks with them in their own language using an interpreter where necessary. From Singh's experience the purpose of the meetings varied but more often than not they served to explain fundamental facts about school organisation, ignorance of which could often lead to misunderstandings. Streaming, transfer according to age, transfer at 11 +, the differences between CSE and GCE courses and the school-leaving age are examples cited by Singh of aspects of school organisation that ethnic-minority parents sometimes fail to comprehend. At the same time, there is a great deal that teachers can learn about such matters as parental backgrounds, child-rearing practices, religious and cultural beliefs and the hopes parents have for their children. Singh suggests that the best way to learn such details is from parent-teacher relationships.

According to Singh, one way that this problem has been tackled in some areas has been through the appointment of home-liaison teachers whose job it is to visit parents in their own homes and encourage from them a more positive contribution towards their children's education. In some instances, schools have appointed immigrant teachers who may fulfil a similar function between teachers and children. They can in particular help to resolve cultural issues. We shall have more to say about black teachers in school in the next chapter.

Singh identifies other examples of initiatives particularly on the part of schools to cement stronger relationships. School buildings, for example, have sometimes been made available to religious groups for the holding of their services, occasions that have sometimes led to the head and his teachers being invited to the subsequent social gathering. English-language teaching for mothers has proved a worthwhile and useful facility; and, occasionally, schools have made use of the knowledge and expertise of parents when teaching particular aspects of the curriculum. This has proved especially useful in the area of religious studies.

One potentially important institution for achieving better home-school relations is the community school, although its role in this respect has not been as fully explored as it might have been. One study that has looked at the possibilities is that of Brazil,[57] who investigated the effect of a community school on parental attitudes to school and education in an educational-priority area. The school in question had a pupil population of some 500 children of whom 64 per cent were from overseas. By including groups from Ireland, Scotland and European countries some twenty nations were represented in all. These included groups of West Indian, Indian and Pakistani origin. There was only a small group of indigenous pupils.

At the outset of the study, measures of pupil-academic attainment and of parental attitudes to school and education were obtained. Thereafter, a programme of community activities was initiated in the school for a period of one year. The school was run in accordance with an adopted definition of 'community school'. After a year the tests of attainment and parental attitude were re-administered. The results were subjected to statistical analysis to determine whether the community-school approach had affected either the academic achievements of the pupils or the attitudes of the parents to school and education. There were a large number of significant improvements in pupil attainment, though these may have been caused by factors other than the programme of activities. Attitudes towards school and education on the part of parents were positive but showed little change except in variables of high personal interest to them. Since we are particularly concerned with the potential effects of the community school on parental attitudes and home-school relations, we might examine this part of the study in a little more detail, especially as it relates to the Indians, Pakistanis and West Indians.

As regards the first attitudinal test, attitudes to education in general, the Indians, Pakistanis and British were the only groups whose mean values improved slightly, but insignificantly. The other groups, including the West Indians who were one of the largest groups numerically, all lowered their means slightly, but insignificantly. The investigator notes that the slightly improved means came from the Indians, Pakistanis and British who supported more actively the events of the year.

The second attitudinal test, attitudes to school in particular, included nine variables. These were: teacher attitudes, content of curriculum, teaching methods, pupil behaviour, discipline and punishment, buildings and equipment, standards, pupil attitudes and home-school relations.

Initial responses from the West Indian families were on the whole relatively high and showed no significant movement one way or the other on any of the variables. Variable 5, attitudes to discipline and punishment, produced a negative response indicating a preference for traditional discipline and corporal punishment. Responses from the Indian families likewise showed no significant changes in either direction. On only two variables was the group clearly positive — teacher attitudes and home-

Box 6.3: Subjective Views of Staff on the Value of the Year's Efforts

	Yes	Undecided	No
1. Has L . . . . Community increased the number of home/school contacts?	11	1	7
2. As a result of this organisation has there been an improvement in the quality of the relationships between home and school?	11	1	7
3. Has there been any improvement in children's work which you think is attributable to increased co-operation between home and school?	4	1	14
4. Were the activities provided of the kind to increase home/school contacts, i.e. were they suitable?	11	2	6
5. Do you think parents really want a home/school organisation?	9	2	8
6. Has the Community brought about increased harmony among multiracial parents?	5	4	10
7. Do you think there is a need for a Community School in this area?	16	1	2
8. Do you think attempts to improve children's work and educational opportunities through increased home/school relations have been:			
A. adequate?	10	1	8
B. successful?	3	6	10
C. of sufficient variety?	11	1	7
D. such that we could be called a Community School?	10	3	6
9. Do you think teachers want a home/school organisation?	9	2	8
10. Do you want a home/school organisation?	17	1	1

Source: Brazil.[57]

school contacts. Like the Indians, the Pakistanis showed a tendency to be neutral or undecided in their attitudes in general. In common with other groups they support the more traditional rigid and formal approach to discipline.

As we shall in the next chapter be examining the teacher's position in the home-school triangle, we conclude by referring the reader to Box 6.3 which gives the teachers' views on the value of the community-school project described by Brazil. On the whole, the results appear to have been favourably received by the teachers, though the enterprise appears to have had little effect on the quality of the pupils' work.

Notes

1. Quoted in A. Little (1978) 'Schools and Race' in Commision for Racial Equality, *Five Views of Multi-racial Britain*, London: CRE.
2. D. Hill (1976) *Teaching in Multiracial Schools*, London: Methuen and Co.
3. S. Tomlinson (1980) 'Ethnic Minority Parents and Education' in M. Craft, J. Raynor and L. Cohen (eds), *Linking Home and School*, London: Harper and Row.
4. Ibid.
5. N. Foner (1975) 'The Meaning of Education to Jamaicans at Home and in London', *New Community*, 4(Summer), 195–201.
6. Ibid.
7. J. Rex and S. Tomlinson (1979) *Colonial Immigrants in a British City. A Class Analysis*, London: Routledge and Kegan Paul.
8. M. Taylor (1981) *Caught Between: A Review of Research into the Education of Pupils of West Indian Origin*, Windsor: NFER-Nelson. In this and the following chapter we draw upon summaries and accounts of research studies contained in this review.
9. Community Relations Commission (1977) *Education of Ethnic Minority Children from the Perspectives of Parents, Teachers and Education Authorities*, London: CRC.
10. A. Richmond (1973) *Migration and Race Relations in an English City*, London: Oxford University Press.
11. M. Pollak (1979) *Nine Years Old*, Lancaster: MTP Press Ltd.
12. Tomlinson, 'Ethnic Minority Parents'.
13. G. Driver (1977), 'Cultural Competence, Social Power and School Achievement: West Indian Secondary Pupils in the West Midlands', *New Community*, 5(4), 353–9.
14. Tomlinson, 'Ethnic Minority Parents'.
15. S. Tomlinson (1981) 'Multi-racial Schooling: Parents' and Teachers' Views', *Education 3–13*, 9(1, Spring), 16–21.
16. Tomlinson, 'Ethnic Minority Parents'.
17. Community Relations Commission, *Education of Ethnic Minority Children*.
18. J. Mack (1977) 'West Indians and School', *New Society*, 8(December), 325.
19. A. G. Davey and M. V. Norburn (1980) 'Parents, Children and Prejudice', *New Community*, 8(3, Winter), 206–12.
20. C. Mabey (1980) *ILEA Literacy Survey, West Indian Attainment*, unpublished.
21. Pollak, *Nine Years Old*.
22. J. Payne (1975) *Educational Priority: EPA Surveys and Statistics. Volume 2*, London: HMSO.
23. Taylor, *Caught Between*.

24. Rex and Tomlinson, *Colonial Immigrants.*

25. J. Tizard, J. Hewison and W. N. Scofield (1980) 'Collaboration Between Teachers and Parents in Assisting Children's Reading, Project Summary', London: Thomas Coram Research Unit.

26. Tomlinson, 'Ethnic Minority Parents'.

27. Ibid.

28. Ibid.

29. A. Little and R. Willey (1981) *Multi-Ethnic Education: The Way Forward,* Schools Council Pamphlet, **18**, London: Schools Council.

30. D. M. Brown (1979) *Mother Tongue to English: The Young Child in the Multi-Cultural School,* London: Cambridge University Press.

31. This section draws upon the review of research by Taylor, *Caught Between.*

32. D. Hill (1968) 'The Attitudes of West Indian and English Adolescents in Britain', MEd. Thesis, University of Manchester.

33. P. Evans (1972) *Attitudes of Young Immigrants,* London: Runnymede Trust.

34. A. John (1971) *Race in the Inner City,* London; Runnymede Trust.

35. J. Marvell (1974) 'Moral Socialisation in a Multiracial Community', *J. Moral Educ.,* **3**(3), 249–57.

36. Rex and Tomlinson, *Colonial Immigrants.*

37. M. M. Jelinek (1977) 'Multiracial Education 3. Pupils' Attitudes to the Multiracial School', *Educ. Res.,* **19**(2), 129–41.

38. Taylor, *Caught Between.*

39. A. Dawson (1978) 'The Attitudes of "Black and White" Adolescents in an Urban Area', in C. Murray (ed.), *Youth in Contemporary Society,* Slough: NFER.

40. L. Dove (1975) 'The Hopes of Immigrant Schoolchildren', *New Society,* **32**, 10 April, 63–5.

41. H. E. R. Townsend and E. M. Brittan (1972) *Organisation in Multiracial Schools,* Slough: NFER.

42. M. Craft and A. Z. Craft (1981) *The Participation of Ethnic Minorities in Further and Higher Education, Summary and Conclusion of a Report,* London: Nuffield Foundation Study.

43. P. Figueroa (1974) 'West Indian School-leavers in London: A Sociological Study in Ten Schools in a London Borough, 1966–67', unpublished PhD thesis, London School of Economics; (1976) 'The Employment Prospects of West Indian School-leavers in London, England', *Social and Economic Studies,* **25**(3), 216–33.

44. G. Gaskell and P. Smith (1981) 'Are Young Blacks Really Alienated?', *New Society,* 14 May, 260–1.

45. D. Beetham (1967) *Immigrant School-leavers and the Youth Employment Service in Birmingham,* London: IRR.

46. J. Hilton (1972) 'The Ambitions of School Children', *Race Today,* March.

47. S. Allen and C. R. Smith (1975) 'Minority Group Experience of the Transition from Education to Work' in P. Brannen (ed.), *Entering the World of Work: Some Sociological Perspectives,* London: HMSO.

48. See, for example: A. Nichol (1971) 'Psychiatric Disorder in West Indian Schoolchildren', *Race Today,* **3**, 1–15; P. Graham and C. Meadows (1967) 'Psychiatric Disorder in the Children of West Indian Immigrants', *J. of Child Psychol. and Psychiatry,* **8**, 105–16; J. Wight and R. Norris (1970) *Teaching English to West Indian Children,* London: Evans/Methuen; C. Bagley (1972) 'Deviant Behaviour in English and West Indian Schoolchildren', *Research in Education,* **8**, 47–55.

49. For example, W. Lambert (1970) *Crime, Police and Race Relations*, London: Oxford University Press.

50. J. Bhatnagar (1970) *Immigrants at School*, London: Cornmarket Press.

51. C. Bagley (1975) 'The Background to Deviance in Black Children in London' in G. Verma and C. Bagley (eds), *Race and Education across Cultures*, London: Heinemann.

52. Ibid.

53. M. Rutter, W. Yule, M. Berger, B. Yule, J. Morton and C. Bagley (1974) 'Children of West Indian Immigrants — I. Rates of Behavioural Deviance and of Psychiatric Disorder', *J. Child Psychol. and Psychiat.*, **15**, 241–62.

54. A. M. Kallarachal and M. Herbert (1976) 'The Happiness of Indian Immigrant Children', *New Society*, **35**(26, February), 422–4.

55. Tomlinson, 'Ethnic Minority Parents'.

56. P. Singh (1974) 'City Centre Schools and Community Relations', *Trends in Education*, May, 27–30.

57. D. E. Brazil (1976) 'The Effect of the Community School on Parental Attitudes to the Multiracial School in an Educational Priority Area', MEd. thesis, University of Birmingham.

58. Ibid.

7 HOME-SCHOOL RELATIONS: II. TEACHERS

Introduction

Having in the preceding chapter reviewed studies on ethnic-minority parents and their children, we come in this chapter to the remaining person who is in a position to exert a powerful influence, positively or negatively, on home-school relations — the teacher in the multicultural classroom. Our interest in the sections following will focus on the following questions: How can teachers themselves become more aware of their own racial attitudes and perceptions, and of the influence they can have on children? If necessary, how can they change their behaviour in these respects? What is known about teachers' attitudes and expectations with regard to ethnic-minority pupils? What are teachers' views on multicultural education? What do they think about pupil behaviour? What is the position regarding black teachers in this country? What is their status, how many are there, and what particular contribution can they make to multi-cultural classrooms? Finally, what guidance can be offered to teachers on the teaching of race in the classroom?

The chapter draws mainly on British, but also American, research studies in an attempt to answer these questions. Often the answers are partial and tentative because the work of the teacher in the multicultural classroom seems to be an area neglected by researchers. Nevertheless, it is hoped that we shall be able to identify at least some of the factors that can influence for good or ill the nature of home-school relations either directly or indirectly as far as teachers are concerned.

Banks[1] considers that to function effectively in multicultural classrooms, teachers need to possess or acquire: (1) democratic attitudes and values; (2) a multicultural philosophy; (3) the ability to view events and situations from diverse ethnic perspectives and points of view; (4) an understanding of the complex and multidimensional nature of ethnicity in society; (5) knowledge of the stages of ethnicity and their curricular and teaching implications; and (6) the ability to function at increasingly higher stages of ethnicity themselves. What Banks means by 'stages of ethnicity' and the ability to function at higher levels is the subject of the section following.

Stages of Ethnicity and the Teacher

In our analysis of the terms used in the literature of race relations in the opening chapter, we saw how the concept of *ethnicity* involves shared customs and cultures within particular ethnic groups. While the contexts in which the term is used tend to imply minority groups, this need not necessarily be the case, so the concept may legitimately be applied to majority groups as well. Although the term itself cannot be measured in precise and quantifiable ways, it does nevertheless possess a developmental aspect and it is this feature that led Banks[2] to suggest a typology that endeavours to outline the basic stages in the development of ethnicity among individual members of ethnic groups. The typology, Banks explains, is a preliminary ideal-type construct constituting a set of hypotheses that are based on existing and emerging theory and research and also on Banks' own work in this field. In this latter respect the typology has an empirical basis.

In presenting the typology, Banks had a number of possibilities in mind. As well as a means of stimulating research and developing concepts and theory related to ethnicity and ethnic groups, he regarded it as a means of suggesting preliminary guidelines for teaching about ethnicity in schools and colleges and of helping both teachers and pupils to identify their own position in the developmental sequence. Thus, having located himself in one of the earlier stages, the individual is in a position to achieve a higher stage of ethnicity, if he so desires. Ford[3] was later to develop an instrument to measure the first five of the six stages about to be described and administer it to a sample of classroom teachers. Her study demonstrated that teachers can be spread into the five stages suggested by Banks. The sixth stage was added to the typology as a consequence of the Ford study.

Stage I: Ethnic Psychological Captivity

This first stage is experienced mainly by members of minority-ethnic groups living in a host society. During it the individual internalises the negative views of his ethnic group that are institutionalised within society at large. Consequently, he experiences ethnic self-rejection and low self-esteem. These characteristics may show themselves in any one of a number of ways. The individual may, for instance, avoid situations which bring him into contact with other ethnic groups, or he may endeavour to become part of the dominant culture, often in an aggressive way. Where his efforts in this latter respect are met by rejection, then some form of anti-social behaviour may result. And the more an ethnic group is stigmatised and rejected by the dominant group, the more are its members likely to experience what Banks terms *ethnic psychological captivity*.

Stage 2: Ethnic Encapsulation

This stage is applicable to both minority- and majority-ethnic groups. It is characterised by what Banks calls *ethnic encapsulation* and *ethnic exclusiveness*, with both terms implying the factor of choice. The individual participates primarily within his own ethnic community believing that his ethnic group is superior to other groups. Many individuals within this stage have internalised the prevalent societal myths about the superiority of their ethnic group and the innate inferiority of other ethnic groups. Examples of 'Stage 2 individuals' may be found in middle-class suburbia in virtually any British town where they lead ethnocentric and encapsulated lives.

The characteristics of Stage 2 appear at their most extreme among those individuals who suddenly begin to feel that their ethnic group and its way of life, especially its privileged and ascribed status, is being threatened by other racial and ethnic groups. As Banks observes, this frequently happens when blacks begin to move into all-white communities.

Stage 3: Ethnic Identity Clarification

Again applicable to all ethnic groups. this third stage in Banks' typology embraces the individual now in a position to clarify his attitudes and ethnic identity, to reduce intra-psychic conflict, and to develop positive attitudes towards his ethnic group. He learns to accept himself, thus developing the characteristics needed to accept and respond more positively to members of other ethnic groups, self-acceptance being a requisite to accepting and responding positively to others. During this stage, the individual develops the ability to accept and understand both the positive and negative attributes of his ethnic group. Ethnic pride is genuine rather than contrived, and is not based on hate for, or fear of, outside groups. Individuals are more likely to experience this stage when they have attained a certain level of economic and psychological security and have been able to have positive experiences with members of other ethnic groups.

Stage 4: Biethnicity

The individual at this stage has a healthy sense of ethnic identity and the psychological characteristics and skills needed to participate successfully in his own ethnic culture as well as in that of others. He also has a strong desire to function effectively in two ethnic cultures. Such an individual may be described as *biethnic*. Banks points out that levels of biethnicity vary greatly. Many Asians and West Indians learn to function effectively in British society during the formal working day in order to achieve social and economic status. In their private lives, however, such people will in all likelihood resort to their own indigenous monoculture.

Non-whites in a white society are more or less forced to become biethnic to some extent in order to achieve social mobility and economic improvement. Members of the dominant group, however, frequently live almost exclusively monocultural and highly ethnocentric lives.

Stage 5: Multiethnicity and Reflective Nationalism

The individual at this stage possesses a clear and positive view of his own ethnic identity and positive attitudes toward other ethnic and racial groups. He is able to function within several ethnic cultures and to understand, appreciate and share the values, symbols and institutions of cultures other than his own. Such multi-ethnic perspectives and feeling, Banks suggests, help the individual to live a more enriched and fulfilling life and to formulate creative and novel solutions to personal and public problems. Individuals at this stage have a commitment to their own ethnic group, an empathy and concern for other ethnic groups and a strong but *reflective* commitment and allegiance to the country as a whole and its idealised values, such as human dignity and justice.

The socialisation that most people experience tends not to help them to acquire the characteristics typifying this stage. Although many indigenous British people participate in other cultures at a superficial level, such as eating ethnic foods and listening to ethnic music, few probably participate at more meaningful levels and learn to understand the values, symbols and traditions of other cultures or to function within them at meaningful levels.

Stage 6: Globalism and Global Competence

The individual within stage 6 is characterised by the features and qualities identified at stage 5, but now extended to encompass a world or global perspective. He is thus able to function competently not only within ethnic cultures in his own country but also in cultures elsewhere. According to Banks, the 'Stage 6 individual' has the ideal balance of ethnic, national and global identifications. Having internalisd the universalistic ethical values and principles of mankind, he has the skills and commitment to implement them in the world at large.

In his discussion of the model, Banks points out that the division between the stages is blurred rather than sharp and that a continuum exists not only between the stages but within them as well. In his subsequent consideration of this model in relation to teachers in multicultural classrooms, he recommends that to become more effective, they should determine their own stage of ethnicity and become sensitive to their ethnic behaviours and characteristics. The individual teacher should not only try to help pupils function at higher levels of ethnicity but should try to operate at higher stages himself. Those teachers who function at stage 2 cannot realistically be expected to help pupils develop positive racial attitudes to different ethnic groups. Once teachers are aware of their own ethnic attitudes, they can begin a programme to change them if necessary. Such a programme, Banks suggests, may consist of individual readings, pursuing suitable courses, or taking part in cross-cultural experiences at home and abroad. Features of teacher behaviour that can be strongly coloured by a teacher's level of ethnicity are his expectations and attitudes towards the pupils he teaches. The section following is concerned with these issues.

Teachers' Expectations and Attitudes

Earlier research in America[4] has clearly demonstrated that teacher expectations and attitudes may have an important part to play in pupil achievement. That this may in turn affect home-school relations has been established in the case of West Indian parents particularly who firmly believe that the performance of their children is affected for good or ill by the expectations their teachers have of them. Unfortunately, little research has been undertaken in this country on teacher expectations of ethnic-minority pupils. This may be so because of the additional problems encountered, for the difficulties researchers have in studying teacher expectations of white pupils are often compounded by racial attitudes when ethnic-minority pupils are involved.

One of the most important studies in this connection was conducted by Brittan.[5] Using a national sample of 510 primary and secondary teachers from 25 schools with between 18 and 84 per cent ethnic-minority pupils, she showed that quite marked differences existed about the ethnic groups in question. There was, however, a considerable degree of agreement on the academic and social behaviour of pupils of West Indian origin. In response to three items on the questionnaire used, more than two-thirds of the teachers indicated unfavourable opinions of West Indian pupils with only a very small percentage expressing the opposite viewpoint. The study also revealed that teachers seemed to be more ready to make generalisations about West Indian pupils as a group from which the researcher concluded that there appeared to be 'large scale stereotyping' of pupils of West Indian origin. A survey by Allen and Smith[6] in which head-teachers and teachers were asked about the achievements and vocational prospects of West Indian pupils support Brittan's findings in this respect. And Tomlinson[7] similarly found that headteachers were likely to have generalised, stereotypical views about West Indian pupils and to respond at greater length about them than Asian pupils. The stereotype that emerged portrayed West Indian pupils as slower to learn than others, lacking in concentration and likely to underachieve. Findings of this nature reveal yet another problem for the researcher: that ethnic-minority pupils cannot be studied in general terms, but only on a strictly racial basis. This means looking specifically at a teacher's expectations of West Indian pupils as distinct from those of Asian origin.

Other evidence on teacher expectations of ethnic-minority

pupils in this country comes from two black researchers.[8] Coard,[9] a teacher of ESN children, considered that most black pupils who had been diagnosed as ESN had been wrongly assessed by their teachers. This had come about, Coard suggested, because the teachers in question were biased towards the pupils and this showed itself in three ways: first, culturally, in that teachers misunderstood the linguistic differences between them and their pupils; second, socially, in that they were middle class and therefore held different values and beliefs; and finally, they were biased in that they failed to understand the temporary upset such pupils experienced as a consequence of moving from the Caribbean to the United Kingdom. Coard further claimed that the black child's performance was affected not only by a teacher's low expectations but also by prejudiced and condescending attitudes that regularly characterised a teacher's exchanges with his black pupils.

The other black researcher was Giles[10] who conducted his study in 15 primary and eight secondary schools in the ILEA. Each school had a significant number of West Indian pupils on roll. Starting from the belief that teachers' attitudes and expectations play an important part in the education of black children, he interviewed headteachers, selected teachers and two groups of black pupils on how they saw life in their schools. He found that in most cases, although stereotyping was in evidence as in the Coard study, the heads and teachers did not perceive black children as being significantly different from the socially-disadvantaged white pupils in the kinds of problems they had. What the study did reveal, however, was the confusion experienced by teachers as to how to treat pupils of ethnic-minority groups in relation to similarly socially-disadvantaged white pupils.

In reviewing the work on teachers' expectations and attitudes with particular regard to West Indian pupils, Taylor[11] considers that overall the evidence does not really permit firm conclusions being drawn as to whether they are a determining influence on black children's school performance. She concludes:

> Whilst it is most likely that some teachers do have negative
> perceptions of and attitudes towards [some] black pupils, it
> would also appear that many teachers are sensitively and
> actively concerned to evolve a consistent and fair policy

towards the treatment of their black pupils both in respect to continuity of school organisation from year to year and in their daily interaction with children of West Indian origin in their classrooms.

The question inevitably arises, where teachers have negative attitudes and expectations towards ethnic-minority pupils, can they be changed? Unfortunately, there is little empirical evidence on which to base an answer. Smith,[12] working in the United States, concluded that the racial attitudes of adults can be modified significantly in a positive way by contact and involvement with minority-group cultures. And Bogardus[13] found that a five-week inter-group education workshop consisting of lectures on racial problems, research projects and visits to local communities, had a significantly positive effect on participants' racial attitudes. Otherwise, the literature suggests that changing racial attitudes of adults is a difficult task.[14]

It has been found in the United States that to be effective, experiences must be designed specifically to change attitudes.[15] Courses that consist primarily or exclusively of lecture presentations have little impact. Neither are courses with general or global objectives likely to be successful. Varied experiences, such as seminars, visits, community involvement, committee work, guest speakers, films, multimedia materials and workshops, combined with factual lectures, are more efficacious than any single approach. More specifically, community involvement and cross-cultural interactions have been found to be among the most promising techniques. Individuals who express moderate rather than extreme attitudes are the most likely to change; and this is encouraging since most prejudiced individuals exemplify an average degree of prejudice.

Another factor in the equation is the particular viewpoint held by teachers. As Banks suggests,[16] there is the need for them to clarify their philosophical positions regarding the education of ethnic minorities and to endorse an ideology that is consistent with the cultural pluralism characteristic of our society. Teachers should be aware of the major ideologies related to ethnic pluralism and be able to examine their own positions and explore the implications of alternative ideologies. Those teachers who endorse a multicultural philosophy naturally respect and value the ethnic characteristics of minority-group pupils but also believe that these pupils need to aquire additional values, skills, attitudes and abilities in order to function successfully within our present society.

We shift our attention now to the broader issues of multi-cultural education and teachers' views on them.

Attitudes to Multicultural Education

If there is one factor pre-eminent in determining directly or indirectly, dramatically or subtly, the quality of home-school relations it is the manner in which teachers perceive the concept of multicultural education, for the way in which it is interpreted and implemented will cut to the very heart of their professional practice. It may be for this reason that there has been an increase in the amount of research in this area in recent years, although, as Taylor[17] reminds us, the findings of Miller's study[18] have tended to inhibit the introduction of race-relations programmes lest they have the opposite effect to the one desired. Miller's study, which found that teaching programmes designed to reduce racial prejudice actually increased it, involved over one thousand male apprentices aged between 15 and 20 who were pursuing courses in liberal studies as part of their day-release studies and who were given from one to three hours teaching about race. It has been suggested that the sample did not really represent the *school* population and that the teaching programme to which the sample was exposed was not long enough. Nevertheless, as Taylor observes, the reaction resulting from the findings also coincided with evidence that suggested that many teachers were unwilling to introduce teaching race or multicultural education in general into the curriculum.

In the national survey of teachers' opinions on aspects of multicultural education referred to earlier, for example, Brittan[19] examined the attitudes of heads and teachers in primary and secondary schools to aspects of the curriculum, cultural adaptation and adjustment, mother tongue teaching and other features arising from the multicultural context. She found that whereas nearly all those questioned acknowledged the responsi-bility of schools in furthering good race relations, about a fifth were either neutral or opposed to the introduction of sessions on the culture and countries of origin of immigrants. Two-thirds of those sampled, however, were in favour of such changes. Brittan also found that more teachers in schools with high percentages of ethnic-minority pupils supported a multicultural curriculum compared with those in low percentage schools, especially those in secondary schools. The studies also showed that whilst 71 per cent of the teachers felt that ethnic-minority pupils enriched the life of the school, the majority found that working in multi-cultural schools was more tiring, though not necessarily more rewarding.

Taylor[20] comments that whilst it is difficult to tell from the publications of the summary and conclusions to the 1978 Schools Council Project 'Studies in the Multiethnic Curriculum'[21] the extent to which teachers' attitudes to a multicultural curriculum have changed over the last few years, and whether they are really 'in advance of action', as is claimed, there is a feeling that a greater awareness of the multicultural nature of British society should be reflected in the curriculum, although it is the teachers in secondary school having sizeable percentages of ethnic-minority pupils who believe that all pupils, irrespective of the composition of the school, should be prepared for life in a multicultural society. Taylor adds that teachers in secondary schools with fewer than 2.5 per cent of ethnic-minority pupils, however, remain unconvinced of the relevance of a multicultural society to their teaching. Inspite of this, nearly 80 per cent of the 525 schools sampled in the project believed that the problems of white children in schools with large numbers of ethnic-minority pupils should receive special attention.[22]

A subsequent study by Widlake and Bloom[23] reveals similar attitudes to multicultural education among some teachers. The researchers were concerned with introducing teaching materials for multicultural education devised by the Centre for Urban Educational Studies in Manchester. They explain that when asked for their opinions on a provocative statement questioning the need for multicultural education, although those teachers already using the Centre's materials disagreed with the statement almost to a man, nearly half of the remaining teachers tended to agree with the view expressed.

Taylor points out[24] that if schemes for multicultural education are considered desirable, there will be no point in trying to implement them until programmes of teacher re-education are first mounted. As she says:

Whether such a policy is either possible or desirable since it appears to override teachers' professional and private attitudes, is, of course, another question, but it does appear to have been acknowledged by the National Union of Teachers who have recently advocated giving express attention to teaching in a multi-ethnic society in all teacher training courses.[25] Since then the National Association of Teachers in Further and Higher Education have argued that initial and in-service teacher training courses should contain a compulsory multicultural element[26] and the Assistant Masters and Mistresses Association has similarly called for improved teacher training to take account of the needs of ethnic minorities.[27]

Attitudes to Behaviour

As we explained at the outset, our concern in this chapter is with the influences that teachers exert, knowingly or otherwise, on ethnic-minority pupils and thereby home-school relations. It is important in this respect to consider the attitudes of teachers to pupil behaviour, especially where such behaviour is clearly deviant, resulting in lower expectations for achievement on the part of the teachers concerned. From the evidence currently available, it does seem that some elements in the black-pupil population would appear to be much more deviant than with white pupils, though this is based almost wholly on the study of West Indian pupils.

In Brittan's study,[28] directed at 171 primary teachers and 339 secondary teachers, the second part of which sought opinions on aspects of school life, 75 of the primary teachers and 78 of the secondary teachers disagreed with the statement, 'West Indian pupils are usually better behaved than English pupils' (compared with 0 and 1 respectively who agreed with the statement). However, whereas 42 primary teachers disagreed with a similar statement with regard to Asian pupils, only 18 secondary teachers so disagreed (compared with 20 and 52 respectively who agreed with the statement). And in response to the statement, 'West Indian pupils resent being reprimanded more than English pupils do', 37 primary teachers agreed with the statement (as opposed to 29 disagreeing) while 72 secondary teachers agreed with the statement (as opposed to 16 who disagreed). In response

to the same statement with regard to Asian pupils, only 9
primary teachers agreed with the statement (with 66 disagreeing)
and only 15 secondary teachers agreed (with 63 disagreeing).

The study by Rutter and his colleagues,[29] to which we referred
in the earlier chapter, investigated among other matters teachers'
attitudes to the behaviour of West Indian pupils. By means of
the Rutter Behaviour Questionnaire, which identifies 26 descriptions of behaviour, the researchers discovered that almost 49 per
cent of West Indian boys were judged by their teachers to be
behaviourally deviant compared with nearly 25 per cent of the
'non-immigrant' boys; and that just over 34 per cent of the West
Indian girls were considered as deviant compared with only just
over 13 per cent of English girls. Thus, in terms of total percentages, more than 41 per cent of the 354 West Indian children
were considered deviant compared with slightly more than 19 per
cent of the 1689 white children — clearly a very significant
difference. Rutter reports that in both boys and girls, the
children from West Indian families were more often rated as
restless, squirming, unable to settle, destructive, quarrelsome,
not liked by other children, irritable, disobedient, more prone to
telling lies, stealing, bullying and generally more resentful and
unresponsive. The West Indian girls were also likely to be rated
as solitary, miserable and fearful compared with either the West
Indian boys or English children.

In an interesting investigation, which endeavoured to relate
teacher responses to West Indian pupils and teacher characteristics, Green[30] studied the attitudes of 87 teachers from primary
and secondary schools in which there were significant proportions of children from ethnic-minority groups. He found that
behaviours on the part of West Indian children that were
described in unfavourable terms included discipline, sulking,
social behaviour, aggressiveness and resentment. And during
unstructured interviews with individual teachers, a characteristic
of West Indian children most often mentioned in favourable
terms was their friendliness. Such positive comments were most
often made by teachers who had been rated as tender-minded,
radical and having naturalistic attitudes. Green also found that
the older, more experienced teachers holding posts of responsibility tended to be less tolerant in their attitude.

In an ethnographic case study directed at the fourth year in a
multicultural school in the West Midlands, Driver[31] set out to

study, among other things, personal experiences of a number of West Indian boys and girls. He discovered that although the staff tried to meet the particular educational needs of the ethnic-minority pupils, their lack of competence in dealing with a range of unfamiliar behaviours from the minority's cultural repertoire led to managerial problems. The resulting confusion for them resulted in the adoption of differing survival strategies. At one extreme, for example, a few teachers took an authoritarian line when challenged and sought to dominate all aspects of the lesson. At the other extreme, many teachers endeavoured to get on with their work with the minimum of confrontation. As Driver says:

> They were forced to accept certain limitations upon their managerial and teaching roles, and this invariably influenced their attitudes towards those individuals who seemed to be the focus of their difficulties.

Driver considers that many of the teachers' difficulties arose from a range of charactertistically non-English social meanings in interaction between pupil and teacher and pupil and pupil. These included distinctive physical features, gestures and other codes of communication. We review here the more significant ones.

First, in the crucial phase of getting to know a class, many teachers persistently mistook and confused the identities of their West Indian pupils long after they had learned the names of faces of English pupils. Even beyond the early stages of contact, an element of uncertainty of judgment lingered in teachers' minds about the West Indian pupils with whom they had to deal.

Second, even when identification was no longer a problem, there was another range of potential difficulties. These had to do with elementary expectations about the ways body movement and posture might coincide with other sorts of expressive behaviour. It was apparent, for example, when teachers often found that the eye movements of their West Indian pupils did not signal an impending message (for example, of some expected verbal initiative or response). Individuals might look away at those moments when conventionally they would not be expected to do so. In this way the expectations of individuals socialised in two cultural settings could give rise both to misunderstandings and heightened ethnic awareness.

On many occasions, a West Indian pupil would turn his eyes away from the teacher, a gesture on his part of deference and respect for the teacher. Yet such behaviour was interpreted by the teacher as an expression of guilt or as a sign of bad manners. Driver suggests that failures of perception at this subtle, yet crucial, level could and did give rise to a code of classroom communication to which the teacher was denied access. The result for the teacher was often increased anxiety.

Third, beyond the reflexive gestures and postures, there were those signs employed by a West Indian pupil to convey specific meaning. The clicking of lips, or pouting them and plucking them with a finger were examples identified by Driver of derogatory expressions which many teachers failed to interpret even when the gestures were directed at them. The impact of the gesture on those children who understood it ranged from disgust to amusement. Sometimes, Driver found, innocent ethnically-exclusive signs could be interpreted as other than innocent. The lack of skills in understanding and responding to these expressions often proved counter-productive to the purposes of the lesson.

Fourth, there was the use of *patois*, which very few teachers understood. Most appeared to discourage its use, some by the imposition of strict penalties. It was noteworthy that among the West Indian pupils who were assessed most highly by the staff there were a number of individuals whom Driver never heard to use *patois* in any circumstances. There could be little doubt, Driver explains, that a number of teachers felt threatened by the persistent use of a dialect they could not understand, and that their anxiety expressed itself in their attitudes and behaviour towards those pupils who used it.

These aspects of communication outside the cultural repertoire of the majority clearly provided the basis for obstacles to confident relations between the West Indian pupils and their English teachers and would inevitably affect the way in which teachers perceived pupil behaviour and their attitude to it.

In conclusion, the evidence to date does seem to suggest that deviant behaviour on the part of West Indian pupils in particular (because they have been subject to the main research thrust) does affect teachers' attitudes and expectations and that this in turn will reflect on the performance of these children.

In the next section we look at the logistics and role of the black teachers in multicultural schools.

Black Teachers

In spite of the 1977 Select Committee Report recommending that statistics should be collected on the numbers of black teachers in schools and training in this country,[32] information on this subject remains incomplete. It has been estimated that the numbers in schools range from the figure of 800 given by the Commission for Racial Equality[33] to 700 suggested by the educational press.[34] Gibbes[35] considers that the figure is probably rather higher than this because the Caribbean Teachers' Association alone knows of approximately 300 teachers of Caribbean origin. These are teachers based mainly in London and the south-east. As many West Indian teachers are not members of the CTA, however, and would not therefore be included in this figure of 300, it is reasonable to estimate that throughout the country there are probably more than 800 black teachers, with West Indian teachers making up a significant proportion of this number.[36] Whatever the precise number of black teachers, however, they are certainly insufficient to match the number of black pupils in schools. Let us take those of West Indian origin as an example. In 1971, the West Indian population as a whole in this country was estimated at just over 300,000, this figure probably increasing slightly by the year 1977. On these figures alone, there is something like one West Indian teacher for every 400 West Indian children of school age. That more black teachers are needed in British schools is self-evident.

But it is more than simply a matter of numbers: there is a qualitative aspect. Given the nature of our pluralist society at the present time, the presence of black teachers in schools and the need for multicultural staffrooms are of paramount importance. Indeed, the Select Committee on Race Relations and Immigration[37] proposed that multicultural schools should employ more teachers from the same ethnic background as the children so that they might facilitate both understanding of the children and the children's identification by their teachers. There are other good reasons for employing more black teachers: they bring to school their experience of what it is like to be black in a racist society; their role and person embody the contradiction of stereotypes and they can achieve the respect of white children and help combat prejudice;[38] in identifying with and understanding black children they can help them feel positively about themselves and their family, and instil in them the values and sense of identity that will equip them to confront rather than accept their predicament; and they can help to combat prejudice among white colleagues by the exchange of ideas and, indeed, their very presence in the staff room. At the very least, as Gibbes points out, the presence of black staff usually forces other staff to reassess their attitudes and views about their black pupils.

One of the very few empirical studies of black teachers in this country is the small-scale case study by Gibbes.[39] A questionnaire on aspects of their role and work in schools was administered to a small sample of teachers of West Indian origin. Over two-thirds of them were teaching in secondary schools; and more than half of the sample were female. Subsequently, eight teachers in the sample worked in London's inner-city schools where black teachers, whether West Indian, Asian or African, were in a very small minority. In some cases, they were the only black member of staff in institutions where the black-pupil population was estimated to be between 25 per cent and 60 per cent of the total population. When asked if they felt that they had any special contribution to make to their schools, the response was overwhelmingly positive. Only three people replied negatively. The majority felt that because they themselves were members of a minority group in a society struggling with multicultural problems they had a definite contribution to make. Particular points they identified are listed in Box 7.1.

Gibbes' study also revealed that the ethos prevailing in many schools was not conducive to frank discussion about pluralism in society and its implications for schools. The West Indian teachers identified a reluctance on the part of school staffs to discuss the more important issues. They also noted a readiness on the part of white staff to see any black staff initiating discussion in this connection as creating disharmony. From the evidence, she concludes that the opportunity for open discussion of critical issues in the multicultural school rarely arises. The black teachers also expressed a need to be in positions of responsibility, yet few were. To be in a position to do something more positive, such as be able to assess the curriculum in terms of its multicultural input, was something yet to be realised for those in the sample.

Box 7.1: Contributions Black Teachers can Make in a Multicultural School

Work with and help those pupils who feel alienated from society and the school system.

Help staff focus on the sensitive issues having to do with race and education, and encourage discussion in this area.

Help in promoting understanding of black pupils and their culture.

Act as models for the pupils and so encourage them to enter one or other of the variety of professions . . . that exist in society and which would enhance the status of black people.

Provide a positive image for white people and so help to eradicate the stereotyped views held of blacks.

Encourage pupils to have confidence in themselves and to help them through discussions to relate to each other, to teachers and to develop a positive attitude to work.

Act as a resource person for staff and be used in an advisory way.

Help black parents, many of whom find it easier to communicate with a black teacher than with white teachers.

Assist in the development of a multi-cultural curriculum.

Source: Adapted from Gibbes.[40]

When asked what societal needs they felt schools should address themselves to, the teachers suggested: the fundamental needs of literacy, numeracy and cognitive development; the changing needs of a technological society; the needs of a pluralistic society including understanding the various ethnic groups and issues, the importance of integration and racial harmony and the need to challenge the stereotyped views prevalent in society; leading pupils to an understanding of themselves so that they are better able to build and maintain happy communities, to care for individuals, to be sympathetic to others and to develop a readiness to seek to understand others; encouraging pupils to take an active interest in the laws and government of this country; and helping pupils prepare for future employment, unemployment and leisure. The teachers also wanted schools to seek ways in which they could help parents to recognise the potential of their children, and to realise that home plays an important part in education and to help parents realise that they need to help their children.

Asked if they felt that their schools were educating pupils to live in a multicultural society, only three of the sample answered positively. But the nature of their comments indicated that those schools felt to be striving to educate pupils in this direction were actually doing very little; what was done was restricted to a very narrow area like language for non-English speaking pupils. As one teacher is reported to have said, 'That the school believes it is doing something does not make this a fact — it is often a false assumption'.

Those who answered that their school was doing nothing to prepare their pupils for living in a multicultural society gave the following reasons: the ethos of the school and the curriculum were too Eurocentric; many courses were not designed or oriented to foster understanding and knowledge of minority groups; white staff were reluctant to face their prejudice and racism and continued to see pupils in terms of deficit models. They still held stereotyped views of minority groups and this was reflected in their discussions; there was much acceptance within schools of the view that if you pretend certain situations and/or problems do not exist, they will go away; insufficient numbers of black teachers (a point we have already established); it was not school policy to do anything and therefore the efforts of individuals hardly caused a ripple; and the prejudice that exists is reflected within schools, therefore, it becomes easy to pay lip service to the needs of minority groups. Prejudice made it difficult to tackle needs objectively.

Interestingly, some of these views would seem to be borne out in Brittan's[41] study. When confronted with the following item on the questionnaire, 'Teachers from immigrants' countries of origin should be used to teach English to immigrant children', teachers were divided on their views, with a majority neither in agreement not disagreement. Approximately 15 per cent more teachers disagreed than agreed, however, the figures being 43 per cent and 29 per cent, respectively. The item attracted quite a lot of comment, much to the effect that the deployment of teachers from minority groups as teachers of English should depend on their proficiency in English and their knowledge of modern methods of language teaching. Some argued that any language is better taught by a native speaker, but others felt there to be a special value in having minority-group teachers in reception centres where they might deal with problems of adjustment and interpretation. One or two teachers believed the greatest contri-bution of such teachers to lie in taking a normal part in school

life and teaching all subjects. A small number of teachers
commented on specific problems which had been encountered
such as resentment on the part of minority-group pupils towards
teachers of the same ethnic origin, and indigenous children who
complained that they did not understand minority-group
teachers.

To return to the professional status of the teachers in Gibbes'
study: their career histories reflect a somewhat depressing state
of affairs. Over half were still holding Scale 1 and 2 posts,
inspite of substantial classroom experience. Having obtained
their first promotion, they found that they could get no further.
Indeed, some had made more than 20 attempts to gain promotion and very few were short-listed for the jobs they had applied
for. But perhaps the position is changing. Taylor reports[42] that
in an attempt to improve employment prospects of black
teachers a new organisation, The National Convention of Black
Teachers, was established in 1981. And that a recent advance
report on one-year foundation courses aimed at preparing ethnic-
minority students for entry to professional training courses like
teaching reveals that 47 per cent of the students on the eleven
courses in 1979–80 were West Indians. Eighty-two per cent of
the West Indian students were subsequently offered places in
higher education. This would seem to indicate, Taylor
comments, that for West Indians at least recently introduced
schemes may be having some success in increasing recruitment to
the teaching profession.[43]

Teaching Race

Stenhouse[44] reminds us that preparing pupils for life in a multicultural society specifically involves teaching race and race
relations. Unfortunately, there is little in the way of theory and
research in this respect to guide the work of teachers. Further,
the subject becomes even more problematic for, as we shall see,
there is some evidence that teachers in both primary and
secondary schools are opposed to the idea of teaching race.

One of the more widely reported experiments in this connection in Britain is that of Miller, to which reference was made
earlier.[45] Working with day-release students in Further Education
and using a wide range of teaching methods to overcome racial

prejudice, he found that prejudice was high in his group and that it increased during the experiment. His results suggest the existence of considerable problems in handling race relations through education. Moreover, they have had some influence in making teachers doubtful of the wisdom of teaching about race relations at all.

Another study on race relations was conducted within the context of the Humanities Curriculum Project.[46] According to Stenhouse,[47] the project proceeded cautiously with a limited experiment. Six schools worked with a mini-pack of teaching materials. The experiment was monitored both by case study and by a small measurement programme. The case study was reported by Parkinson and MacDonald.[48] Pupils in general maintained that their attitudes had *not* been modified as a result of the study, although many added that their understanding had been enhanced. In reporting on the measurement results, Verma and Bagley[49] say that 'this experimental study has shown that teaching designed to enhance inter-ethnic attitudes in the school setting can at least be moderately successful'. In summing up, Verma and MacDonald say:

> The combined picture of the results seems to indicate that there was no general tendency towards intolerance after a seven- to eight-week teaching programme. There is no evidence to suggest that the students generally became less sensitive to or tolerant of other racial groups. These results cannot be considered as constituting proof.[50]

At a more theoretical level, Hall[51] identifies four sets of problems inherent in teaching about race: the difficulties centring specifically on the teaching of race, and the clusters of problems stemming from the economic, political and ideological aspects of race, respectively. In Hall's view, the pedagogical difficulties are particularly important because race is an area about which people feel very strongly indeed. What is essential, Hall suggests, is that the strong emotional charge attached to the concept is recognised and brought out into the open: it is not an issue to be side-stepped. And this applies to the teacher just as much as his students. Whatever the teacher's own commitments and feelings on the matter, they have to be made clear in the way he handles the topic and the kinds of things he says about it. It is not an area where traditional academic neutrality is to be encouraged. This means that the teacher has to create an atmosphere which allows people to say unpopular things. As Hall puts it:

> The 'commonsense' racism that is part of the ideological air we breathe must be allowed to surface in the classroom, no matter how unpalatable this might be to those listening: it is better to hear it than not to hear it. We are not talking here about an abstract topic with which we are entertaining ourselves or over which we are stretching our minds. We are talking about very real, concrete, social, political and economic issues which touch the students' lives, and which they experience. So we have to consider the problems of how to create an atmosphere in which those questions can be openly and honestly discussed — one in which your own position can emerge without people feeling over-weighted by its authority.

What Hall is careful to stress is the great complexity of the subject and the consequent dangers of over-simplification. Being very complicated, the subject is difficult to teach clearly. The paradox is that whereas people know what they feel and where they stand on matters of race, it becomes much more difficult when it comes to *explaining* racial issues. And this is so, Hall explains, partly because the task involves putting together explanations from different areas of knowledge. So, Hall concludes, all attempts at a simple explanation must fail.

In spite of the fact, then, that there is something really intrinsically difficult and complicated about the whole area of race, it is essential that the teacher sets out to *teach* as well as he can without recourse to crude over-simplification or caricature. This leads naturally to the question, How can the problem of race be approached in teaching terms? Hall suggests two ways. First, there is a kind of liberal commonsense way of approaching the topic which fastens on to questions of discriminating attitudes between people from different ethnic populations, prejudicial actions, beliefs and opinions, and so on. One tendency in teaching, Hall explains, is to take these immediate surface manifestations of the problem at face value and to look at how these prejudices arise through a kind of attitudinal or social-psychological explanation of whatever the phenomenon is. The second strategy would say that all this is just a surface approach and that we should go rather to the structures which generate particular kinds of relations or racial structures. Hall expresses a preference for the second of these two approaches.

So what does this involve? Hall explains that we have to uncover for ourselves in our own understanding, as well as for the students we are teaching, the often deep structural factors which have a tendency not only to generate persistently racial practices and structures but reproduce them through time in a way that accounts for their extraordinarily immovable character. Racism has a *deep base* in the way it manifests itself in a particular society and is deeply resistant to attempts of amelioration, good feeling, gentle reform, and so on. For this reason, it is important to turn to the structural questions although it would be a mistake not to bring whatever explanations one is dealing with back to the surface phenomena. No matter how deep one goes into structural factors one needs to show that they do generate particular interactions between groups of people but one has to be able to show that a deeper understanding of those surface relations is possible. Hall subsequently goes on to examine the economic, political and ideological aspects of these deeper structures.

Hall refers to two other factors that need to be borne in mind when teaching race. The first is the difficulty that teachers may encounter if they try to change prejudices by counterposing 'good prejudices' to bad ones. He says in this respect:

> Teaching strategies which engage people's most obvious, uncomplicated, unreflexive apprehension of the problem are important but if having engaged them at that level you try to change attitudes and prejudices by putting good attitudes and good prejudices against them, what you get is a kind of 'ding-dong' of: "Well you believe that and I believe this, you see it that way and I see it this way", and it becomes very difficult to move on in any sort of productive way.

The crucial question for Hall then is how do you begin to make a move away from the level of prejudice and belief. The answer, he contends, is for us to take a leaf out of the social scientist's book: we must question the obvious. As he says, 'Social science . . . is about showing people that the things they immediately

feel to be "just like that" aren't quite "just like that".' One has
to show that there are social and historical processes. These are
deep conditions that are not going to change merely by our
tinkering with them. He warns us that we must not give our
students that kind of illusion. We can, however, begin the
process of questioning what the structures are and how they
work. In stressing an approach to teaching race that emphasises
cognitive factors and the acquisition of the necessary empirical
data, Ferguson, in a sequential article to Hall's, would seem to
be endorsing this view.[52]

The second factor considered by Hall to be of importance in
teaching race is the notion that it is some kind of moral duty. As
he says:

> Instead of thinking that the questions of race are some sort of
> moral duty, moral intellectual academic duty which white
> people with good feelings do for blacks, one has to remember
> that the issue of race provides one of the most important ways
> of understanding how this society actually works and how it
> has arrived where it is. It is one of the most important keys,
> not into the margins of the society, but right into its dynamic
> centre.

Unfortunately, both of these factors inform and structure the
approaches of much teaching. As Ferguson[53] puts it, they lead
one to the impasse where intellectual debate, acquisition of
further information or a closer examination of one's terms of
reference are irrelevant and annoying. In these circumstances,
Ferguson suggests, the classroom can become the site for emotive
and often aggressive regurgitation of learned values.[54]

We conclude by referring again to the study by Brittan[55] which
provides some empirical evidence to support points made by Hall
regarding the difficulties and complexities associated with
teaching race and race relations. In response to the item,
'Lessons on race relations should be given in schools', only 43
per cent of the teachers agreed with the statement whilst 35 per
cent disagreed. In primary schools, 7 per cent more teachers
expressed disagreement than agreement. There was, however,
more agreement in secondary schools, especially those with high
percentages of minority-group pupils. About one-fifth of the
sample added to their replies, roughly half of these expressing

opposition not to the general principle but to the idea of formal lessons, preferring an 'informal', 'incidental', or 'oblique' approach. As one said:

> I do not think 'race relations' is a specific subject — rather a continuous subject which has to be worked at, at all times, in any situation, by all the staff . . . it should not be necessary to hold formal lessons.

Some raised points which seemed to indicate a more fundamental opposition to the idea: racial differences should be ignored not emphasised; lessons on race relations would create problems where none exist at present; lessons would be counter-productive; and the problem should be dealt with as the need arises.

Notes

1. J. A. Banks (1981) *Multiethnic Education: Theory and Practice*, Boston: Allyn and Bacon.
2. Ibid.
3. M. Ford (1979) 'The Development of an Instrument for Assessing Levels of Ethnicity in Public School Teachers', Ed.D dissertation, University of Houston.
4. For example, R. Rosenthal and L. Jacobsen (1968) *Pygmalion in the Classroom*, New York: Holt, Rinehart and Winston.
5. E. Brittan (1976) 'Multiracial Education 2. Teacher Opinions on Aspects of School Life. Part Two: Pupils' and Teachers', *Educ. Res.*, **18**(3), 182–92.
6. S. Allen and C. R. Smith (1975) 'Minority Group Experience of the Transition from Education to Work' in P. Brannen (ed.), *Entering the World of Work: Some Sociological Perspectives*, London: HMSO.
7. S. Tomlinson (1979) 'Decision-making in Special Education (ESN-M) with Some Reference to Children of Immigrant Parentage', Unpublished PhD thesis, University of Warwick.
8. Reported in M. Taylor (1981) *Caught Between: A Review of Research into the Education of Pupils of West Indian Origin*, Windsor: NFER-Nelson.
9. B. Coard (1971) *How the West Indian Child is Made Educationally Subnormal in the British School System*, London: New Beacon Books Ltd, for Caribbean Education and Community Workers' Association.
10. R. Giles (1977) *The West Indian Experience in British Schools. Multiracial Education and Social Disadvantage in London*, London: Heinemann.
11. Taylor, *Caught Between*.
12. F. T. Smith 'An Experiment in Modifying Attitudes Towards the Negro', summarised in A. M. Rose (1947) *Studies in the Reduction of Prejudice*, Chicago: American Council on Race Relations.
13. E. S. Bogardus (1948) 'The Intercultural Workshop and Racial Distance', *Sociology and Social Research*, **32**, 798–802.
14. Banks, *Multiethnic Education*.

15. Ibid.

16. Ibid.

17. Taylor, *Caught Between*.

18. H. Miller (1969) 'The Effectiveness of Teaching Techniques for Reducing Colour Prejudice', *Liberal Education*, **16**, 25–31.

19. E. Brittan (1976) 'Multiracial Education 2. Teacher Opinion on Aspects of School Life. Part One: Changes in Curriculum and School Organisation', *Educ. Res.*, **16**(2), 96–107; E. Brittan (1976) 'Multiracial Education 2. Teacher Opinion on Aspects of School Life. Part Two: Pupils and Teachers', *Educ. Res.*, **18**(3), 182–92.

20. Taylor, *Caught Between*.

21. A. Little and R. Willey (1981) *Multi-ethnic Education: The Way Forward*, Schools Council Pamphlet, **18**, London: Schools Council.

22. Taylor, *Caught Between*.

23. P. Widlake and D. Bloom (1979) 'Which Culture to Teach Immigrant Pupils?', *Education*, 14 December.

24. Taylor, *Caught Between*.

25. NUT (1980) *The Achievement of West Indian Pupils*, Union evidence to the Rampton Committee of Inquiry into the education of children of ethnic minority groups, London: NUT.

26. NATFHE (1981) 'The Written Evidence to the Race Relations and Immigration Sub Committee of the Home Affairs Committee of the House of Commons', London: NATFHE, January.

27. AMMA (1981) *Education for a Multicultural Society*, A submission to the Inquiry into ethnic minority groups, London: AMMA.

28. Brittan, 'Multicultural Education'.

29. M. Rutter, W. Yule, M. Berger, J. Morton and C. Bagley (1974) 'Children of West Indian Immigrants — I. Rates of Behavioural Deviance and of Psychiatric Disorder', *Proc. First Intern. Conference on Special Education*, London.

30. P. A. Green (1972) 'Attitudes of Teachers of West Indian Immigrant Children', unpublished MPhil. thesis, University of Nottingham.

31. G. Driver (1977) 'Cultural Competence, Social Power and School Achievement: West Indian Secondary Pupils in the West Midlands', *New Community*, **5**(4), 353–9; G. Driver (1979) 'Classroom Stress and School Achievement: West Indian Adolescents and Their Teachers' in V. S. Kahn (ed.), *Minority Families in Britain: Support and Stress*, London: The Macmillan Press, Ltd.

32. Great Britain, Parliament, House of Commons, Select Committee on Race Relations and Immigration (1977) 'Report with Minutes of Proceedings and Appendices to Report. Session 1976–7: The West Indian Community', Volume 1, London: HMSO.

33. *Observer*, 6 August, 1978.

34. *Teacher*, 2 November, 1979.

35. N. Gibbes (1980) *West Indian Teachers Speak Out: Their Experiences in Some of London's Schools*, Lewisham, London: Caribbean Teachers' Association and Lewisham Council for Community Relations.

36. Ibid.

37. Great Britain, Parliament, House of Commons, Select Committee on Race Relations and Immigration (1969) 'The Problems of Coloured School Leavers. 1968–9, Volume 2, Minutes of Evidence, London: HMSO.

38. D. Milner (1975) *Children and Race*, Harmondsworth: Penguin.

39. Gibbes, *West Indian Teachers*.

40. Ibid.

41. Brittan, 'Multiracial Education'.

42. Taylor, *Caught Between*.

43. Ibid.

44. L. Stenhouse (1975) 'Problems of Research in Teaching about Race Relations' in G. Verma and C. Bagley (eds), *Race and Education across Cultures*, London: Heinemann.

45. Miller, 'Teaching Techniques'.

46. Humanities Curriculum Project (1970) *The Humanities Project: An Introduction*, London: Heinemann Educational Books.

47. Stenhouse, 'Problems of Research'.

48. J. P. Parkinson and B. MacDonald (1972) 'Teaching Race Neutrally', *Race*, **13**(3), 299–313.

49. G. Verma and C. Bagley (1973) 'Changing Racial Attitudes in Adolescents: An Experimental English Study', *International Journal of Psychology*, **8**(1), 55–8.

50. G. Verma and B. MacDonald (1971) 'Teaching Race in Schools: Some Effects on the Attitudinal and Sociometric Patterns of Adolescents', *Race*, **13**(2), 187–202.

51. S. Hall (1980) 'Teaching Race', *Multiracial Education*, **9**(1), 3–13.

52. B. Ferguson (1981) 'Race and the Media: Some Problems of Teaching', *Multiracial Education*, **9**(2), 27–40.

53. Ibid.

54. Ibid.

55. Brittan, 'Multiracial Education'.

8 THE MULTICULTURAL CURRICULUM

Introduction

Most of the responses of 510 men and women teachers in primary and secondary schools to an NFER questionnaire about multicultural education evoke little surprise.[1] One would perhaps expect an overwhelming endorsement of the statement that schools have a responsibility to promote good race relations amongst pupils. In fact, 94 per cent of the sample did agree with this.

The NFER analysis is more revealing of teachers' sentiments when Brittan, the researcher in question, touched upon questions that threatened the traditional identity of the school and where she searched out the extent to which teachers are prepared to make changes in their curriculum planning and teaching in the light of the multicultural composition of contemporary British society. It seemed that it was all right to impart information about the religions and homelands of minority groups. Beyond this, however, the teachers were divided in their opinions, and Brittan detected an overall assimilationist viewpoint among her respondents, that is the viewpoint that dominated official and educational policy in the early days of immigration in the 1960s. This sought to help immigrants accommodate to the host society by giving them a working knowledge of the English language and of the indigenous culture. Given the emphasis on English-language teaching during the early years of immigration and the widely-held belief that once English-language proficiency had been acquired all other problems would diminish, it is perhaps hardly surprising that the majority of teachers in the study should have espoused an assimilationist objective for Britain as a multicultural society.

The research further revealed that a sizeable proportion of the sample appeared to be unaware of the ways in which school books may, and in fact did, reinforce stereotypes and negative, derogatory images of ethnic minorities. Only 43 per cent of the teachers supported the view that lessons on race relations should be given in school, many feeling that such formal instruction was unnecessary and, indeed, likely to be counterproductive. One wonders, Brittan asks, how many teachers are prepared to accept the far-reaching and fundamental curricular changes that are necessary to meet the needs of preparing pupils for life in a multicultural society, changes that cut across most subject divisions and across all age groups?

What would such changes entail? We begin this chapter by outlining a recent proposal for a multicultural curriculum that, according to its author, is a perfectly natural response to the altered nature of British society and, for many teachers, to the cultural composition of the classes that they now teach. We then go on to consider ways of planning a multicultural curriculum and follow this with a number of guide-lines for such an under-taking. In conclusion, we examine the problem of racism and bias in the curriculum with particular reference to books and other teaching materials.

The Multicultural Curriculum

Jeffcoate defines a multicultural curriculum as one in which choice of content reflects the multicultural nature of British society and the world and draws significantly on the experiences of British racial minorities and cultures overseas.[2] He justifies it on the following grounds.

First, there is what Jeffcoate calls a 'pathological' foundation for developing a multicultural curriculum premised on the assumption that British society suffers from an endemic disease, racism. Because the influence of racism is so pernicious and pervasive, schools have a clear duty to make a concerted response by promoting racial self-respect and inter-racial understanding. Second, a multicultural curriculum may be justified on the notion of minority-group rights. This is to say, racial minorities are entitled to expect that their cultures will be positively and prominently represented in the school curriculum. Third, there is the traditional view that a fundamental task of the school is to present an accurate picture of society to its pupils; it goes without saying that other races and cultures are important elements in that picture. Fourth, a multicultural curriculum involves pupils in more interesting, stimulating and challenging learning experiences than one which is not.

Having thus justified the need for a multicultural curriculum,

Box 8.1: Criteria for the Selection of Learning Experiences

(a) An insular curriculum, preoccupied with Britain and British values, is unjustifiable in the final quarter of the twentieth century. The curriculum needs to be both international in its choice of content and global in its perspective.

(b) Contemporary British society contains a variety of social and ethnic groups. This variety should be made evident in the visuals, stories and information offered to children.

(c) Pupils should have access to accurate information about racial and cultural differences and similarities.

(d) People from British minority groups and from other cultures overseas should be presented as individuals with every variety of human quality and attribute. Stereotypes of minority groups in Britain and of cultures overseas, whether expressed in terms of human characteristics, life styles, social roles or occupational status, are unacceptable and likely to be damaging.

(e) Other cultures and nations have their own validity and should be described in their own terms. Wherever possible they should be allowed to speak for themselves and not be judged exclusively against British or European norms.

Source: Jeffcoate.[3]

Jeffcoate draws on his experience with the Schools Council to identify some problems and limitations in the organisation of materials and methods for multicultural classrooms.

There is, for example, little to be said for isolating topics on India, Africa or the Caribbean which are not part of a comprehensive multicultural-curriculum policy. Where schools have poor relations, such efforts are likely to be counterproductive. In terms of curriculum tactics, a sounder approach is to construct a learning programme around regular themes drawing on a variety of cultures for source materials with which all pupils can identify. That said, the need still remains for some kind of overt, systematic study since themes of themselves cannot provide pupils with an appreciative understanding of the logic and integrity of a way of life different to their own. The humanities curriculum should divide its attention evenly between local and international studies, these serving to complement one another in the process whereby the pupil makes sense of his world. It is particularly important that having decided to incorporate minority cultures into their curricula, schools should avoid defining those cultures solely in terms of patterns of life and experience in countries and continents of origin. It may be far more meaningful for children to look at those minority cultures as they are evolving and taking shape here in Britain. Finally, Jeffcoate has a word or two about development studies, those types of investigation of the Third World that are particularly popular in secondary schools. Too often, it seems, they are too dependent on European concepts and categories for their operation. The multicultural curriculum involves a change in perspective as well as a change in content, an end, in effect, to ethnocentrism which views other cultures in a disparaging or, at best, condescending light.

In Box 8.1 we list the set of five criteria for the selection of learning experiences in the multicultural curriculum that Jeffcoate has put forward. We shall return to this aspect of the multicultural curriculum in the next section.

Jeffcoate identifies two contrasting functions of the school that might be served by the multicultural curriculum: *transmitting culture* or *transforming culture.*

Those who support the view that the primary purpose of the school is to transmit culture would argue that despite the bewildering complexity of knowledge and the variety of beliefs that are available to curriculum planners, it is still possible and desirable to winnow out the best that can be identified by criteria of excellence and pass this on to the next generation. While Jeffcoate supports the view that the curriculum should constitute the school's attempt to 'sift out' all that is excellent, he does not believe that it is the school's primary purpose to transmit a curriculum so constituted since central to that concept is the idea of learning as passive reception. He therefore advances the alternative *transformationist* position, arguing that if a new viable common culture is to emerge, then what has previously served as the 'cultural heritage' must be open to critical revaluation. The prime task of the school in this process is to develop those skills in its pupils which a child-centred philosophy of education regards as indispensable to children becoming autonomous. Besides presenting pupils with its version of excellence, then, the school should also ensure that when its pupils leave, they are equipped with the ability to decide for themselves 'which knowledge is most worth'. But this, Jeffcoate observes, involves the multicultural school in particular difficulties because it serves not one society or culture, but a diversity of cultures whose beliefs and values may not only differ, but at times be in conflict.

Consider for a moment the case of Muslim pupils who attend Quran schools in the evening where they are taught the tenets of Islam. There they will certainly not be encouraged to regard what they are told in a critical light whereas during the day they may well find themselves engaged in curriculum studies which require them to form their own opinions and arrive at their own decisions. In other words, some children could be placed in the dilemma of attending a daytime school which interprets its function as transformationist and an evening one which sees its purpose as transmissionist. But here, Jeffcoate asserts, so far as maintained schools are concerned, while the cultures of racial minorities should be represented prominently and positively, it is no part of their task to represent those cultures uncritically. The preservation of minority cultures in a fossilised form is not what multicultural schools should be about. Rather, their aim for minority-group pupils should be to make them critically aware of their culture and equipped to decide themselves how much to retain. The school's duty is to ensure that its philosophy, its policies and its curricula are such as to enable and accommodate as many choices as are feasible.

Planning the Multicultural Curriculum

In a paper on the phenomenological approach to the multicultural curriculum, McEwen[4] writes of the weakness inherent in the topic approach to the multicultural curriculum that Jeffcoate had identified and to which we made reference in the preceding section. McEwen writes:

> Although there are some very successful examples, attempts to construct a multicultural curriculum in British schools have tended to exist as topics tacked on to the traditional curriculum which are assumed to be of interest to the students and are presented in a didactic fashion. Such an approach cannot succeed because firstly, it fails to recognise that multiculturalism represents a challenge to teachers and students to re-appraise the nature of education and the curriculum and secondly, the pedagogic and curricular strategies which have

been employed have tended to alienate students from whichever cultural or ethnic groups has felt threatened or neglected.

If, on the other hand, an effective multicultural curriculum must set out to transform culture, if it must make use of pupils' own experiences, and if it must encourage pupils 'to articulate their own ideas, to question, to listen to each other, to co-operate rather than compete, and . . . to take an increasing part in democracy',[5] how is this to be achieved? What strategies and tactics can be employed to bring this sort of curriculum into being? A difficult question you may say; certainly there are no easy answers. What we shall do in this section, therefore, is to present three possible approaches to the problem. The first begins at a global level by defining the kind of society deemed desirable and then proceeds to tease out the curricular implications of the definitions arrived at. The second presents a flexible model based on a philosophical and conceptual stance. And finally, the more familiar objectives model is outlined.

For our first approach to the multicultural curriculum, then, we turn to the two models proposed by Banks.[6] Both reflect a societal perspective and are characterised by power-sharing. Banks considers that to create the sort of *open society* that most would regard as desirable, it will be necessary *either* to redistribute power so that groups with different ethnic and cultural features will control entry to various social, economic and political institutions, *or* to modify the attitudes and actions of individuals who will control future institutions so that they will become less ethnocentric and permit people who differ from themselves culturally and physically to share equally in society's reward system on the basis of the *real* contributions they can make to the functioning of society. These two means to an open society can be conceptualised as models, Banks explains.

Thus Model I Banks calls a *shared power model*. The goal of this model, he explains, would be to create a society in which currently-excluded ethnic groups would share power with dominant-ethnic groups. They would control a number of social, economic and political institutions, and would determine the criteria for admission to these institutions. The methods used to attain the major ends of this model would be an attempt to build group pride, cohesion and identity among excluded ethnic groups, and help them to develop the ability to make reflective political decisions, to gain and exercise political power effectively and to develop a belief in the humaneness of their own group.

The alternative means to an open society would be reflected in Model II which Banks terms an *enlightening powerful groups model*. He explains that the major goal of this model would be to modify the attitudes and perceptions of dominant-ethnic groups so that they would be willing, as adults, to share power with excluded ethnic groups. They would also be willing to regard excluded ethnic groups as humans, unwilling to participate in efforts to continue their oppression, willing to accept and understand the actions by excluded groups to liberate themselves and willing to take action to change the social system so that it would treat powerless ethnic groups more justly. The major goals within this model focus on helping dominant ethnic groups to expand their conception of who is human, to develop more positive attitudes towards ethnic minorities, and a willingness to share power with excluded ethnic groups.

Banks then goes on to trace out the curricular implications of these two models. They can help the curriculum specialist, he explains, to determine the kind of emphases that are necessary for the curriculum for different pupil populations. While the curriculum for excluded- and dominant-ethnic groups should have many elements in common, the central messages these groups receive in the curriculum should in some cases differ.

In his philosophical approach to the idea of a multicultural curriculum, Walkling[7] asks how should the curriculum of general education be changed to reflect the multicultural nature of society. This in turn, Walkling explains, generates three sub-sidiary problems. First, which of any group's valued beliefs or practices ought to be included? Second, if education is the development of reason, then it is necessary to consider whether there are fundamental conceptual or procedural differences in the thoughts of different groups and, if there are, whether these should be 'opposed, ignored, tolerated, or encouraged'. And third, should a multicultural education confirm the child in a particular way of life, or give him independence within a wider, transcultural form of life?

In order to clarify these three questions, Walkling takes three central aspects of the multicultural curriculum — the *substantive content*, the *procedural content* and its *educational purposes*. In each case, he identifies two extreme positions. Thus, with regard to substantive content, he considers the extremes of *tolerance* and *selection*. A 'tolerant' view holds that whatever an ethnic group claims to value has an equal right to a place in the curriculum with all else; whereas the view that not all candidates for inclusion in the curriculum are of equal worth is a 'selective' one. The contrasting extremes of procedural content Walkling terms *relativism* and *absolutism*. By procedural content, he means the logical structures and styles of thought which the substantive content illustrates. Thus an absolutist view in this connection would hold that the criteria of meaningfulness and truth in our logically distinct forms of knowledge have universal applicability. A cultural relativism, on the other hand, would contend that rationality may be defined only in terms of particular cultural contexts. The final pair of opposed categories focusing on educational purposes we have already encountered — *transmission* and *transformation*.

Box 8.2: Eight Alternative Attitudes

1. Tolerant, Absolutist, Transmissionist
2. Selective, Absolutist, Transmissionist
3. Tolerant, Relativist, Transmissionist
4. Selective, Relativist, Transmissionist
5. Tolerant, Absolutist, Transformationist
6. Selective, Absolutist, Transformationist
7. Tolerant, Relativist, Transformationist
8. Selective, Relativist, Transformationist

Source: Walkling.[8]

These three sets of polar opposites will, if combined, produce eight alternative styles of, or attitudes to, curricula which respond to a multicultural society. These we have listed in Box 8.2. As Walkling says, 'The purpose of this very crude scheme of analysis is that it should be of some assistance in giving a preliminary shake out of the tangled issues which plague this field of interest.'

In his conclusion, Walkling writes:

The possibility of a pluralistic society depends upon the possibility of understanding people and their beliefs. It must, if it is to be worth anything at all, provide a dynamic context in which people's beliefs are exchanged, defended, argued about, converted, retained, assessed, ignored ostentatiously, and so on: all the reactions people have to the beliefs of other people whom they take seriously. Extreme relativism or transmissionism in a curriculum imply a sort of cultural protectionism. When encouraged by the wider society outside the particular minority group they imply either blank hostility or a patronising refusal to take the group seriously.

Withdrawal from society, in the forms of alienation, anomie or cultural isolationism, is the greatest threat to a multicultural society. It is avoided by engagement, which, in education, involves the pursuit of responsibility and individuality.

In Box 8.1, we listed Jeffcoate's criteria for choosing learning experiences in the multicultural curriculum. In an earlier paper,[9] he outlined a *modus operandi* for curriculum planning in the multicultural school based on the traditional objectives model. His expressed intentions in the paper were to establish the primacy of objectives in curriculum planning in multicultural education, to explore the factors governing their selection and to suggest, in a general way and in the form of a Bloomsian classification, what they might be. The latter we have included in Box 8.3. He justifies his preference for the objectives model because, as he explains:

> We share the basic assumption of the objectives school that the function of formal education is to bring about desired changes in children. We want them to have acquired certain identifiable knowledge and skills and developed certain identifiable attitudes and behaviours by the time they leave school. We must be prepared to make these knowledges, skills, attitudes and behaviours the starting point and focus for our curriculum planning.

While recognising that the objectives model has certain weaknesses, he is careful to defend his own particular taxonomy. For him, multicultural education is *primarily affective*, being concerned with attitudes and dispositions, and only instrumentally cognitive. But, as he goes on to explain:

> It is a different sort of affectivity from the affectivity of

Box 8.3: A Classification of Objectives in Multiracial Education

(A) *Respect for others:*

Cognitive (knowledge)

All pupils should *know*:
the basic facts of race and racial difference;
the customs, values and beliefs of the main cultures represented in Britain and, more particularly, of those forming the local community;
why different groups have immigrated into Britain in the past and how the local community has come to acquire its present ethnic composition.

Cognitive (skills)

All pupils should *be able to*:
detect stereotyping and scapegoating in what they see, hear and read;
evaluate their own cultures objectively.

Affective (attitudes, values and emotional sets)

All pupils should *accept*:
the uniqueness of each individual human being;
the underlying humanity we share;
the principles of equal rights and justice;
and value the achievements of other cultures and nations;
strangeness without feeling threatened;
that Britain is, always has been and always will be a multicultural society;
that no culture is ever static and that constant mutual accommodation will be required of all cultures making up an evolving multicultural society;
that prejudice and discrimination are widespread in Britain and the historical and socioeconomic causes which have given rise to them;
the damaging effect of prejudice and discrimination on the rejected groups;
the possibility of developing multiple loyalties.

(B) *Respect for self:*

Cognitive (knowledge)

All pupils should *know*:
the history and achievements of their own culture and what is distinctive about it.

Cognitive (skills)

All pupils should *be able to*:
communicate efficiently in English and, if it is not their mother tongue, in their own mother tongue;
master the other basic skills necessary for success at school.

Affective (attitudes, values and emotional sets)

All pupils should have developed:
a positive self-image;
confidence in their sense of their own identity.

Source: Adapted from Jeffcoate.[10]

creative work or aesthetic judgment. Even though the over-riding objectives, respect for self and others, stipulated in the classification could hardly be called 'correct', they are ones we believe to be necessary for children and for society, and we could go some way to justifying their selection; equally, they are not objectives that could be said to be open to negotiation. Many of the objectives in the classification are knowledge objectives, and I have called these 'instrumental'. In order to come to respect themselves and others, I am suggesting children must be in possession of certain facts. The first three specific knowledge objectives are, then, a necessary [but not, of course, a sufficient] condition of the overriding objective of respect for others. It is at this point that we find ourselves at odds with the dominant progressive ideology. We do not dissent from the importance they attach to skills but we also attach importance, in a way they would not, to specific items of knowledge which we feel to be predicated by our overall affective targets.

In stressing the need for the acquisition of distinctive knowledge, Jeffcoate concedes he may be adopting a somewhat unfashionable stance.

He goes on to discuss factors governing the selection of objectives. In particular, he reviews the way in which they are significantly affected by a school's value system (its philosophy of education) and its definition and analysis of the situation (problems, needs and so on).

Each of these three models is sufficiently open-ended and contains sufficient principles to be used as a suitable starting point for the construction of a multicultural curriculum.

Curriculum Guidelines for Multicultural Education

The following broad guidelines for a multicultural curriculum are adapted from Banks.[11] These are predicated on a democratic ideology in which ethnic diversity is viewed as a positive, integral ingredient. A democratic society protects and provides opportunities for ethnic pluralism and this, according to Banks, is based on the following four premises:

1. Ethnic diversity should be recognised and respected at individual, group and societal levels.
2. Ethnic diversity provides a basis for societal cohesiveness and survival.
3. Equality of opportunity should be afforded to members of all ethnic groups.
4. Ethnic identification should be optional for individuals.

The guidelines are as follows:

1. *Ethnic pluralism should permeate the total school environment.*

Banks considers that effective teaching about ethnic groups can best take place in an educational context that accepts, encourages and respects the manifestation of ethnic and racial diversity. To achieve this kind of educational ambience, the total school environment should be reformed. This will mean the informal as well as the formal; the hidden as well as the explicit curriculum.

In order to establish ethnic pluralism, it is essential that pupils have access to resource materials that provide accurate information on all aspects of different ethnic groups. Learning centres, libraries and resource centres should provide comprehensive resources on the history, literature, music and the arts of different ethnic groups.

Ethnic diversity in the school's informal life should be reflected in assemblies, classrooms, corridors, entrance halls and extracurricular activities. Participation in activities should be open to all pupils with participation by ethnic-minority pupils being particularly encouraged. Such activities, according to Banks, can provide invaluable opportunities not only for the development of self-esteem, but for pupils from different ethnic backgrounds to work and play together.

2. *School policies and procedures should foster positive multicultural interactions and understandings among pupils, teachers and ancillary staff.*

Every school requires rules and regulations to guide behaviour and achieve its specified goals. As such, they should encourage harmony and understanding among different ethnic groups. In Banks' view, school harmony was often sought in the past through efforts to 'treat everyone the same'; however, experience in multicultural schools indicates that the same treatment of everyone is unfair to many pupils. Instead of thus presenting an ideal model of behaviour, schools should recognise and accommodate individual and ethnic-group differences. Banks explains that this does not mean that some pupils should obey school rules while others should not; it means simply that different ethnic groups may have different ways of behaving that should be honoured providing they are not disruptive or clash with school objectives.

3. *School staff should reflect the ethnic pluralism within society; and staff development programmes should be a mandatory feature of school life.*

Although there may be good reasons why it may not be so, it is desirable that members of different ethnic groups be part of the school life. This means not only among the teaching staff but also among the administrative and ancillary staff, for all can make an important contribution to multicultural environments. Pupils can learn important lessons about living in a multicultural society by observing how older, more mature people conduct themselves with others of differing ethnic backgrounds.

Particular attention should be given to the training and retraining of teachers. This should begin at the pre-service stage and continue as in-service as teachers are employed by schools. Banks considers that the focus should be on helping staff to (1) clarify and analyse their feelings, attitudes and perceptions to their own and other ethnic groups; (2) acquire knowledge and understanding of the historical experience and characteristics of ethnic-minority groups; (3) improve their instructional skills with particular reference to multicultural contexts; (4) develop their skills in creating, selecting and evaluating appropriate instructional materials; and (5) develop curricula in so far as they relate to multicultural needs.

4. *The curriculum should reflect the ethnic learning styles of the pupils within the school community.*

A school's culture and its teaching programmes should be modified where necessary to reflect the cultures and learning styles of children of ethnic-minority groups. Banks bases this recommendation on recent research in America which indicates that the teaching and learning methods that are most often favoured in American schools are inconsistent with the cognitive styles and cultural characteristics of some groups of minority pupils.[12] Such findings, Banks considers, should thus alert educators to the need to become more sensitive to pupil differences based on ethnicity and to the implications of these findings for planning and organising the school environment.

5. *The multicultural curriculum should provide pupils with continuous opportunities to develop a better sense of self.*
The multicultural curriculum should help pupils to develop a better sense of self. Banks considers that this should be an ongoing process, beginning when the child first enters school and continuing throughout his school career. This development should include at least three areas:

1. Pupils should be helped to develop accurate self-identities. Who am I? and What am I? are questions with which pupils must deal in order to come to grips with their own identities.
2. The multicultural curriculum should help pupils to develop improved self-concepts.
3. The multicultural curriculum should help pupils to develop greater self-understanding. This will help them to deal more effectively with future situations in which ethnicity may be a factor to be dealt with.

6. *The multicultural curriculum should promote values, attitudes and behaviours that support ethnic pluralism.*
Banks points out that pupils should learn that to be different does not necessarily mean to be inferior or superior, and that the study of ethnic-group differences need not lead to ethnic polarisation. They should also learn that while some conflict is unavoidable in ethnically- and racially-mixed societies, it does not necessarily have to be destructive or divisive. Conflict is an intrinsic part of the human condition, especially in a pluralistic society where values differ. Multicultural programmes should thus explore ethnic pluralism in positive and realistic ways that present ethnic conflict in proper perspective. As Banks adds, pupils will be helped to understand that there is strength in diversity and that co-operation among ethnic groups does not necessarily spring from their having identical beliefs and values.

7. *The multicultural curriculum should help pupils develop the skills necessary for effective inter-personal and inter-ethnic group interaction.*

Good relationships between members of different ethnic groups can sometimes be difficult to achieve. As Banks observes, attempts at cross-ethnic interaction are often thwarted by ethnocentrism. The problems in this respect can at least be partially resolved by helping pupils recognise consciously the factors that facilitate or impede the development of inter-personal relationships. By developing the appropriate skills and acquiring relevant concepts, pupils can be helped to overcome potential obstacles. These could include the danger of stereotyping, clarification of ethnic attitudes and values, the development of cross-ethnic communication skills and the ability to see the dynamics of inter-personal interaction from the perspective of other people.

8. *The multicultural curriculum should be comprehensive in scope and sequence and should present holistic views of ethnic groups and be an integral part of the total school curriculum; further, interdisciplinary approaches should be used in designing and implementing the multicultural curriculum.*

Banks recalls that pupils learn best from well-planned, comprehensive, continuous experiences. In an effective multicultural curriculum, the study of ethnicity should be integrated into all subject areas and courses throughout the whole gamut. This study should be carefully planned in order to encourage the development of increasingly more complex concepts.

He rightly observes that no single discipline can adequately explain all of the components of the life-styles, cultural experiences and social problems of ethnic groups. A concept such as racism, for example, has many dimensions and to elucidate these requires the concepts and perspectives of such disciplines as the social sciences, history, literature, art and music. Single-discipline analyses, Banks explains, can result in misleading or distorted evaluations. A promising way to avoid these pitfalls is to employ regular interdisciplinary approaches in studying experiences related to different ethnic groups.

9. *The school should provide opportunities for pupils to participate in the aesthetic experiences of various ethnic groups.*

Banks considers that ethnic groups should not be studied only at a distance. Theoretical approaches to the study of ethnic-minority groups needs to go hand in hand with participation in the experiences of ethnic-minority groups. To this end, it is necessary to include the arts of ethnic-minority groups in the curriculum. Ethnic music and literature, art, architecture, folklore and dance all provide avenues for experiencing, often at first hand, the cultural heritage and achievements of other ethnic groups. In studying multicultural literature and arts, pupils should become acquainted with what has been created in local ethnic-communities. Local people should be invited to discuss their viewpoints and experiences with pupils. The immersion of pupils in multicultural experiences is an effective way of developing an understanding both of self and others. A useful introduction to the arts of ethnic minorities in Britain may be found in Khan.[13]

Racism and Bias in School Books and other Materials

Racism has been defined as 'the belief in, and practice of, the domination of one social group, identified as a "race", over another social group, identified as another "race" '.[14] Hicks[15] considers that on this basis, racism can be seen to involve: (1) the belief that people can be grouped according to discrete races; (2) the belief that some such races are superior to others; and (3) the belief that self-proclaimed superior races should control allegedly inferior ones, a definition that closely parallels our use of *maximum racism* that we outline in the initial chapter.

There are indications from recent research[16] that British attitudes are quite often ethnocentric and even racist. Since, therefore, schooling is a reflection of a nation's culture, ethno-centricity and racism will be characteristics of the curriculum. As we have earlier made reference to these, the particular focus in this section will be on books and teaching materials and the extent to which these reflect society's racist attitudes. A recent Schools Council Report[17] has indicated that the evaluation of books and materials from a multicultural perspective has taken one of two forms in Britain: lists of books for the multicultural curriculum, and critiques of racial bias and stereotyping. Their weaknesses, the authors suggest, lie in not making explicit the criteria by which they are evaluated and in expressing them in terms too general to be operational. As they say, 'if the selection of teaching materials is to become more consistent and effective, it is to the definition of precise, operational criteria that attention should now be directed'.[18]

As an indication of the kind of content and level of specificity that such criteria require, the report refers to the *Guidelines for Evaluation of Instructional Materials for Compliance with Content Requirements of the Education Code*, published by the California Education Department in 1975 in response to Federal and State legislation designed to guarantee to American-ethnic minorities just treatment in school curricula and materials.[19] The section on ethnic and cultural groups itemises three essential criteria that have to be met if the materials concerned are to meet with approval. These are:

1. Reference in the form of labels which tend to demean, stereotype or be patronising toward minority groups must not appear.
2. When diverse ethnic or cultural groups are portrayed, such portrayal must not depict differences in customs or life-style as undesirable and must not reflect an adverse value judgment of such differences.
3. Instructional materials that generally or incidentally reflect contemporary American society, regardless of the subject area, must contain references to, or illustrations of, a fair proportion of diverse ethnic groups.

Other criteria include the following:

4. The portrayal of minority characters in roles to which they have been traditionally restricted by society should be balanced by the presentation of non-traditional activities for characters of that race.
5. Minority persons should be depicted in the same range of socio-economic settings as are white persons.
6. Depiction of diverse ethnic and cultural groups should not be limited to the root culture, but rather expanded to

include such groups within the mainstream of American life.

7. Whenever developments in history or current events, or achievements in art, science, or any other field, are presented, the contribution of minority peoples, and particularly the identification of prominent minority persons, should be included and discussed when historically accurate.

The thinking behind these guidelines coincides with thinking on these matters in this country and particularly with the Schools Council project already referred to.[20] Three issues the Schools Council is particularly concerned about are stereotyping, racial bias and the need for books and materials to reflect the multicultural nature of Britain.

Stereotyping, according to the Report, over-categorises, over-generalises and over-simplifies. At the same time it carries an evaluative component. The British appear to operate more negative stereotypes than even those European countries who shared the experiences of empire and the slave trade from which so many of the stereotypes originated. With school materials, stereotypes are to be located in the text and visuals of readers, picture books, children's fiction and topic and information books, the latter two being the sources where children are most likely to encounter stereotyping.

The Report considers that *racial bias* is distinguished by its irrationality — its failure to take into account all the facts and its reluctance to acknowledge other points of view. As it says in these respects:

Racial or ethnic bias selects only those events supporting a belief in the overriding importance or superiority of a particular race or culture, and dramatises the encounter with other races and cultures without any kind of recognition of the integrity or the value of their perspectives.

The Project's inspection of school books found that racial bias in the form of Eurocentrism was prevalent especially in history and geography books on Africa.

The books and teaching materials used in schools ought to reflect the *multicultural nature of British society,* yet it is not uncommon to discover that racial minorities are not represented in the factual and fictional materials about British society. The Report comments:

> Although there has been some improvement in recent years
> . . . qualitatively and quantitatively, in the presentation of
> blacks and Asians in text and illustration, it is still possible to
> speak of the 'all-white world of children's books' in a way
> that it is not in the United States. They continue to be
> excluded from information books covering even those areas —
> productive industry, public transport, the National Health
> Service — to which they incontrovertibly contribute.[21]

Some authors and publishers are guilty of *tokenism* in this respect — making superficial gestures by introducing one black character in a story or including a solitary black face in an illustration. As such, the Report notes, they can hardly count as reflecting the truly multicultural composition of contemporary British society.

We conclude this section with nine guidelines recommended by the Council for Interracial Books for Children, New York, as reported in Hicks.[22] They are recommended as a starting point in evaluating children's books from the perspective of racism:

1. *Check the illustrations.*
Look for stereotypes. A stereotype is an over-simplified generalisation about a particular group, race or sex which usually carries derogatory implications. The stereotypes of blacks as happy-go-lucky, water-melon-eating Sambos, or the inscrutable, slant-eyed 'Oriental' are typical examples here. While stereotypes may not always exist in such blatant forms as these, one should look for variations which demean or ridicule individuals because of their race or sex.

Look for tokenism. If there are non-white characters in the illustrations, do they look just like whites except for being tinted or coloured in? Do all minority faces look stereotypically alike; or are they depicted as genuine individuals with distinctive features?

Who's doing what? Do the illustrations depict minorities in subservient and passive roles or in leadership and action roles?

2. *Check the story line.*
The following checklist suggests some of the more subtle forms of bias to watch out for in stories.

Standard for success. Does it take 'white' behaviour standards for a minority person to 'get ahead'? Is 'making it' in the dominant white society projected as the only ideal? To gain acceptance and approval, do non-white persons have to exhibit extraordinary qualities — excel in sports, get As, etc.? In friendships between white and non-white children, is it the non-white who does most of the understanding and forgiving?

Resolution of problems. How are problems presented, conceived and resolved in the story? Are minority people considered to be 'the problem'? Are the oppressions faced by minorities represented as casually related to an unjust society? Are the reasons for poverty and oppression explained, or are they accepted as inevitable? Does the story line encourage passive acceptance or active resistance? Is a particular problem that is faced by a minority person resolved through the benevolent intervention of a white person?

3. *Look at the lifestyles.*
Are minority persons and their setting depicted in such a way that they contrast unfavourably with the unstated norm of white middle-class suburbia? If the minority group in question is depicted as 'different', are negative value judgements implied? Are minorities depicted exclusively in ghettoes or migrant camps? If the illustrations and text attempt to depict another culture, do they go beyond over-simplifications and offer genuine insights into another life-style? Inaccurate and inappropriate representation of other cultures should be looked for, as should instances of the 'quaint-natives-in-costume' syndrome.

4. *Weigh the relationship between people.*
Do the whites in the story possess the power, take the leadership and make the important decision? Do non-whites function in essentially supporting roles?

How are family relationships depicted? In black families, is the mother always dominant? If the family is separated, are societal conditions — unemployment, poverty — cited among the reasons for the separation?

5. *Note the heroes and heroines.*

For many years, books showed only 'safe' minority heroes and heroines — those who avoided serious conflict with the white establishment of their time. Minority groups today are insisting on the right to define their own heroes and heroines based on their own concepts and struggles for justice.

When minority heroes and heroines do appear, are they admired for the same qualities that have made white heroes and heroines famous or because what they have done has benefited white people? The question to ask is: whose interest is a particular figure really serving?

6. *Consider the effects on a child's self image.*

Are norms established which limit the child's aspirations and self-concept? What effect can it have on black children to be continuously bombarded with images of the colour white as the ultimate in beauty, cleanliness, virtue, etc.? Does the book counteract or reinforce this positive association with the colour white and negative association with black.

In a particular story, is there one or more persons with whom a minority child can readily identify to a positive and constructive end?

7. *Consider the author's or illustrator's background.*

Analyse the biographical material on the jacket or the back of the book. If a story deals with a minority theme, what qualifies the author or illustrator to deal with the subject? If the author and illustrator are not members of the minority being written about, is there anything in their background that would specifically recommend them as the creators of this book?

8. *Check the author's perspective.*

No author can be wholly objective. All authors write out of a cultural, as well as a personal context. Children's books in the past have traditionally come from authors who are white and who are members of the middle class. This can result in a book being dominated by a single ethnocentric perspective. With the book in question, look carefully to determine whether the direction of the author's perspective substantially weakens or strengthens the value of his or her written work. Are omissions

and distortions central to the overall character or message of the
book?

9. *Watch for loaded words.*
A word is loaded when it has insulting overtones. Examples of
loaded adjectives (usually racist) are *savage, primitive, conniving,
lazy, superstitious, treacherous, wily, crafty, inscrutable, docile*
and *backward.*

Books on minority themes — usually hastily conceived —
suddenly began appearing in the mid 1960s. There followed a
growing number of 'minority experience' books to meet the new
market demand, but most of these were still written by white
authors, edited by white editors and published by white
publishers. They therefore reflect a white point of view. Only
very recently, in the late 1960s and early 1970s, has the children's
book world begun even remotely to reflect the realities of a
multicultural society.

The copyright date, therefore, can be a clue as to how likely
the book is to be overtly racist, although a recent date, of
course, is no guarantee of a book's relevance or sensitivity. The
copyright date only means the year the book was published. It
usually takes a minimum of one year — and often much more
than that — from the time a manuscript is submitted to the
publisher to the time it is actually printed and put on the market.
This time lag meant very little in the past, but in a time of rapid
change and changing consciousness, when children's book
publishing is attempting to be 'relevant', it is becoming
increasingly significant.

Notes

1. E.M. Brittan (1976) 'Multiracial Education 2', *Educational Research*, **18**(2),
96–107.
2. R. Jeffcoate (1979) 'A Multicultural Curriculum: Beyond the Orthodoxy',
Trends in Education, **4**, 8–12.
3. Ibid.
4. N. McEwen, 'A Phenomenological Approach to the Multicultural
Curriculum', unpublished paper.
5. A. James (1979) 'The Multicultural Curriculum', *New Approaches to
Multiracial Education*, **8**(1), 1–6.
6. J. A. Banks (1981) *Multiethnic Education: Theory and Practice*, Boston:
Allyn and Bacon.

7. P. H. Walkling (1980) 'The Idea of a Multicultural Curriculum', *Journal of Philosophy of Education*, **14**(1), 87–95.

8. Ibid.

9. R. Jeffcoate (1976) 'Curriculum Planning in Multiracial Education', *Educational Research*, **18**(3, June), 192–200.

10. Ibid.

11. Banks, *Multiethnic Education*.

12. J. Kleinfeld (1975) 'Effective Teachers of Eskimo and Indian Students', *School Review*, **83**, 301–44.

13. N. Khan (1976) *The Arts Britain Ignores*, London: Commission for Racial Equality.

14. J. L. Hodge, D. K. Struckman and L. D. Frost (1975) *Cultural Bases of Racism and Group Oppression*, Berkeley, California: Two Riders Press.

15. D. Hicks (1981) 'Bias in School Books: Messages from the Ethnocentric Curriculum', in A. James and R. Jeffcoate (eds), *The School in the Multicultural Society*, London: Harper and Row.

16. T. S. Bowles (1978) *Survey of Attitudes towards Overseas Development*, London: HMSO.

17. Schools Council (1981) *Education for a Multiracial Society: Curriculum and Context 5–13*, London: Schools Council.

18. Ibid.

19. Ibid.

20. Ibid.

21. Ibid.

22. D. Hicks (1981) *Minorities: A Teacher's Resource Book for the Multiethnic Curriculum*, London: Heinemann Educational Books.

LANGUAGE IN THE MULTICULTURAL CLASSROOM

Introduction

In 1968, Derrick[1] observed that for native or immigrant children 'English is the key to their future in this country, thus the teacher has to see that they acquire language for the full range of communication within the school'. Clearly, a child can neither learn specific skills nor develop his potential ability until he can learn to speak, understand, read and write the language that is used in school. Regrettably, she was subsequently to report[2] that as far as immigrant pupils were concerned, the overall picture of language education was not encouraging. Indeed, in the early '70s it had been estimated that 24 per cent of all ethnic-minority pupils were weak at English, a percentage considered by Derrick to be a gross underestimate. As she writes in this respect:

> On all sides there are complaints that the immigrant child who learns English as a second language reaches too low a level of proficiency before he leaves school. This raises questions both about the effectiveness and quality of present practice in the initial teaching of English to such pupils, as well as about the later stages of the pupils' language learning.

Some of the specific language problems of immigrant pupils at this period were identified by Derrick in her article. These we have included in Box 9.1.

Language provision for ethnic-minority pupils then left quite a lot to be desired, so what was the response of those responsible for the language education of these children? Earlier, in the early and middle 1960s, the ideas of Bernstein[4] on the ways in which types of language (i.e. the *elaborated* and the *restricted* codes) affect modes of thinking had been influential in the setting up of compensatory language programmes for children who were said to be culturally and linguistically deprived. Many of Bernstein's ideas are thought to be applicable to the education of ethnic-minority pupils who, although born in Britain, do not speak standard English. What then are the particular linguistic

Box 9.1: Language Problems of Immigrant Pupils in the Early Seventies

Many observers have commented on the deceptive fluency in English of immigrant pupils who have been in secondary school here a couple of years or more. Certain grammatical forms seem forever to have eluded their grasp; they handle only a limited number of English verb forms, rarely in the past tense. Sentence connectives are limited to 'and', 'then' and 'because'. They are unable to sustain a piece of narrative or descriptive writing, or if they do so, lack flexibility and variety in the syntactical forms and in the vocabulary they have at their disposal. Such limitations may pass relatively ignored in speech; in writing they are at once apparent. It is as if the student, having mastered a minimum of English grammar and syntax for the purposes of communication, sticks at that point (possibly between 1,500 and 2,000 words) and never goes beyond it. This disability is at once apparent when faced with the linguistic requirements of the Certificate of Secondary Education or O-level subject teaching. As more demands are made upon him to follow oral exposition, to read for extensive information, and to write, he senses his own failure and possibly regresses rather than progresses in his command of English.

Source: Derrick.[3]

limitations of these children? Taylor[5] suggests the following:

1. *Total language deficiency*, where not only is a foreign language spoken, but the written script is alien also.
2. *Partial language deficiency*, where some, but very little, English is spoken in the home or where the child has acquired some English from having lived in Britain for a longer period of time. The vernacular script may or may not be based upon the Western alphabet.
3. *Dialect impediments*, where some children may speak English fluently but dialect interposes, or a 'pidgin' English is spoken, so that problems of listening, interpreting and later reading and writing are present. This is a particular problem for some West Indian children where Creole dialects are present. We shall have more to say about this specific difficulty later in the chapter.

The Schools Council Development Projects[6] for teaching English to immigrant children were a direct response to the urgent need voiced by teachers up and down the country to find ways of helping immigrant children attain linguistic proficiency in English. The specific objectives of the Schools Council

Programmes were first, to prepare materials and carefully graded schemes to meet the needs of teachers of non-English-speaking children in order to help such pupils achieve an adequate command of English for school and society. Second, the programmes were intended to support the provision of in-service training in order to explain the purposes of the new materials to teachers and to give them opportunity both to use and criticise the materials and to offer positive suggestions for their improvement. In the absence of research evidence showing that there were distinctive problems attached to the teaching of particular ethnic-minority groups, the Schools Council Projects aimed, initially, to produce a general package of teaching materials for all non-English-speaking children. Full details of each of the SCOPE programmes are available in Taylor[7] and Hill.[8] As time went on, specific language kits were developed for use with particular ethnic-minority groups.

The Schools Council Curriculum Development Projects were but one of a number of programmes of activity attempting to come to grips with the language problems of immigrant and ethnic-minority children. Others include pre-school language research, language teaching in multicultural infant classrooms, the work of the NFER in its five-year project for disadvantaged children and the findings of the Educational Priority Area Action Research as they specifically relate to the needs of ethnic-minority children.

For the most part in this introduction we have spoken in fairly general terms of the language problems of ethnic-minority pupils, but what of the needs of the two groups that are our primary concern in this book — the Asians and West Indians? As Derrick[9] has observed, the language needs of Asians are more easily recognised than those of West Indian pupils. In the case of the former, the position is relatively clear-cut in that the concern is to develop bi-lingualism, the ability to achieve some command over English as well as retaining skills in the original native language, an aim that can be achieved through the policy of extraction during normal school lessons and the setting up of special centres for the purpose. What complicates the language issue for the West Indian pupils is that they already speak a variety of English, though not the standard form. The need for them then is to develop skills in bidialectism, a challenge greater for both pupils and teachers than that presented by bilingualism.

Derrick[10] puts it like this:

> Although West Indian pupils speak a variety of English, they
> ultimately perform less well than the non-native English
> speakers. Learning to use a second *dialect* and learning to
> learn through it, may be a more difficult task for most
> children than learning a second language.

For this reason, as well as the problem of limitations of space,
we intend to devote the remainder of this chapter to the needs of
West Indian pupils.

Specifically, the problems for the West Indians have been set
out by Taylor.[11] In terms of accommodating to the school
situation in this country, a West Indian speaker of Creole dialect
is likely to encounter problems of hearing, because the sounds he
is familiar with are Creole, not English; he is likely to impute
different meanings to the sounds he hears, so there is likely to be
the problem of understanding; and reciprocal communications
problems between pupils and teachers as each group fails to
understand the dialect of the other.

We begin by looking at features of the historical background
of Creole and related matters.

Creole: The Background

The language spoken by most people in the West Indies and,
indeed, by many second and even third generation West Indians
is known as 'Creole' by linguists and is a dialect form of
standard English. Occasionally, it may be a dialect form of
French. It is termed 'patois' or 'dialect' by the West Indians
themselves. Edwards[12] describes the linguistic position in the
West Indies in terms of a continuum with broad Creole at one
pole and standard English at the other. Each speaker will tend to
draw from a section of the continuum rather than limiting himself to one particular point on it. Social class and social context
are the principal determinants of just where the particular section
is located. Thus, working-class speakers will tend to draw on the
Creole end of the continuum, as will speakers engaged in
informal exchanges. Middle-class speakers, on the other hand,
will utilise the other end, as indeed will speakers involved in

more formal social discourse. Edwards is careful to point out, however, that it would be misleading to think in terms of specific varieties occurring at different points along the continuum. A brief example of Creole given by Edwards may be found in Box 9.2.

Box 9.2: An Example of Creole

Edwards[13] quotes the following short transcription of a story told by a Jamaican girl. A particularly interesting feature is her use of 't' and 'd' for the English unvoiced 'th' and voiced 'th' respectively.

Once upon a time, Miss Annancy and Brother Annancy go buy pork. When Miss Annancy go buy de pork and come back and come se Miss Annancy sit down. So den Miss Annancy go back and carry pork come put down, Miss Annancy come come, take you time, 'cos for fry it. And when she go in her batroom go bed first, when him done Miss Annancy come and den him come in upon him and cut off him bottom and put it in a pot for fry. And him go back and come back and come back and do de same ting.

Source: Edwards.[14]

Variations in the spoken language existed not only among individuals but also from one Caribbean island to another, the reasons for this being historical. France, Spain, Holland and Britain had all colonised different territories, some changing hands on more than one occasion. Thus the linguistic influences on the islands differed according to both time and place. The Creole dialects were developed by the West African slaves working on the islands' plantations during the colonial period. The dialects used, as Taylor informs us,[15] derived from both African languages and from the model languages of the European planters. She further explains:

The proportion of Europeans to Negroes determined the orientation of the model languages so that as Le Page[16] explains, in those islands such as Barbados where there was a high proportion of Europeans to Negroes the influence of the model language — in this case English — was considerable, and brought the Creole dialect much nearer to it. On the other hand, in those islands, like Jamaica, where Europeans were easily outnumbered by Negroes, the influence was far less.

African slaves to the islands would initially have developed a kind of pidgin, that is a simplified form of English in which the grammar and vocabulary would have been considerably reduced.[17] Eventually parents would teach it to their children and subsequent development of grammar and vocabulary resulted in Creole. As Edwards comments:

> Where it is possible to argue that pidgins are inadequate linguistic systems, Creoles are fully developed languages, capable of expressing the whole range of communicative needs of a population. They are logical and regular and it would be quite wrong to consider them in any way 'broken' or 'inferior'.

Whether Creole should be accorded the status of a separate language or whether regarded simply as a dialect of English has been a matter of some contention. Those adhering to the former view would hold that it is very different from English both in terms of its grammar and sound system; whereas those seeing it as a variant of the mother tongue would stress the common vocabulary. Whether Creole is termed a language or a dialect, however, it remains, as Edwards notes, a perfectly adequate linguistic system in its own right.

Much of the discussion on Creole tends to concentrate on British opinions of it, these tending to take on a pejorative flavour, mainly because it is at variance with the standard variety. But what do the West Indians themselves think of their own language? In general terms, their attitude tends to be ambivalent. In one respect, as Edwards points out,[18] they are among its most severe critics. She says:

> This pattern is one of the more unpleasant aspects of the domination of one group by another; the dominated are persuaded that they, their language and their culture are inferior and that the stigma attached to them is deserved.

There is another perspective, however. Although West Indians can perhaps concede the criticisms made of Creole, especially in comparison to the standard language, it does in fact play a crucial role in the social and communicative system of West Indian culture. As Edwards informs us, it remains the language of sincerity and the means by which strong feelings are expressed.

It can be an extremely private and personal utterance and a most telling means of excluding outsiders. But perhaps most important of all, it symbolises West Indian identity in the sense that it defines membership of a particular group with particular values and provides the means whereby a specific culture can be transmitted.

A particularly distinctive feature of West Indian culture in respect of its language is the oral skill possessed by West Indians. Considerable importance is attached to verbal dexterity and their traditions in this connection are highly regarded. By way of example, Edwards[19] identifies some of the directions in which these reveal themselves. Verbal interchanges between both adults and children can take on a competitive and bantering flavour which can be as racy as it is humorous. Likewise among adolescents, their skills in this respect find expression in 'rhyming' — a highly formalised exchange in which banter and insults of a playful kind are improvised and given expression in rhyming couplets. In contrast, the 'good talker' is found among adults — the person who can hold the floor at social and community events like weddings and political meetings. Finally, their gifts as story-tellers are well known, the fecundity of everyday themes providing ample points of departure.

Such oral skills and traditions need to be borne in mind whenever limited writing skills are considered.

The Home and the School: Creole Influence in Second-generation Immigrants

It is difficult to know the extent to which children of West Indian origin use Creole dialect, especially in the home or social situations. Edwards[20] considers that, in the light of the small amount of information available, the popular belief that Creole is reserved for the home and English for the school appears to be an oversimplification. Indeed, research to date presents something of a conflicting picture. In her review of studies in this connection, Taylor[21] refers to the work of Essen and Ghodsian[22] who found that few respondents in their national sample spoke English at home. She considers that the extent to which West Indian parents encourage or discourage their children from speaking Creole at home can only be a matter for speculation, although conflicting inferences can be drawn from two studies, one by Rex and Tomlinson[23] and the other by Stoker.[24] In the case of the former, the researchers found that West Indian parents appeared not to acknowledge any linguistic difficulties on the part of their children; only 1 per cent of the sample considered their children had difficulties in speaking English on starting school. Stoker, by contrast, on seeing the problems that infant pupils of West Indian origin had in their first contacts with school, suggested that they needed to preserve their native dialect for home but that some accommodation was needed at school between how they speak at home and the language used by the teacher in the classroom. That there is a decade between these two studies might indicate that the problem is not now quite as acute.

Taylor also refers to the point that, although questioned by some, there is evidence to show that the language used in the West Indian child's home can in fact be handicapping in some respects. In one study[25] of 150 black children aged ten to eleven matched with a similar number of white children from four schools in working class areas in London, attitudes to home and school were investigated. In addition, parents were interviewed in their homes. Among a variety of factors studied, it was found that the use of Creole in the home correlated with underachievement in reading for children of West Indian origin. The researchers subsequently suggested that it seemed that:

> What is educationally handicapping is the language in which parents and children converse, not the language which children use in school. And parents who tend to use Creole at home are those who do not converse with their child in ways which stimulate him to achieve in school.[26]

In her examination of the occasions and circumstances for the use of Creole, Edwards[27] refers to the work of Sutcliffe,[28] who interviewed nearly 50 British- and Caribbean-born West Indians. They disclosed the following patterns of language use:

Low use of Creole	*High use of Creole*
to siblings	from parents
to parents	to peers

These claims, it appears, were corroborated by recordings made in a wide range of social settings. It seems that only two of the sample said that they used no Creole at all, while 88 per cent of the Caribbean-born and 79 per cent of the British-born subjects conceded that they spoke Creole as broad as the following example:

me asks di man fi put me money eena him pockit

These findings were replicated by Hadi[29] using a modified version of Sutcliffe's questionnaire with first-year children in a multicultural comprehensive school in the Midlands. Three-quarters of a sample of 22 West Indians said they sometimes used Creole having a broadness similar to the example quoted. Although it was not clear just who spoke most Creole at home, the study did disclose that the dialect was frequently used among peers at school, often in moments and situations having a high emotional change — anger, excitement, amusement, and the like.

The comparative responses from British and West Indian children on the use of standard English were also illuminating. When asked what their friends would think if they spoke in the standard form (viz. whether they would be considered 'posh', or as 'imitating someone for fun', or as being 'nice to listen to'), the British children thought they would be regarded as 'posh' for the most part, rather than simply imitating others. The West Indian children, on the other hand, thought they would be regarded as imitating others. Some, indeed, thought they would be accused of showing off, being English or being mad. These findings suggest that the West Indians regard standard English as an alien form and that using it regularly with their peers would mean surrendering their identity.

Edwards concludes that Creole appears to be used widely by both Caribbean- and British-born West Indians and that in many cases it is likely to influence both the production and understanding of standard English. She says:

There is, however, great sensitivity as to when and to whom speech from the Creole end of the continuum should be used and there is considerable linguistic adjustment from one situation to another. There is certainly no justification for the opinion often voiced by some teachers that West Indians do not know when to use standard English. A study of the whole range of a child's speech shows considerable flexibility and versatility. Nor should it be in any way surprising that Creole is widely spoken amongst second-generation West Indians.

She goes on to explain that because accent and dialect indicate that we belong to a particular group with its own values, the only occasions such features can be changed is when an individual wants to identify with another group. The need of West Indian children to identify with speakers of standard English is, however, slight. As she comments, 'Their feelings of alienation and rejection are such that the urgency for young blacks to establish their own separate identity cannot be over-estimated and one of the ways in which this identity can be manifested is in their speech.'

It would appear that this feature of West Indian children is becoming more apparent. It has been noticed by teachers, for instance, that the speech of some West Indian children becomes noticeably more West Indian in character as they move through the system. Indeed, a study by Edwards and Sutcliffe[16] found that second-generation blacks who persisted in using fairly broad Creole were discouraged from so doing by their parents. Furthermore, teachers' efforts to teach children to speak the standard form ended in failure. The researchers comment:

> The links between language and identity are so strong that attempts to 'correct' non-standard speech are likely to be interpreted by the children as criticism or rejection of themselves, their family and friends.

Creole Interference

We have established the point that Creole is a valid language in its own right and as such is a suitable medium for learning. Nevertheless, because it is derived from standard English and, therefore, similar to it in many respects, it may 'interfere' with both the production and understanding of the standard form. Indeed, it is the fact that they are so similar that is the cause of the difficulty.

The concept of interference in the sense we are using it is of course common to other areas of human behaviour and endeavour. Interference theory, for example, plays an important part in the theory of forgetting in the psychology of memory. In effect, old and new associations compete, as it were, with one association interfering with the retention of others. And at the level of motor skill, one readily recalls how much more difficult it is to learn a particular skill correctly when one has learned it incorrectly on an earlier occasion. At the linguistic level English people have great difficulty in pronouncing the Welsh voiceless 'll' because the only 'l' available in the English language is the voiced one.

In briefly identifying some of the ways in which interference can result in difficulties, we are not implying that these are necessarily experienced by all West Indian pupils. Indeed, as Edwards recalls,[31] the extent of Creole interference will be seen to vary greatly among individual West Indians.

The manner in which Creole can affect *speech* is very important indeed. Edwards observes that very few children in this context are truly bidialectal in that they have complete control of two different language systems, Creole and standard English. If interference in speech is important, then equally so are the teacher's reactions for, as we have seen, a child's language is intimately tied up with his identity and any criticisms of the way he talks will be interpreted as a criticism of himself as a person.

It is often taken for granted that because the West Indian speaks 'English', he fully *understands* what is being said to him. Quite often, however, this is not the case for there are many occasions when there is either complete or partial misunderstanding. The problems stem from different grammar, different vocabulary and, initially, different sound systems. The latter is particularly significant because, as Edwards notes, we all learn to distinguish only those sounds that are meaningful in our own language or dialect. She says of the early stages of contact between pupil and teacher:[32]

A period of considerable adjustment for both teacher and child is bound to arise. And even when the child perceives the words correctly they may have different meanings, and certain constructions may prove puzzling. Nor do difficulties have to be very numerous to cause confusion. One key word or expression can completely 'throw' the listener. One West

Indian describes vividly her frustrations during a schools broadcast on moths shortly after her arrival from St. Kitts:

'The teacher thought I was thick, but I didn't know what a moth was. If she had said butterfly or something it would have been different.' Consequently, she only understood a word here and there in that lesson — 'the sound was pouring over my ears but I couldn't catch the sense of it.'

Glaring examples of Creole interference can be observed in the written work of West Indian children (see Box 9.3 for examples). Edwards says in this respect:

Interference is to be seen both in the transfer of Creole grammar to the children's written work and in the spellings which reflect Creole phonology. Dealing first with the question of spelling, we find many of the features of the Creole sound system in the writing of West Indian children, though the extent of this kind of interference varies enormously from child to child, and is certainly more marked in younger children.

These problems place a particular responsibility on the teacher, as Edwards explains:

The teacher's familiarity with the West Indian child's sound system and his reaction to dialect-based misspellings are, however, crucial. If the teacher does not recognise the source of the child's difficulties he is likely to imagine that his literacy problems are far greater than they are in fact, and to be ready to label him as 'dyslexic', 'slow', or 'hopeless'.

Examples of grammatical interference identified by Edwards which tend to be the most persistent features of children's written work include plurals, the use of past tenses and subject-verb agreement. She gives the following examples to illustrate these points:

One day their live a witct and her husband and five little <u>girl</u> (Karen, 8)

Don't stand they Alfred and let this woman call me <u>name</u> (Jennifer, 13)

Box 9.3: Examples of Interference in Writing

Creole /t,d/; English /th/

He was very tin and he was very dirty (Alison, 9)

There is about tree (three) kinds of zebra are left in Africa (Donna, 10)

Creole /θ/; English /ð/

One day Michael set out fram (from) home to look far (for) advencher (Gary, 8)

Shrimps are about 6cm. lang (long) (Kevin, 9)

Creole /a/; English /o/

'How dear (dare) she,' said Hilda (Jennifer, 13)

I went downstiars (downstairs) (Paula, 7)

Reduction of consonant clusters at the end of words

I will fine (find) them (Alison, 9)

He forgot wher she lived and had to go pars (past) a vicar (Kevin, 9)

Source: Edwards.[33]

One Christmas day father Christmas he give me a present for Christmas (Sharon, 6)

He had six wifes and he chop of the head of the sicth one (Gillian, 8)

Minerva know all about spiders (Lloyd, 8)

Mary usually sleep on my bed (Valerie, 14)

Edwards comments on the fact that these features are so persistent in spite of the fact that they have been corrected by generations of teachers in the West Indies and more recently by teachers in British schools. She considers that there are two possible reasons. First, all West Indians do use the -s suffix of the plural and the -ed suffix of the past tense on some occasions, these being characterised by formality. Second, they express a semi-conscious need to preserve their separate identity: 'Adoption of standard forms acknowledges acceptance of the values of those who use the standard language; retention of Creole features indicate membership of a particular cultural and linguistic group and rejection of the values associated with standard speakers.'[34]

Attitudes Towards Language and Educational Achievement

As important as the differences between Creole and standard English are the attitudes that people hold towards these differences. Indeed, the strong links that exist between attitudes to language and attitudes towards the speakers of the languages prompted Edwards[35] to investigate the attitudes of various groups to both West Indian and British speech, believing that teachers' attitudes to linguistic differences may play a bigger part in children's underperformance than the differences themselves.[36] The groups in question were teachers, West Indian children and their British middle- and working-class peers.

Recordings were made of four children in their first year at secondary school. One was a British-born Barbadian girl who was completely bidialectal. She spoke first with a working-class Reading accent which she used in school and secondly in Creole. The latter recording had phonological features of Creole, though not a great number of grammatical features. The effect was a type of speech recognisable as West Indian but at the same time comprehensible to native British listeners. The remaining speakers were an English boy having a working-class Reading accent, a professor's son who used Received Standard English and a recently arrived Jamaican girl who spoke with a strong Creole accent that was barely understandable to native British listeners. All spoke fluently for 30 seconds on the subject of going to the dentist.

The questionnaire used by the researcher consisted of two semantic differential scales, one relating to the children's speech and the other to their behaviour (see Box 9.4), along with two questions dealing with potential academic achievement and attitudes to the children, thus:

How far do you think this child will get in school? CSE/O-levels/A-levels

and

Do you think this child would be interesting to have in the class? Yes/No

The first group whose attitudes to speech and behaviour were considered consisted of 20 student teachers. Edwards regarded

Box 9.4: Semantic Differential Scales

Using the semantic differential technique, two sets of scales were used in the questionnaire. The first set related to the children's speech, thus:

valuable :___:___:___:___:___:___:___: worthless

bad :___:___:___:___:___:___:___: good

careful :___:___:___:___:___:___:___: careless

smooth :___:___:___:___:___:___:___: rough

negative :___:___:___:___:___:___:___: positive

sharp :___:___:___:___:___:___:___: dull

strong :___:___:___:___:___:___:___: weak

clever :___:___:___:___:___:___:___: stupid

The remaining scales relate to the child's behaviour:

shy :___:___:___:___:___:___:___: friendly

moody :___:___:___:___:___:___:___: cheerful

nervous :___:___:___:___:___:___:___: confident

helpful :___:___:___:___:___:___:___: unhelpful

lazy :___:___:___:___:___:___:___: hardworking

naughty :___:___:___:___:___:___:___: well-behaved

Source: Edwards.[37]

them as an obviously important group because of the effect that teacher attitudes may well have on West Indian behaviour and performance. Evaluations were compared on four separate counts to see if the respondents would distinguish between (1) the two working-class speakers; (2) the two guises of the West Indian girl (working-class Reading and Creole); (3) the working-class and middle-class boys; and (4) the two West Indian girls.

The results showed that the student teachers did not distinguish between the working-class speakers or the two West Indian girls, but there was a significant difference in their evaluations of the working-class and middle-class boys and, more importantly, between the two guises of the West Indian girl, both in speech and behaviour. Edwards detected extensive evidence of stereo-typing behaviour in the results. As she expresses it:

> The high status assigned to the middle class speaker, for instance, suggests that this social stereotype evokes a gross classification and that little attention has been paid to individual characteristics. More striking still is the fact that the same girl is judged less favourably when speaking in a West Indian accent than in a Reading working class accent. It is also notable that the evaluations of speech are similar to those of behaviour.[38]

The two other factors considered were the relative academic potential of the speakers and their desirability as members of a class. The results proved to be consistent with the ones just noted. The middle-class boy is felt to have the highest academic potential and the working-class guise is viewed more favourably than the West Indian. Evaluations of the children's desirability as members of a class, however, proved to be more surprising. The researcher had at the outset hypothesised that there would be no significant differences here. And this indeed was the case with the working-class speakers, the working-class and middle-class speakers and the two West Indian girls. However, there was a highly significant difference between the two West Indian guises, that is working-class Reading and Creole, which reflected the student teachers' negative feeling about West Indian children or, as Edwards puts it, children using language that is recognisably West Indian.

With regard to the British children's attitudes to speech and behaviour, the results disclosed that both working-class and middle-class judges agree with the student teachers in assigning high status in both speech and behaviour to the middle-class boy. Edwards notes, however, that there is an interesting variation in their evaluations of West Indian and working-class guises. The working-class judges, like the student teachers, view the West Indian guises less favourably. The middle-class judges, in contrast, do not distinguish between the two guises. Edwards interprets this as indicating that the middle-class judges regard working-class and West Indian speakers equally favourably.

Similar patterns emerged in the children's evaluations of the academic potential and social desirability.

The West Indian judges agree with both student-teacher and child judges that the middle-class boy has highest status in terms of both speech and behaviour. They did not distinguish between West Indian and working-class in speech, but they did regard West Indian behaviour less favourably than the working class.

As regards the evaluation of academic potential and social desirability, the West Indian responses resemble those of the working-class and middle-class children. Like them, they assign highest status to the middle-class boy whom they regard as having the greatest academic potential and being the most desirable member of the class. Edwards concludes that the overall picture which emerges from the West Indian evaluations is that of a group of children with a depressed self-concept.

There are two particular aspects of these findings that give cause for concern. First, it appears that teachers differ little from the rest of society in the stereotypes they hold of ethnic-minority groups. Second, and perhaps more significant, West Indians view themselves very negatively and these views reflect to a large extent the stereotype of West Indians that is prevalent in Britain. The educational and social implications of this are pin-pointed by Edwards;

It seems highly probable that a child's ability to learn is affected by his motivation and that his motivation is affected by the feedback he receives from society concerning his probability of success. If this is the case, the plight of West Indian children in British schools is likely to continue to give rise to concern; not only is there evidence of extensive under-performance, but there are indications of far-reaching social malaise.[39]

Practical Approaches to Language in the Multicultural Classroom

Edwards[40] has pointed out that the arrival in recent years of ethnic-minority children from quite different backgrounds to native children has provided teachers with the opportunity to look afresh at the whole approach to educating young people, methods no less than content, and that this will be to the advantage not only of the ethnic-minority children but also to the native pupils as well. Although most teachers have had to deal with the problems created by regional dialects such as Geordie and the like, the West Indian dialect has been particularly difficult for them because it is further removed from standard English than local dialects and for most teachers was a completely new experience. Because the educational system in the United States has had to deal with a similar problem in the case of black Americans speaking a dialect similar to Creole (Black English Vernacular, or BEV), Edwards considers that an examination of what has been done in that country could be informative.

For a long time the policy in teaching blacks in America was to attempt to eradicate their dialect. Initially, it was felt that BEV was a limited and illogical system that did not measure up to the needs of abstract thought. However, it has been demonstrated by linguists like Labov[41] that such criticisms were unfounded and that like all other languages and dialects, BEV was a valid language in its own right and perfectly capable of meeting the communicative needs of its speakers. A subsequent reason for believing that dialect should be eradicated was that it put those speaking it at a disadvantage because educational achievement and social mobility depended on the acquisition and use of a standard form of language.

The experience of blacks in America, then, showed that dialect eradication is just not feasible. Indeed, as Edwards makes clear, insistence on constant correction of dialect is harmful for at least two reasons. First, because of the connection between language and identity, attempts to belittle dialect reflect on the individuals using it and this will eventually affect the relationship between the person using the dialect and the one attempting to 'correct' it, in other words, the pupil and teacher. Second, dialect eradication can result in confusion and lack of confidence.

An alternative to which Americans resorted was the bidialectal approach. By this, the differences between the dialect in question and the standard form are brought out into the open and freely discussed. The child is then taught how to translate his own speech patterns into standard form. *Bidialectalism* is thus aimed at helping the child to produce a standard *written* English without insisting that his spoken language should change. Because the emphasis is thus on written work, there is less likelihood of provoking a hostile reaction from the child.

A bidialectal approach would thus permit children to use their own dialect in speech, reading and writing in the early years of school without any intervention from the teacher. The latter would only subsequently draw a child's attention to differences and the advantages of learning to write standard English when reading and writing in the child's own dialect had been mastered. Edwards considers that of the two methods, dialect eradication and bidialectalism, the latter would appear to be the more ethically acceptable and also the one amost likely to succeed, in spite of difficulties. Indeed, it is seen as more attainable than the final approach discussed by Edwards — dialect appreciation.

From a linguistic point of view, language and dialects ought to be of equal standing with none being regarded as in any way superior to others. In practical terms, however, the picture is somewhat different for the weight of tradition attached to the use of standard English more or less ensures for a long time to come that dialects will be regarded as inferior to it. Edwards points out that there are great difficulties in persuading teachers that all dialects are of equal standing. But even if this were not the case, what goes on in real life points to the virtual unassaila-bility of the standard form of language — at least as far as the medium term is concerned. In identifying the consequences for children, she quotes from the work of Crystal,[42] thus:

> The children being taught now are going to have to grow up in a society where the formal standard English language and its various varieties retain considerable prestige. Its practitioners still, in several walks of life, call the tune . . . We may wish to change society to remove some of the stigma that attaches to certain language forms. But it seems unreasonable to expect the child to do it for us, and unfair to give him the impression that anything goes, as long as it is 'sincere and expressive', when we know full well that in real life there are other linguistic standards which educated people are expected to live up to.

Edwards considers that the difficulties of implementing the bidialectal approach are formidable, explaining that the traditional views towards Creole and all non-standard forms are so deeply embedded that the process of change is likely to take some considerable time. She refers to the controversy, by way of illustration, that arose over the Language Arts syllabus published by the Trinidad and Tobago Ministry of Education and Culture in 1975 and discussed by Carrington and Borely,[43] as a good example of the problems involved. This syllabus questioned the traditional assumption that Creole is slovenly and unacceptable and put forward the view that, since it is the only means of communication available to children on entry to school, they should be allowed to express themselves in it in the early years. The argument put forward was that such an atmosphere of acceptance, alongside a more systematic approach to teaching standard English, is likely to be more successful than earlier methods. The publication of the syllabus resulted in a hostile reaction from a significant section of the community and a heated debate ensued for some time in the local press.[44]

Box 9.5: Writing by a Young West Indian

'De blackman' by Meryl Philip:

De blackman workin all night,
De blackman trousers fittin tight.
De blackman working eight day week,
de blackman na getting no sleep.
De blackman cleanin all you streets,
De blackman can't even buy a sweets.
De blackman doin all de cookin,
de whiteman standing der just lookin.
De blackman only wearing red,
de blackman gonna dead.

Source: Edwards.[45]

In identifying similar moves in this country, Edwards refers to the Inner London Education Authority which has undertaken a radical reappraisal of its policies for multicultural education, bringing it into line with the European Economic Community directive which obliges governments 'to promote, in co-ordination with normal education, teaching of the mother tongue and culture of the country of origin'. Although, as Edwards explains, this does not go as far as actually teaching Creole, it is nevertheless hoped to achieve greater understanding of the language by teachers, and encourage its use in the more creative aspects of the curriculum like poetry and drama (see Box 9.5). She also compares the response to the proposals with that referred to in Trinidad. One London headteacher was sufficiently provoked to write the following to the *Sunday Times* (16 October, 1977):

> Should I create a black curriculum? Should I put Creole on the time-table? Over my dead body and the majority of my parents would cheer me to the skies. They want their children to get jobs. I will not even allow patois in the school. It must not be elevated to linguistic status at the expense of English.

Like those who contributed to the *Trinidad Guardian*, the letter's author has failed to understand the purpose of the new curriculum. There was no suggestion, for example, that Creole should take the place of standard English; it was simply recognised that a child's own language and culture is likely to have a positive effect on his school work where these are acknowledged. As Edwards comments, the strength of prejudice against Creole should not be underestimated.[46]

Notes

1. J. Derrick (1968) 'The Work of the Schools Council Project in English for Immigrant Children', *Times Educational Supplement*. 25 October.

2. J. Derrick (1973) 'The Language Needs of Immigrant Children', *London Educational Review*, 24 September, 25–30.

3. Ibid.

4. B. Bernstein (1958) 'Some Sociological Determinants of Perception', *British Journal of Sociology*, 9, 154–74; B. Bernstein (1960) 'Language and Social Class', *British Journal of Sociology*, 11, 271–6; B. Bernstein (1961) 'Social Class and Linguistic Development: A Theory of Social Learning' in A. H. Halsey, J. Floud and C. A. Anderson (eds), *Society, Economy and Education*, Glencoe, Ill.: Free Press; B. Bernstein (1965) 'A Socio-linguistic Approach to Social Learning' in J. Gould (ed.), *Penguin Survey of the Social Sciences*, London: Penguin Books.

5. F. Tayor (1974) *Race, School and Community: A Study of Research and Literature*, Slough: NFER.

6. Schools Council *English for Immigrant Children*, Curriculum Development Project, Leeds: E. J. Arnold: (1969) *Scope 1: An Introductory Course for Pupils 8–13 years*; (1971) *Scope Handbook 2: Pronunciation for Non-English Speaking Children from India, Pakistan, Cyprus and Italy;* (1972) *Scope Senior Course for Non-English Speaking Students 14 years and over*; (1972) *Scope 2 for Pupils 8–13 years at 2nd Stage of English* (Longmans); (1973) *Scope 3 Handbook 3: Language Work with Infant Immigrant Children*; (1973) J. Taylor and T. Ingleby, *Scope Story Book 5–12 years*; (1973) D. Manley, *Scope Supplementary Plays and Dialogues*.

7. Taylor, *Race, School and Community*.

8. D. Hill (1976) *Teaching in Multiracial Schools*, London: Methuen.

9. Derrick, 'Language Needs'.

10. Ibid.

11. M. J. Taylor (1981) *Caught Between: A Review of Research into the Education of Pupils of West Indian Origin*, Windsor: NFER-Nelson.

12. V. K. Edwards (1979) *The West Indian Language in British Schools*, London: Routledge and Kegan Paul.

13. Ibid.

14. Ibid.

15. Taylor, *Caught Between*.

16. P. C. C. Evans and R. B. Le Page (1967) *The Education of West Indian Immigrant Children*, National Committee for Commonwealth Immigrants.

17. Edwards, *The West Indian Language*.

18. Ibid.

19. Ibid.

20. Ibid.

21. Taylor, *Caught Between*.

22. J. Essen and M. Ghodsian (1979) 'The Children of Immigrants: School Performance', *New Community*, **1**(3), 422–9.

23. J. Rex and S. Tomlinson (1979) *Colonial Immigrants in a British City. A Class Analysis*, London: Routledge and Kegan Paul.

24. D. Stoker (1969) *The Education of Infant Immigrants*, a report prepared for the Schools Council Project in English for Immigrant Children, Leeds: The Institute of Education.

25. C. Bagley, M. Bart and J. Wong (1978) 'Cognition and Scholastic Success in West Indian 10-year-olds in London: A Comparative Study', *Educational Studies*, **4**(1), 7–17.

26. Ibid.

27. Edwards, *The West Indian Language*.

28. D. Sutcliffe (1978) 'The Language of First and Second Generation West Indian Children in Bedfordshire', MEd thesis, University of Leicester.

29. Hadi, quoted in V. K. Edwards, *The West Indian Language*, p. 37.

30. V. K. Edwards and D. Sutcliffe (1978) 'Broadly Speaking', *Times Educational Supplement*, 13 October, p. 19.

31. Edwards, *The West Indian Language*.

32. Ibid.

33. Ibid.

34. Ibid.

35. V. K. Edwards (1978) 'Language Attitudes and Underperformance in West Indian Children', *Educational Review*, **30**(1), 51–8.

36. Edwards, *The West Indian Language*.

37. Edwards, 'Language Attitudes'.

38. Ibid.

39. Ibid.

40. Edwards, *The West Indian Language*.

41. W. Labov (1972) 'The Logic of Non-Standard English' in P. P. Giglioli (ed.), *Language and Social Context*, Harmondsworth: Penguin Books.

42. D. Crystal (1976) *Child Language, Learning and Linguistics*, London: Edward Arnold.

43. D. Carrington and K. Borely (eds) (1977) *The Language Arts Syllabus, 1975: Comment and Countercomment*, Trinidad: University of Saint Augustine.

44. Ibid.

45. Edwards, *The West Indian Language*.

46. Ibid.

INDEX

Index